AUSTRALIA
Law Book Co.
Sydney

CANADA and USA
Carswell
Toronto

HONG KONG
Sweet & Maxwell Asia

NEW ZEALAND
Brookers
Wellington

SINGAPORE and MALAYSIA
Sweet & Maxwell Asia
Singapore and Kuala Lumpur

A GUIDEBOOK TO INTELLECTUAL PROPERTY

FIFTH EDITION

by

The Rt. Hon. Sir Robin Jacob
A Lord Justice of Appeal

Daniel Alexander, Q.C.

Lindsay Lane, Barrister

LONDON
SWEET & MAXWELL
2004

First Edition (1970)
Second Edition (1978)
Third Edition (1986)
Fourth Edition (1993)
Fifth Edition (2004)

*Published in 2004 by Sweet & Maxwell Limited of
100 Avenue Road, London, NW3 3PF
Typeset by Interactive Sciences Ltd, Gloucester
Printed in England by Ashford Colour Press Ltd,
Gosport, Hants*

No natural forests were destroyed to make
this product; only farmed timber was used and replanted.
A CIP catalogue record for this book is available
from the British Library.

ISBN 0 421 799 803

© Sweet & Maxwell
2004

PREFACE TO THE FIFTH EDITION

This is the fifth edition of a book whose nature and style was devised by Thomas Blanco White Q.C. as long ago as the 1940s, when he produced three small pamphlets on patents and designs, trade marks and copyright that formed the basis of the first edition. As ever it is different to other books on intellectual property law. We have never really even been sure which market it is aimed at. The original pamphlets were aimed at business-men, for there were no IP students then. We like to think that students will buy it (or, in these hard times, at least read someone else's copy) but we rather think, and hope that it has a wider market. This is because one of its principal objects is to give the reader an overview—a feel for the subject. There is now so much legislation and case law that it is all too easy not to see the wood for the trees. So we have left lots out. There are no detailed discussions on almost any of the myriad of fancy and difficult points of law. There are just glimpses of these and there are deliberately no footnotes which impede an easy read.

No-one can take this book and reliably look up the law on a particular detailed point. But they can do something quite different—something that other books do not try to do — that is, understand the structure and practical workings of the sub-ject.

Why do we write it? Sweet and Maxwell are generous but no-one could suggest it is for the money. We are not quite sure: it has something to do with our love of the subject and a desire to communicate its excitement. There was a lot of work involved—much has changed since the last, 1993 edition. The trade mark section is wholly new—not only did the new law come into force about 10 years ago, but the flood of cases in recent years (just look at how many are post-2000) shows just how uncertain the new law is.

A few words of thanks: to Trevor Thompson of Boult Wade Tennant for providing current figures as to the various cost figures we mention and to Jessie Bowhill, of 8 New Square, who helped with the final stages of getting the book into shape.

Our most special thanks are to the Arsenal Football Club for allowing the use of their new and old crests on the front cover. We wanted to do this not merely because one of us is a well known Arsenal fanatic but because it illustrates the significant Arsenal trade mark case discussed in Chapter 9. Arsenal have never licensed the use of their copyright and trade marks before. Sweet and Maxwell readily agreed to give what they would have paid (and more) for a cover design sum to Arsenal's nominated charities. We decided to match them.

Rt. Hon. Sir Robin Jacob
Daniel Alexander, Q.C.
Lindsay Lane

CONTENTS

CONTENTS

CONTENTS

TABLE OF CASES

xvii

TABLE OF CASES

PART I

INTRODUCTION

1. IMITATION, MONOPOLY AND CONTROL

This book is about the law of commercial and industrial monopoly and imitation: imitation by one manufacturer of another's products, imitation by one trader of the names and badges by which another's goods or business are known; imitations, deliberate or not, accidental or on purpose. It is about how the law deals with the appropriation of the fruits of other people's labour. It is also about how people can acquire monopoly rights to do certain profitable things (such as make certain products or sell them under particular names) and how those monopolies are protected and kept from getting out of hand. Thirdly, it is about how people can keep control over the use other people make of their creative work. These three subjects overlap to the point of inseparability in much of what follows.

Kinds of Intellectual Property

"Intellectual Property" ("IP") is the umbrella phrase now used (but only since about the 1970s—before that it meant only copyright and like rights) to cover all the various rights that may be invoked to prevent imitations of various sorts. But contrary to quite a lot of current woolly terminology and thinking, actually the rights are quite distinct. For legal purposes, the rights have to be considered individually. In practice, the kinds of imitation and the applicable rights often overlap. There are numerous examples of such overlap. The manufacture of a particular industrial item might infringe a rival's patent, but may also infringe design rights of various sorts, some of which come into play if there has been copying, others even if there has not. For another example, industrial designs are given protection in theory to protect the work of the designer—to protect the artistic element in manufacture. In many cases, however, the main value of design protection is to supplement the manufacturer's trade marks by securing to him exclusive rights in the "get-up" of the goods—a function that in legal theory belongs rather to the law of passing-off or registered trade marks. For a third example, patent protection can be used to build up the reputation of a trade mark for the patented goods such that the effect of the monopoly that the patent gave can be felt long after the patent has expired because the trade mark has by then become so well established.

Exactly how to go about using, reinforcing and challenging the various monopoly rights to best commercial advantage is a matter for complex strategic assessment. Quite often it is possible to do almost as much with an unchallenged monopoly (such as a subsisting patent) as with one that is secure (such as a *valid* subsisting patent) because the costs for a competitor of breaking the monopoly by legal action are often very high. The mere possession of a patent, however rubbishy to a lawyer's mind, may be of real value for commercial purposes and it will encourage others to think of ways of "designing round" the monopoly rather than face an action for infringement once substantial resources have been committed. Because of the substantial costs for people of finding out exactly what it is they can do, by going to court to get a judge to tell them, a great deal of intellectual property law in practice involves not squabbling in court over the existence or scope of rights but getting into the best position for reaching agreement on who should be allowed to do what.

"Exclusive rights"

Most of the legal rights with which this book is concerned are rights to stop other people doing things—what an old cynic called "the grit in the wheels of industry". For some reason (or possibly none), Acts of Parliament and EU legislation do not put it like that: thus the proprietor of a registered industrial design is said by the Act to have "the exclusive right" to do certain things with the design, and the other rights are expressed in similar language. But what is meant is, not that the owner of the design, patent, or copyright concerned has, by that ownership, the right to do anything he could not otherwise do, but that he has the right—subject to questions of validity—to decide whether other people shall be permitted to do certain things or not. This point is worth emphasising, because the position is too often not understood. In particular, many, if not most, of the people who take the trouble to secure patents for inventions believe that, somehow, possession of the patent secures to them the right to manufacture their inventions without interference. It does nothing of the sort: the thing such an inventor wants to manufacture may well incorporate other people's patented inventions, and the only way the inventor can be sure that he or she has the right to manufacture is by searching to find what patents other people have. The inventor's own patent (if it is valid, and the specification is properly drawn up—points discussed later) confers the right to stop other people using the particular device that is the subject of the patent—and nothing else. In principle, the position is much the same with the other rights considered in this book, although ownership of a registered trade mark, exceptionally, gives a limited freedom from infringement of other people's registered marks.

A related misconception about IP rights is that they can readily be treated as items of property independent of the underlying business that they protect. IP rights can, of course, be bought, sold, or licensed. This has led to a tendency by accountants to want to value IP rights independently of any associated business, thereby "increasing" net asset value. Such an approach overlooks the fact that the IP rights merely provide the business with protection from competition; so to value the rights and business separately is likely to involve a significant element of double-counting—absent the rights the business would be worth less.

Registered and unregistered rights

Most IP rights have to be applied for and registered to take effect, but there are some important ones that arise automatically as a matter of law. Of particular importance are: copyright and related rights; the right to prevent goodwill being undermined by deceptive conduct in the market ("passing-off"); unregistered design rights; and the right to stop misappropriation of trade secrets ("the action for breach of confidence").

Civil and criminal law

The enforcement of IP rights is largely by action in the civil courts. This must be initiated and paid for (at least until he wins and gets and enforces an order for costs) by the right owner. In some cases (particularly with "counterfeits"—near exact copies of things such as CDs, DVDs, perfumes and "designer" clothes), criminal enforcement is used. Sometimes the prosecutions are then paid for by the State—either via local authorities or, exceptionally in the case of big dealers, by the DPP. Criminal courts have the power to punish by fines and/or imprisonment, but not to order payment of damages.

The civil courts—their functions and acronyms

A violation or a perceived violation of an IP right brings the right holder into conflict with an infringer. If the infringer will not stop after being notified of the rights (care must be taken to avoid "threats" in the case of many IP rights), ultimately he must be sued. It is a fact of life (sometimes ignored) that many IP rights are apt to be rather indistinct at their edges (*e.g.* what is a "substantial part" of a copyright work?) or uncertain in their very nature (*e.g.* the value judgement as to whether a development said to be an invention is so close to a prior idea that it is "obvious"). So where there is a lot of money at stake, it may be rational for both sides to fight. Even weak cases may be worth a long shot if there are many millions at stake. It is principally in the civil courts that such fights take place.

For patents and registered designs there are specialised courts for England and Wales (where most patent disputes take place). They are the Patents Court (forming part of the Chancery Division of the High Court) and the Patents County Court. Each has specialised judges—the principal judges having spent a career in IP and having science degrees. Those same judges are apt to deal with other IP cases too, but these can also be dealt with by other judges of the Chancery Division. It is possible to sue in Scotland too and it occasionally happens. There the judges (and lawyers), though very good indeed, are less specialist. Northern Irish cases are very rare.

Of increasing importance is the European Court of Justice ("ECJ") in Luxembourg. A lot (pretty well all trade mark) of IP legislation is EU based. If there is a problem with the meaning of the law based on a "Directive" (requirement to bring national law in line with its requirements), then a national court can "refer" a question to the ECJ. This has been happening regularly and many of the cases that we mention were references to that court. A reference can take up to two years—the case has to pause meanwhile. If, as sometimes happens, a lot of other cases depend on the same point, they are often paused (the lawyers say "stayed") at the same time.

It is also possible for some sorts of disputes, essentially about whether a right should be or has validly been granted, to take place in offices that grant IP rights. Thus trade mark oppositions can take place before the European Trade Mark Office, which forms part of the Office for Harmonization of the Internal Market ("OHIM") based in Alicante. OHIM has boards of appeal, from which one can appeal further to the Court of First Instance ("CFI") of the ECJ with a possible appeal to the full ECJ or a chamber of it. Soon there will be appeals from OHIM in the case of Community designs too, the EU registered design system having started in 2003. The British Patent Office can hear trade mark oppositions or attacks upon the validity of patents—the former is used a lot, the latter hardly ever happens. The European Patent Office ("EPO") has its own system for dealing with post-grant disputes about the validity of patents.

Costs

The cost of litigation, particularly IP litigation, has always been a running sore with users. They want all of the following in combination: speed, low cost, and certainty. The last (which is often under-rated) is very important—if both sides get the same advice about their respective prospects then there is room to settle. But if both sides think they are going to win, or that anything can happen, then settlement is much less likely.

That being said, the problem of legal costs has become even worse in recent years—mainly because large firms of solicitors appear to put too many "bodies" on a case. It is not actually necessary to use a solicitor: the Patents County Court was created mainly so patent agents could instruct a barrister direct or even appear themselves. It is rather a pity that more use is not made of such teams but, unnecessarily, clients, or perhaps their patent agents, are a bit frightened by the image of the big battalion law firms. They need not be—a good patent agent with a good barrister can be a formidable fighting team for small and even medium size cases. Even larger cases do not need more than the addition of a good solicitor and perhaps one assistant. As things are, quite a number of cases in the Patents County Court are fought with much the same teams as would be used in the High Court—so the costs are much the same. Sensible parties will question why their lawyers want to use so many people on their case. A slim team is usually more effective than teams twice the size—and billing by the hour alone almost inevitably drives up costs, even though it is the fashion.

Partly because of increasing costs, but also because of the increasing internationalisation of IP problems (with room for parallel actions in different countries and a patchwork of results), people are increasingly turning to mediation or arbitration as ways of dealing with their IP conflicts. Mediation involves the parties getting together (usually in separate rooms) with a trained mediator who is there to help them settle their disputes. Mediations are often successful in the IP field—a good mediator will point out to each side that their position is not quite as strong as they may think and will help the parties find common ground. There are even cases where English courts have "punished" (by withholding some or all of an award of costs) a winner who has unreasonably refused to mediate. There are limits to this, however—if the parties have negotiated "without prejudice" (*i.e.* so that their discussions cannot be used in court) then the court cannot tell whether one side or the other was unreasonable and thus "punish" the winner (*Reed*, 2004).

The Patent Office have come up with an idea (enacted in the Patents Act 2004), which may help—the Office can be asked to give a non-binding opinion on the case. This should at least be relatively cheap—it may help both sides to form a realistic opinion of their chances, thus helping them to settle. Whether the idea will work remains to be seen.

Other things

Although this book is mainly about exclusive rights themselves, it also deals with other matters, for instance systems of licensing and the action to prevent threats of certain types of IP litigation.

Remedies

Spatial and temporal monopolies

Many IP rights are limited in time (*e.g.* 20 years for patents) and exist only for certain territories (mainly countries). The fact that the exclusive rights are limited by space and time causes a whole series of problems of international and particularly EU law. For example: two of the key objectives of the Common Market are first to achieve free movement of goods and services by reducing or eliminating the effect of national boundaries, and second to ensure that healthy competition takes place. Both objectives stand in opposition to the structure of IP law which carves up the EU by national boundaries (rights are, by and large, nationwide rather than EU-wide). So one of the most practically important sources of law in recent years in this area has been decisions of the ECJ and, increasingly since the 1980s, European legislation, taking direct effect via a Regulation or via one of our Acts of Parliament passed to comply with a Directive. It is now mainly these that determine what the subject matter of IP law is and places limits on its exploitation.

The scheme of this book

This book is divided into sections broadly along the lines drawn by the main Acts of Parliament and EU legislation dealing with these branches of the law. The basic division is into three parts: the first part is concerned with the copying of the product and deals mainly with the law of patents and of industrial designs; the second part is concerned with the way things are sold and deals mainly with the law of passing-off, and trade marks and other rules preventing unfair competition or unfair selling techniques; and the third part deals with the law of copyright (apart from its use to protect industrial designs) and certain related issues such as rights in perform-ances and "moral" rights. It also deals with the law of con-fidential information.

It should be clear that this division into three sections is merely a matter of convenience. Commercial strategies and disputes often cut across these lines. It is one of the functions of this book to show the interrelations between the different subjects in a way that more specialised works cannot easily do. There is a large amount of academic writing, some of it by lawyers and some by economists, on the value of particular IP rights and the ways in which they are protected. For example, doubts are often expressed by industrialists about the value of patents at protecting the competitive advantage that their sci-entific innovations produce, and some companies prefer to keep their inventions secret rather than disclose the details to the world, albeit in exchange for a limited monopoly. Often these concerns are industry specific; depending in part on how fast innovation occurs and can be commercially exploited. So a form of protection that might suit the biotechnology indus-try might be useless for heavy engineering. For another exam-ple, doubts are also often expressed by economists and industry analysts concerning the importance of the intellectual property system in providing incentives to research and inno-vate. The importance of providing proper incentives is one of the (several) justifications most frequently offered for giving people IP rights in the first place. As with most laws affecting industry, the legislation, which is the source of most of the law with which this book deals, is a mishmash of compromise, some of it the result of effective lobbying by particular interest groups, some a result of muddled thinking or appalling draft-ing by legislators and some that is actually sensible and prac-tical. There is not space in a book of this kind, which is devoted to describing how the system works, to give those arguments or the empirical work that has been done to sup-port them, any detailed consideration.

Since most of the various rights here discussed are similar in nature, they are enforced in essentially the same way—by an action in the courts for "infringement" of the right. The real point of most such actions is that in this country, once the owner of the right has made it clear that he or she insists on it and once the court has declared that the right exists, few reputable business people will want to argue the point any further. Although the owner of the right usually asks for, and usually gets (if victorious) an injunction against further infringement—a formal order, that is, from the court to the infringer, forbidding infringement for the future—it is the decision that really matters, not the formal order. Indeed, such an order is so rarely disobeyed in commercial cases (where the defendant is almost always a company) that no really effective method of dealing with real disobedience has ever been worked out. In practice, the thing to do against individuals who are determined infringers is to sue not only any companies, which are controlled by them that are infringing for the time being, but also the individuals themselves. This prevents these individuals from forming new companies for the purpose of infringing—disobedience of an injunction by an individual means, ultimately, imprisonment.

When to sue

An action for infringement can be brought either when infringement has already started, or even earlier, when it is merely threatened. In general, the law allows one whose rights are infringed to choose when to sue. If infringement has already taken place, a successful plaintiff (we prefer this intelligible word to the trendy but official word "claimant") will be entitled to damages for what has already occurred as well as an order for the future, and an order that any goods or materials whose use would infringe the claimed rights be delivered up or rendered innocuous. In many cases, instead of damages it is possible to claim the profits the infringer has made from the infringement. However, litigation is expensive, and although the losing party will be ordered to pay the winner's costs, the amount paid will fall well short of covering the bills the winner will have to pay. Even if damages are reckoned in with the costs the loser pays, there is seldom money to be made by this sort of litigation. Actions are often brought to punish the infringer, to stop further infringement by him or others and to establish the legal position for the future; very seldom are they brought for the sake of the damages. It follows that, in almost all cases, the right time to start an action for infringement (if an action is to be started at all) is when infringement first starts—or even better, when infringement is first threatened. This is especially true of actions for infringements of trade marks and of actions to stop passing-off, since in these cases the right to sue may be lost by delay.

There are other reasons why actions for infringement are best brought quickly if they are to be brought at all. The best way to win an action is not to have to fight, so the best sort of action to start is the sort that will not be defended. Whether an action is defended or not naturally depends in large degree on whether the case is important enough to the defendant to make it worthwhile going to the trouble and expense of fighting—and facing the uncertainty of not knowing what the result will be. The defendant in an infringement action faces the prospect of an injunction against continuing the offending business, and it is not easy to plan ahead not knowing whether such an injunction will be issued or not. Accordingly, just as few people start infringement actions unless they feel they must, so few people defend them unless they feel they must. If an infringer is allowed to infringe in peace for years—to spend money advertising a new business or a new product; to develop a new market to the point where it becomes profitable, perhaps even to build a new factory or re-equip an old one—there may be no real option but to fight; yet if the action had been brought earlier on, before there was so much at stake, the offending activity would probably have been dropped rather than waste time and money fighting. There are always other products and other markets. In trade mark cases this is especially so: it is very rarely worth fighting for a new mark, even if the chances are in your favour.

Although the various rights with which this book is concerned are all enforced by actions of much the same nature, the cost and complexity of litigation varies widely between the different cases. Actions for infringement of patent are in a class by themselves: in complexity, in cost, in the time needed to bring them to trial. Few patent disputes are finally settled inside a year (though the courts are faster than they were and are making a determined effort to speed things up), so that an infringement that will have ceased to be commercially important within a year or so is often hardly worth suing over at all, whilst an infringer who can be sure of stopping infringement within a year or so can often face the possibility of an action with comparative equanimity. This considerably reduces the practical value of patents for short-term products. A copyright, trade mark or passing-off action may be brought to trial in a matter of months, and the cost and trouble are much less, too. Actions for infringement of industrial designs are intermediate in character; whether they are more like patent actions or more like copyright actions depends on how the parties (and the court) handle them.

Interim ("interlocutory") injunctions

There are cases in which to wait a matter of months is to wait months too long. In these cases, the court may be asked to act at once, and to grant at the outset an injunction against infringement—not a permanent injunction, but an interim one, lasting until the trial of the action. In particular, many trade or service mark infringements, many cases of passing-off (especially where there is a suggestion that the defendant is dishonest), and many infringements of copyright are best dealt with in this way. A plaintiff who is granted an interim injunction must give what is called a "cross-undertaking in damages": that is, the plaintiff must undertake that, if in the end the action fails, he will compensate the defendant for the interference to the defendant's business caused by the injunction. In most cases, this is not an important matter; but an interim injunction in a patent case may well stop a production line, and the damage caused to the defendant may be very great. At the same time, the final result of the action is seldom entirely certain. So the risk to the plaintiff involved in asking for an interim injunction may be too great and should be carefully considered before an application for an interim injunction is made. Provided the plaintiff acts as soon as the infringement is brought to light—this is essential—an interim injunction will often be granted by the court in order to preserve the status quo until the trial. Unless the evidence fails to disclose that the plaintiff has any real prospect of success at the trial, the court will consider whether the balance of convenience lies in favour of granting or refusing an interlocutory injunction. An important consideration in weighing the balance of convenience is whether the plaintiff or the defendant will be adequately compensated in damages if an interlocutory injunction is either wrongfully refused or wrongfully granted. The court tries to make an order at the interim stage, which will put the trial judge in the best position of being able to do justice at the end of the day.

Following the *American Cyanamid* case in the mid-1970s, interim injunction applications became common in intellectual property cases. This was partly because it took such a long time before cases could be fully heard at trial. There are many fewer now—partly because the courts are much quicker than they were before. With determination, it is possible to get even a pharmaceutical patent case to trial in about 12 weeks—only a few weeks longer than it would take to get an interim injunction application heard. A plaintiff will ask the court for a speedy trial instead, shortly after the action has started with a view to getting the case heard very quickly (a few months or weeks). This can be rather effective in cases where one's opponent has a weak case and piles on the pressure. Of course, defendants with strong cases also use this tactic—often very effectively—at dealing with cases that should not have been brought.

Inspection and disclosure ("discovery") orders and freezing injunctions

Since about the 1970s, cases of piracy have become much commoner in many different fields of commerce. Partly in response to this, the courts have held that in extreme cases, orders can be made upon the application of the plaintiff alone requiring the defendant to permit the plaintiff's solicitors to inspect his documents and premises immediately. They are now formally called "search orders" but the name *Anton Piller* order is used, after one of the early cases in which one was granted. The purpose of this is of course that an unscrupulous defendant is given no time to destroy incriminating documents or evidence. The courts have also held that even innocent persons who have become "mixed up" in the wrongdoing (*e.g.* the Customs, or innocent warehousemen and the like) can be compelled to disclose at least the name of the wrongdoer. Such persons (save, possibly, the Customs who are in a special position) can also be restrained from permitting pirate goods from leaving their possession until at least there has been time for the case to come properly before the court. Defendants are protected against abuse of search orders by stringent conditions governing their grant and particularly by the appointment of a neutral "supervising solicitor".

Another remedy which is particularly useful in obvious piracy cases is the "freezing injunction" (*Mareva*—after the first case when such an injunction was granted). This freezes a pirate's assets and bank account: it might not work against a dishonest pirate who is prepared to take a chance as regards contempt of court, but will be obeyed by honest third parties such as banks.

Foreign Law

This is a book mainly about UK law. In many cases this is now the same as IP law throughout the EU (and, in the cases of patents, some other European countries too). Almost all foreign legal systems have something corresponding more or less to the various rights discussed in this book, but outside the EU the correspondence is seldom close. Commonwealth countries, and to some extent the United States too, have legal systems that work like ours; but their patent law is in some respects like our old patent law, not the present one. Other countries, including European countries, have legal systems that work in a different way, so that even where their law is supposed to be the same as ours—as with European patent, trade mark and some design law—it is sometimes works differently in practice from ours.

Note: Compensation for Infringement

The usual procedure in any action for infringement is that the issue of liability is decided first: only if the plaintiff wins does the issue of how much compensation the defendant must pay him arise. The successful plaintiff has then a choice: to be compensated according to the damage the infringement has done to his own business, or, instead, to have paid over to him the profits made by the infringer from the infringement. In either case, only the damage suffered or profits made in the six years immediately prior to the issue of the writ in the action and since the issue of the writ can be awarded. In exceptional cases, where the court for some reason disapproves of the plaintiff's conduct, profits can be refused, but damages can be refused only in special cases discussed below. Of course, neither problem may arise in some cases—for example, where the infringer merely made samples of an infringing article to see what would happen.

What happens in practice is this: the defendant must, if the plaintiff asks, make a preliminary disclosure of his infringing activities so that the plaintiff can make an informed choice about whether to take damages or profits (*Island Records*, 1995). The court orders a corresponding investigation. Before the investigation takes place (before, therefore, the plaintiff and defendant have seen each other's books in detail and sometimes at all), the infringer usually makes an offer (he may even have made this offer earlier, before the issue of liability was determined). If the plaintiff accepts, well and good; if the plaintiff refuses, the investigation takes place, but at the plaintiff's risk as to costs. If the amount found due is less than was offered, the plaintiff pays for the investigation; if it is more, the infringer pays. Normally, the infringer pays "into court" (into an official bank account) the amount offered.

Damages

If the plaintiff elects to have damages, the court orders an inquiry into just how and how much the infringement has injured the plaintiff. There is an exception to this, however, in the case of patents, designs and copyright where an infringer can escape the payment of damages if, at the time of the infringement, he was not aware, and had no reasonable grounds for supposing, that the monopoly infringed existed. (Such innocence is not unknown in patent and design cases: it is rare in copyright cases, since most "works" of recent origin are pretty well bound to be copyright and the infringer who copies them ought to have known that. Note that in any case, the infringer who goes on infringing after warning can no longer be innocent. Any manufacturer, is unlikely to have an innocence defence because manufacturers are expected to make a reasonable check via the Patent Office that what they want to do is all right.)

As to the measure of damages, the plaintiff is entitled to exact compensation for any monetary damage he has actually suffered that can be fairly attributed to the infringement. Thus, if an infringing book or machine has sales of so many, the author or inventor will have lost so many royalties. A plaintiff who is a manufacturer or publisher can ask the court to assume (unless the infringer can show that this was not so) that each infringing sale has cost him a sale, and so lost him the profit on a sale. There may be other heads too: the owner of a trade or service mark that is infringed may have to pay for additional advertising to restore the position; the owner of an infringed patent or design may be forced, whilst waiting for the action to be tried, to reduce profit margins in order to retain any share of the market; a patentee may have lost sales of spare parts or other goods, which normally are expected to follow the sale of a patented machine—so-called "convoyed goods" (*Gerber* 1997). All that can go in, or the matter may be approached in a different way: pirating of a copyright work may render the work valueless, or passing-off may partly or wholly destroy a goodwill.

Damages may be assessed by estimating the value of the copyright before and after the infringement and taking the difference. Some cases are complicated of course; but it is seldom difficult to make a rough estimate of the sum likely to be involved. The key question, when dealing with a manufacturer-plaintiff, is: what is his profit on a sale?

In the case of particularly serious infringements of copyright, the court may award a plaintiff additional damages. In deciding whether they are appropriate, particular regard must be had to the flagrancy of the infringement and any benefit accruing to the defendant by reason of the infringement. One example of a situation in which such damages might be awarded is where a journal publishes material believing that the profits (or enhancement of reputation) to be gained from publication would exceed the compensation that a plaintiff would be likely to recover.

Profits

When it comes to taking an account of profits, it is the infringer's profits that matter, not the plaintiff's. They are harder to assess. For one thing, it is difficult to judge the extent to which (in assessing the profit from infringement) that particular part of the business can properly be loaded with overheads, or even promotion expenses. In addition it is the profits from infringement that matter, and they may or may not be separable from other matters giving rise to profits. For example, a book of which only part infringes; or a stocking, of which all that was patented was the way the toe was made. It may be very difficult to say what part of the profit is attributable to that. It is often even harder for a plaintiff to guess what the answer is going to be before he has seen the defendant's books in fine detail. Accordingly, it is usually too risky to ask for an account of profits and it is seldom asked for in practice. Not always, however. Suppose that the inventor of the stocking toe can say: "Making the toe my way saves, on average, per dozen pairs of stockings, so many minutes of operatives' time at so much an hour"—then an estimate of the profit from the invention is directly available for comparison with estimates of damages before the plaintiff makes his election.

In copyright cases, innocence is no defence to a claim for profits. In other cases, it probably usually is a defence.

Note: Self-help in Copyright Infringement

There is a partial self-help remedy for copyright infringement only to be exercised with great caution. This is in addition to the inspection and discovery orders referred to above. After notifying the local police station, a copyright owner can seize infringing copies found exposed or immediately available for sale (such as in a street market). Adequate notice must be left for the alleged infringer to challenge the seizure in the courts. An alternative, and safer route, is to apply to court for an order that the offending articles be delivered up.

Note: Exclusive Licensees

An exclusive licensee is someone who is given rights under a patent or copyright exercisable *to the exclusion of the right holder* as well as anyone else. They are given special rights to sue. In the case of copyright and patents, an exclusive licensee of a copyright or the patent has concurrent rights with the right holder to sue and can pursue an action as if he or she were the copyright owner or patentee. There are certain formalities (registration at the patent office) that must be observed in the case of exclusive patent licensees in order not to lose rights to damages. A licensee of a registered trade mark can, unless his license says not, sue, but he or she must first call upon the proprietor to do so. If the proprietor does not take action within two months, the registered user can sue. In each case, the proprietor of the right must be joined into the proceedings but the court can dispense with this requirement in the case of copyright.

2. PATENT, COPYRIGHT OR DESIGN?

In considering protection of a new product against imitation, the first question is whether the case calls for patenting, can be left to copyright or design right, or is one of the special cases where design registration is advisable

Patents

A patent is granted to protect an article that is essentially better in some way than what was made before, or for a better way of making it. The monopoly a patent gives can extend to any other improved article or process that is better for the same reasons as that on which the patent is based. In an extreme case, a patent can be wide enough and represent a big enough advance over earlier ideas to give its owner a complete monopoly of an industry. For instance, there have been patents giving for a time a monopoly of telephones, a monopoly of pneumatic tyres or a monopoly of transistors. Very few patents are as important as that, but the existence of almost any patent (if it is, or is thought to be valid) will make it necessary for a competitor to do design work or even major research of his own rather than copy the actual product he wishes to imitate.

When patents suffice

Whether in a particular case the law of patents can give a manufacturer the protection he needs, depends mainly on three things: how new his product is, how important it is, and for how long he needs protection. The degree of novelty will decide whether he can get a patent, and if so how wide a monopoly this patent may be made to give him. The importance of the product will decide how much trouble it will be worth a competitor taking to get over the monopoly and how big a risk of legal attack a competitor will be prepared to face. The time factor may decide whether it is practicable to carry out the design or research work needed to avoid a monopoly whose validity cannot safely be challenged.

If, then, a manufacturer needs freedom from competition while he builds up a new business of substantial size, only a patent of unusually wide scope with a really important invention behind it will do: any ordinary patent could be got over by

18

competitors long before the business was firmly established. If what is wanted is a monopoly in a new line of goods not of great importance, a patent of comparatively narrow scope should suffice, for it will usually be less trouble for competitors to produce something different than to risk trouble with patents. In intermediate cases, it may be very hard to get proper protection: where goods are markedly more successful than what was made before without being very strikingly different, it is doubtful whether any patent can prevent imitation. This point is important and will be considered more fully in the course of the next two chapters.

Designs, Registered and Unregistered

Design rights are basically about rights over the shapes or decoration of articles. There are no less than four different sorts of right.

Unregistered design right

Unregistered design right is a useful short-term means of protection for designs for industrial articles. Like copyright, it arises without the need for any special registration or application. Although free in the sense of no official fees, a sensible designer will incur the internal costs of keeping records of all stages of the design process. This will include all drawings, models or prototypes, as well as records as to who did what and, if they are employees, their employment contracts, and if freelance, the terms of engagement and preferably a proper assignment of all rights in the design. Like copyright, unregistered design right does not give a complete monopoly, it only prevents copying, so if others come up with the same design independently they cannot be stopped. Almost unbelievably, there are now two sorts of unregistered design right, one arising under our own Copyright, Designs and Patents Act 1988 and the other under an EU Regulation.

Registration of designs

The registration of a design involves some expense and must be done before the design is shown to anyone other than in strictest confidence. But sometimes it could be worthwhile. In particular, the sort of design that someone else would be sure to come up with fairly soon may call for registration, to deal with competitors who reach the same design independently. A copyright is not infringed except by actual copying, but a registered design (if validly registered) is infringed by anyone using the same design even if he thought of it independently. Inevitably, though, it is much easier to persuade a court that someone else's design is the same as yours if you can show that he actually copied it. Unbelievably (again!), there are two sorts of registered design, British and EU with minor differences between them.

Copyright

Copyright is principally designed to protect literary, artistic, and musical works as well as other products of what may loosely be called the entertainment industry—films, sound recordings, broadcasts and the like. It arises automatically as soon as a work is physically recorded, without the need for any formalities, application or registration. (Some people think that "to copyright" a work, you have to put a little "c" in a circle on it but this is not so.) Copyright had an important role to play in protecting industrial designs, but at the same time as the introduction of the unregistered design right, this was much diminished.

Copyright gives a right to prevent copying. It does not give a complete monopoly in the sense that a patent does.

Computer software

One thinks of copyright as mainly relevant to the "creative industries"—artistic and literary works. But there are other kinds of work of a more functional nature that attract copyright protection—of which the most important kind is probably computer programs. Computer programs are, in general, copyright; and the copyright is infringed both when a listing of the program is copied (copied as a listing, or recorded as a runnable program) and when an object-code or assembly-code version is reproduced. Programming techniques, as distinct from actual programs, call for patent protection: neither are programs as such supposed to be patentable, but ingenious patent agents have found ways in which this can be done—so far, anyway. There is an ongoing debate about whether the exception to patentability of computer programs should be removed. The Americans do not have it, but there is not much evidence that having programs patentable has done any good—except, of course, to lawyers and perhaps the big companies such as IBM and Microsoft.

Periods of Protection

The periods of protection given by patents, copyrights and design registrations are all different.

Patents

A patent lasts—so long as renewal fees are paid—for 20 years from the date when the full specification of the invention is filed at the Patent Office (this need not be the date of first application for a patent). Patent protection, however, does not become fully effective until the Patent Office grants it, although once granted, damages can be had for the period between publication of the specification (to 18 months from the date when the patent is applied for). How long it takes to grant depends partly on the applicant (how quickly he responds to queries from the Office) but mainly on the Office. In this respect, the British Office is much faster than the European. But whichever Office one uses, patenting of a quickly produced and short-lived line of goods will normally be useless: the patent may have lost its importance before it comes fully into force.

Of course, the delay in publication may sometimes be an advantage, for the invention can be kept secret until publication date.

Copyright

Copyright in an artistic work arises when the work is made so that the owner of the copyright gets immediate protection and there is no period of waiting for registration. In general, the period of copyright is the life of the author plus 70 years, but there are many exceptions.

Unregistered design right

UK design right lasts for at most 15 years from the year in which the design was made. But it expires after 10 years if the design is first marketed within the first five years of the life of the design right. Also, five years after first marketing by the designer, it is possible to apply for a compulsory licence. An EU unregistered design right lasts for three years from first marketing of the product.

UK *registered designs*

The registration procedure for a design may take about six months, and until then there is no registration and no protection. (So, with articles that are very quick and easy to copy—many Christmas "must-have" toys for example—registration ought to be applied for some six months before they are first shown to the trade, and then copying can be stopped at once.) The registration lasts for five years from the application, and can be kept alive on payment of further fees for four further five-year periods, 25 years in all. Few design owners find this worth doing.

EU *registered designs*

EU registered designs also last for 25 years on payment of renewal fees.

Registered trade marks

Registered trade marks last indefinitely, provided renewal fees are paid. They can be lost, however, if they are not used (see later).

"Imitations" and Copying

In an action for infringement of a patent or a design registration, it makes, in theory, no difference whether infringing goods are copied from those of the owner of the patent or design, or the makers of the infringements worked entirely on their own. In practice, a defendant who has copied is always more likely to lose the action; but in theory the only questions to be decided are first: whether the patent or design registration is a valid one; and, second, whether the monopoly given by it is wide enough to cover the alleged infringement. Even if the "infringer" did not know of the existence of the patent or registration concerned, this will not make any difference to the giving of an injunction against him; nor even in most cases to his liability to pay damages and to pay the costs of the action. In an action based on copyright, the position is different: the action will only succeed if it can be shown that the alleged infringement was copied (directly or indirectly) from the copyright work.

It follows that a new product, developed entirely by the staff of the company that makes it, may well be an infringement of patent or registered design rights belonging to a competitor. Throughout this book, when we speak of "imitations" we mean to include such independently developed products. In the case of registered designs, the risk is not usually very serious and can be easily avoided by a proper search. The risk of innocent infringement of patents, however, in any industry where there is appreciable technical progress will usually be serious if the new product is noticeably different from the old. There is no way of avoiding this risk except thorough acquaintance with or thorough search of all existing patents in the branches of industry concerned. In fields such as electronics, these may number thousands. No attempt is made in this book to suggest any other way, and discussions in later chapters on avoiding patents refer only to patents whose existence is already known. A thorough search of a field of any size is difficult and rather expensive. A good patent agent will do it as cheaply as it can be done—and not even a genius can find patents until they are published—so you are always at risk against an inventor who is slightly ahead of you.

The essence of a patent is that the inventor gets a monopoly in return for full disclosure of his invention in the specification which he files at the Patent Office and the Patent Office publishes. (These published specifications are an extremely valuable source of information in many fields; in some fields they are almost the only reliable source of information about recent developments.) Sometimes, however, technical knowledge is best protected by not publishing it at all. Even where an invention is patented, those who work it soon acquire special knowledge of how to work it. The law will sometimes protect such unpublished information by way of an action for breach of confidence. This is discussed in Chapter 24.

PART II

PROTECTING THE PRODUCT

3. PATENTS AND HOW TO GET THEM

The European System of Patent Law

The modern patent system

In order to understand patent law properly, it is helpful to understand a bit about the current system for getting patent protection. The current European system of patent law started in 1978. Its basis was harmonisation of the patent laws of different European countries. Until then each country had its own patent office and own independent laws. By the EPC (European Patent Convention) of 1973, the participating countries (now 26, and not just EU countries and with expansion planned) agreed to bring their own laws into conformity with the Convention and to set up a common system for granting patents. Each country then enacted a new national patent law to bring it in line with the EPC. Our own Patents Act 1977 was part of that process. No country was willing to give up its own patent office and so a compromise was reached.

An inventor can apply for his patent either through a national patent application ("the national route") or through the EPC route. This latter route involves an application to the EPO ("European Patent Office") in Munich, the inventor choosing ("designating") the European countries in which he wants a patent and paying fees accordingly. Subject to one complication (so-called "oppositions"—see below), once a patent is granted by the EPO it takes effect in each designated country just as if it had been granted by that country's national patent office. We call a patent granted by this route a "European Patent (UK)" but it is not, as its name may suggest, really European. It is a British patent with corresponding sister patents in other European countries. There is no common European patent court and you can get different results when the "same" patent is litigated in different countries. This is not just because the facts might come out differently in different courts; there is no "top" patent court for Europe, and so the views of the "top" courts of each country as to what the EPC actually means can, and do, differ. Most notably this is the case in relation to the rules for deciding what the scope of a patent is (see below).

We should also mention the PCT ("Patent Co-operation Treaty"). This is procedural only: although an application made by this route is called an "international application", it in fact leads to parallel national patents in different countries. An application is made to our own Patent Office or the EPO, the office checks formalities and then sends the application to the appropriate searching office for that type of invention (this will usually be a foreign office). If the applicant wants (he generally will), the searching office will reach preliminary conclusions on novelty and obviousness. Some countries' patent offices are apt to accept these. Thus the applicant is able to get a fairly early indication of how good his patent might be, and, if things do not look good, quit before he has spent too much money. If all is well, the application is then passed to the patent offices of the countries where he wants patents and proceeds as ordinary applications there. The system is administered by WIPO ("World Intellectual Property Organisation," a UN agency) in Geneva. The procedure is complex (with some risk, therefore, of things going wrong) but patent agents have now got used to it and it is increasingly being used. Sometimes it has financial advantages: for instance, it treats all the EPO countries as one, which saves fees at an early stage. They have to be paid later, of course, but then the application may never get that far. Most countries are now parties to the PCT.

More ambitious plans for the internationalisation of patent law exist. Until March 2004, one seemed actually to be about to happen, nearly 30 years since the first, unimplemented Treaty for it. This was the plan for a single EU patent. Originally proposed in the Community Patent Convention of 1975, talks were on and off for many years. In March 2003 the EU took the plunge and decided to create an EU patent—by 2010. There are real problems with making such a system, for instance, the question of a competent court to administer the law outside national systems of law (called "judicial arrangements")—and questions of language. Politicians agreed a basic framework in March 2003. There was to be a European Patent Court (staffed by experienced patent lawyers assisted by court assessors), and an appeal court. The court was to be based in Luxembourg but would have the power to sit elsewhere in Europe. The patents themselves were to be in one of the three basic languages of the EPO (English, French or German). But the claims would have to be translated into all EU official languages (20 after enlargement). The politicians may have liked their "common political approach" but industry did not. Major companies said they would not use the system. One of the problems was that the defendant had to be sued in his language—scarcely attractive if he is Hungarian and you are Italian, for instance. In March 2004, a failure to agree some of the detail (*e.g.* what happens if the claims are mistranslated) halted the project. This may mean that another idea, the European Patent Litigation Protocol ("EPLP") may be taken forward. Under this, just those countries interested in forming a common court for themselves would do so. They could make their own rules about languages and courts. The scope for petty difficulties would be much reduced—and a system could be created which industry would accept. Finally, we should mention another plan under discussion in Geneva at WIPO: a world treaty for bringing the laws of different countries (principally the USA, Europe and Japan) more into line with each other. This keeps bumping into the fact that Americans want a "first to invent" rule (as they have at home) whereas the rest of the world works on a "first to file" rule.

What route, European or British?

Since he can get a patent here either via the EPO in Munich or via the British Patent Office (in Wales), an inventor can choose which system to use. Indeed he can, initially, choose both, though once the EPO grants a patent with the UK as a designated country, any British patent disappears. A number of factors will influence the inventor's choice of route. He can possibly use the "international route" of the PCT rather than applying directly to the EPO or British Office.

First, cost; obviously there are official fees. Official fees are not the only factor, however. If one uses the EPO, one can use just one patent agent. Moreover there is no need in the EPO at an early stage for translations. The application can be filed in just one of the official languages (English, French or German) and the whole application proceeds in that language. Only later, when and if the patent is granted, is there need for translation into other European languages (there are proposals to limit the need for this). If one uses the national route, then translations are needed from the beginning of applications for protection abroad that will be, under the International Convention (mentioned in the next chapter), a year from the initial application. Generally speaking, if a patent is wanted in more than three countries, then the EPO is cheaper. Three countries is about break-even. The following is a rough indication of cost for a reasonably simple-to-explain, invention. A patent agent's fees for an initial draft would be about £2,000. Then come official fees along with further agent's fees depending on what happens. In the UK there is no fee for just filing the application but to go all the way to grant, the official fees amount to £700. In the EPO, official fees to grant (for all EU countries) are £3,000 to EPO grant—it is less if some countries are dropped. There will be translation fees on top (which can be rather large) if the patent is granted—and also further agent's fees along the way, typically about £2,000. Patent agents have devised ingenious ways of delaying the time when fees need to be paid. This can be important, since it gives the inventor more time to see whether what he has got is actually a good idea commercially and whether his patent is likely to be any good.

Next, speed; the British Office is markedly faster than the EPO. For instance, in the case of the hepatitis-C testing kit, both our High Court and Court of Appeal had heard the case (and held the patent valid) within two-and-a-half years of grant by the British Office. The corresponding EPO application (made at the same time) was still pending several years later and the opposition in the EPO was still going some eight years after grant. Much the same has occurred in many other important cases. The lesson is obvious: if you think you will need to enforce your monopoly soon, go British.

Third, validity and scope; a patent drawn up to suit the practice of one country will seldom be fully suited to others. So international applications (for the whole world) using a single specification for all countries may not be as good as individually tailored applications.

Fourth, there is the "eggs in one basket" versus the "gap in protection" problem. If the inventor goes the European route and something goes wrong (*e.g.* the Office holds the patent invalid and an appeal fails), then he loses for all designated countries (unless he has also gone via national routes also). This is particularly important in relation to "oppositions" in the EPO—see below. On the other hand, if he goes only via national routes then, if the application fails in one country, he will have a gap in his European protection. If he goes via both routes, it will cost a lot more, but he will have the maximum flexibility and security against things going wrong, even though he will ultimately have to choose between the patent granted by the EPO and that granted by the British Office.

Who Applies

The right to apply for a patent belongs to the owner of the invention—the inventor himself, or anyone who can claim the invention from him. Other people can join in the application.

Most inventions are made by employees, as part of their job:

in such cases, the employer owns the invention (see Note at the end of this chapter) and can apply to patent it, although he needs the inventor's signature (unless the invention is a foreign one, and he is patenting it here under the International Convention mentioned below). Or the inventor can make the application (in which case he will be a sort of trustee of it for his employer); or they may both apply together (when the inventor will still be a sort of trustee of his half-share).

The Specification and the Claims

The applicant must file at the Patent Office a document called a specification. This must contain a description of the apparatus or process or article, or whatever is to be the subject of the patent. It must contain instructions that will enable a skilled person to work the process, or make the apparatus or article as the case may be. Often patents will contain a series of drawings as well. Most important of all, it must contain what are called "claims": that is, statements defining the precise scope of the rights of monopoly that the patent will give. There is only one way of finding out whether the owner of a patent can prevent the manufacture and sale of a particular imitation of his patented product, and that is by looking up his specification and seeing whether the words of the "claims" describe that imitation. Note that the form of the specification which matters is the "B" specification. This is the one with "B" after the patent number. The specification with an "A" after the number is the application as filed by the patentee. In other words the "A spec." is what he asked for, the "B spec." what he got.

Claims

Claims are central to a patent—they defines the territory that is reserved to the patentee. Claims are usually written in special jargon (to make them as general as possible without being invalid), and a good deal of practice is needed to understand exactly what they are saying. Likewise, a good deal of practice is needed to write them. The heart of a patent agent's craft lies in claim-drafting.

Patents usually have several claims. These are a bit like concentric or overlapping circles with the largest territory or most general claim first of all. This is so that if the broader claims are held invalid, the patentee can fall back on narrower claims. So Claim 1 might read: "1. A motor vehicle powered by an internal combustion engine". Claim 2 might read "2. A

motor vehicle according to Claim 1 wherein the internal combustion engine is turbo charged". Claim 3 might read "3. A
motor vehicle according to Claim 3 [2] which has four wheels."
Some patents have product claims (to a machine or a chemical,
for example). Some have process claims (to a method such as a
chemical synthesis process). Some have both.

The reader is invited to read a few real patents—which are
available online at the Patent Office (or EPO) website to get a
feel for them and how they are structured.

Most patent disputes include an argument about the meaning
(what the lawyers call "construction") of the claims. Generally
the patentee says they are wide enough to cover the thing he is
complaining about, and the defendant denies it. Often the
defendant adds that if they are wide enough to catch him, they
also cover something old or obvious and so are bad. We in
Britain are reasonably careful about patent claims. After all, they
are there for telling people not only what they cannot do but
also, by converse, what they can. It is the patentee (or at least his
patent agent) who draws the line in the first place. Although
foreign countries have claims in their patents, and in theory
might seem to use them as we do, this is sometimes not so in
practice.

Parties to the EPC are indeed supposed to treat claims in
exactly the same way and there is a special "Art.69 and
Protocol" that tries to achieve this. But all they say is that the
claims should be construed in the context of the description and
drawings (which we have always done anyway) and not used as
a "guideline." Our House of Lords has just confirmed that it is
only the meaning of the words in context which defines the
monopoly (Kirin – Amgen, 2004). In practice it seems that some
mainland European countries still treat claims rather more
liberally than we do, particularly in relation to so-called "equivalents" (*i.e.* the court making the patent cover something, which
is not but which is very close to, what the language of the patent
claim, read in context, means). An amendment to the Protocol
will come into force shortly. It says courts are to take equivalents
into account in applying Art.69. Typically, this being a diplo-
matic comprise, it does not say how. For instance, you could take
the view that if a patentee uses a specific term ("screwed", say)
then he must have meant what he said and intended to leave out
other methods of fixing *e.g.* nailed. Or you could take the
opposite view. The Americans also have a more liberal doctrine
of equivalents. But no-one seems to know exactly where it is
going. In recent years the uncertainty it leads to is causing the US

courts to apply it more and more restrictively. It may end up as just covering equivalents unforeseeable at the time of the application.

Two examples

The patent in *Catnic v Hill & Smith* (1982) was for a "box lintel"—a building component for going over doors or windows. Old lintels were made of reinforced concrete. The Catnic idea was to use a hollow steel box appropriately shaped. The patent claim called for two horizontal plates "substantially parallel" to each other, an inclined support member, and a "second rigid support member *extending vertically*" from one horizontal plate to the other. The row was over the meaning of "extending vertically". What the defendant did was to use a support member that was six degrees off true vertical but that was good enough to work. He said that the claim meant true vertical—emphasising his point by contrasting the way the claim dealt with the horizontal plates. It was enough for these to be "substantially parallel" whereas the word "vertical" was not qualified. The House of Lords had no difficulty in dismissing this argument as a lawyer's quibble. A practical person would regard any member vertical enough to work as "vertical." The only wonder of the case is how the Court of Appeal ever thought otherwise.

On the other hand, in *Improver v Remington* (1989), the patent was for a device for removing hair from women's legs—in the refined language of the patent, a depilator. The patentee had the idea of using a helical spring bent in a curve. One end was fixed to a small high-speed electric motor and the other to a fixed bearing. The spring rotated at high speed and its windings opened and closed rapidly, catching and pulling out the hairs. The patent claim called for a "helical spring." The wily defendant substituted for this a rubber rod with transverse slits. When this was rotated the slits opened and closed just as in the case of the windings of the helical spring. But, both here and in Hong Kong, the courts held there was no infringement. True it was that the rod had all the necessary properties of the helical spring (it was appropriately "bendy" and "slitty"), but it was not a helical spring. To find infringement it would have been necessary to ignore the word "helical" altogether, or regard it as no more than a kind of shorthand for a component having the necessary properties.

Interestingly, the corresponding German court took a different view, for in Germany there is a doctrine of infringement by exact and obvious equivalents of items specified in a claim. Quite how that was reconciled with the requirement that the invention be specified in the claim we are not sure and the Germans have tightened up somewhat recently. From the point of view of a student of comparative patent law (apart, of course, from the lawyers involved), it is a great pity that this case was not fought all over the world because its facts are easy to understand and the legal approaches of different countries would have been easy to study. From the point of view of a British lawyer or patent agent, the case is an excellent example of the danger of being too specific in the widest patent claim. If it had said in Claim 1 "means for removal of hair" and by a Claim 2 "wherein said means is a helical spring" there would have been no difficulty. But then it is always easy to be wise after the event. Some good patent agents do favour the "means for" approach. It forces the patentee to think about the function of each item making up his invention. On the other hand, some patent offices (*e.g.* the US) do not like this type of approach, holding that it is apt to give the patentee more than he really invented.

Securing Priority

Preparation of a specification is usually a long job, and it is often important that the patent should be applied for at the earliest possible moment. But the Act allows the applicant to secure a right of priority by filing an informal application in the first place (here or abroad); he then has a year to prepare and make a proper application. So long as the invention is well enough described in the original application to "support" the claims of the final one, the novelty of his invention will be judged as of the earlier date. The original application can simply be dropped: but there are snags; see "Delay in application" below. If it is dropped, the only penalty for getting the original specification wrong is loss of priority. The specification of the application that is finally proceeded with, however, not only has to pass detailed scrutiny by expert examiners at the Patent Office but also must be proof against the destructive criticism of hostile lawyers and experts: for if the patent is ever the subject of legal proceedings, the wording of the specification may determine the validity and scope of the patent.

Just what is necessary for an earlier specification to "support" the claims of a later one is not clear. As is coming to be more usual in IP legislation, the draftsman has been careful not to use words that mean anything very definite, either to a lawyer or to anyone else.

Patentability

Not every bright idea is patentable. A patentable invention has to be "capable of industrial application"—including exploitation in agriculture, but excluding plant or animal varieties and "essentially biological processes for the production of animals or plants". Microbiological processes, though, can be patented; they are rather important, since many antibiotics are made by fermentation, as are many drinks. Although genes as they are in nature cannot be patented, stretches of DNA containing the essential code can, a matter of controversy both because some of the patents are particularly important and because it is normally impossible to design round. Medical and veterinary treatments are not patentable; but drugs are (even if the materials used are old; see Note to Ch.5).

There is also a list of matters excluded from patentability as being essentially intellectual: scientific theories; mathematical methods; computer programs; aesthetic creations of all sorts. It used to be possible to "dress up" a claim to a computer program as some sort of device claim (a computer organised to run the program) but this has become harder. For instance, a chip containing a novel and inventive program for finding square roots was held unpatentable (*Gale*, 1991). The EPO has evolved a test: whether there is a "technical effect" for patentability, but it is not clear what this means. Borderline cases in this area will always be improved by ingenious framing of claims, another reason why the services of an experienced patent agent can be so valuable. Currently, there is a big debate within Europe about computer programs and patents. Should we follow the American "anything goes" approach or should we stick to our exclusion or even tighten it up? Another area where controversy rages now is the patentability of genetically engineered animals (there is no problem over bacteria). The EPO has taken ages over the point in the "Harvard mouse" case—a mouse that develops cancer so it can be used in cancer research. The EPO has finally (July 2004) decided in favour of patentability in this area in principle, although, because of the odd practice of not giving reasons at the time, we do not yet know why. Astonishingly, the patent was applied for in 1984 and took until 1992 to be granted. Then the EPO "opposition" ran until 2004. The patent was very nearly expired. For the particular case, the delay hardly matters because the mouse was a commercial flop, but more generally the case shows the EPO "opposition" procedure at its worst. Even though the EPO has now decided the point, the strenuous

35

opposition means that the argument is far from over—it could for instance go on in national courts as well as in the political arena. The American office granted the Harvard mouse patent years ago.

Search, Publication, Examination

If it is intended to proceed with a patent application, the next step is to request (and pay for) a preliminary examination and a search of earlier patents. The preliminary examination goes to the formal correctness of the application and specification; the search, in the first place at least, will be through earlier published British specifications for the same sort of invention. At the same time, the application and its specification will be published, probably 18 months after filing. This means that if the inventor wants to avoid publication (as he may: see below, under "Delay in application"), the application must be withdrawn.

The next stage is for the applicant to request (and, as usual, pay for) a full examination. Here the examiner considers whether what is claimed is the sort of thing that is patentable at all; whether the specification is clear and complete enough to enable a skilled reader to work the invention; and above all, whether, when compared with what appears in earlier specifications, the invention appears new and not obvious. It is reasonably easy to decide whether a supposed invention is new—the examiner has only to read the claims of the specification and look in the earlier documents for anything falling within those claims. Deciding whether an invention is obvious, on the other hand, is always difficult, and with nothing to go by except what appears in patent specifications becomes almost impossible. Naturally, then, examination for obviousness produces some odd objections: the only thing an examiner can do is turn the application down and see whether the applicant's patent agent can produce a convincing answer to the objection.

When examining for obviousness, the examiner considers only earlier specifications already published at the date when the application was filed (or the date of an earlier application giving priority, if there is one). But in considering whether the invention is actually new, he must look also at specifications published after but already on file at that date: in relation to novelty only, these are treated as if already published. This makes things complicated, see below.

36

Delay in Application

If a reasonable specification was filed with the application for a patent (either the application actually proceeded with, or an earlier one made here or abroad—see above, "Successive applications") nothing after that counts in deciding on the validity of the patent. This is the main reason for getting an application in as soon as enough is known about the invention for a specification to be drawn up. If there is delay, some competitor, here or abroad, working along the same sort of lines may in the meantime publish some description, or market something, or make some patent application, that will make it difficult or impossible to get a valid patent at all. Or the inventors themselves may let out enough information to invalidate their own patent: by samples shown to the trade perhaps, or by some note in a trade journal. Too often, inventors let the cat out of the bag too soon. Even a single non-confidential disclosure to one person anywhere in the world is enough to destroy a subsequent patent. A single use from which it is possible, without undue effort or skill, to work out the nature of the invention is also enough.

There is a particularly acute problem in the case of inventions which need some sort of public trial. There is no special protection for such trials, so if you can work out the nature of the invention from such a trial there will be prior disclosure. Public trial, which does not enable a skilled person to know the secret of the invention is, in itself, all right (*Quantel,* 1991). There are proposals to ameliorate this rule—so that the inventor has a "grace period" following disclosure by him in which he can file for a patent—his prior disclosure not counting for this purpose. The trouble with this would be uncertainty. The Americans have a similar (and even more generous) scheme in place. There, provided an inventor applies within a year from the time he has "reduced his invention to practice", no intervening disclosure counts. The rules leads to much litigation, quite apart from meaning that trade rivals may not know for several years (the one-year period plus office processing time) about the patent.

The problem of priority can be dealt with (as has been explained) by getting on file an informal patent application that is good enough to support the claims in a proper application filed in due course. But getting priority in this way will not stop a competitor working along similar lines—and it is remarkable how often competitors are found to have been working along similar lines—from getting his own patent. If a competitor has a patent covering the same thing, it may be impossible to work the invention without a licence from him. To invalidate rival patents, it is necessary either to have made the invention public or to have filed a patent application (in this country, or an international or European one "designating" this country), which is in due course published. But it will seldom be safe to allow publication of an application intended only to give priority: it might anticipate the inventor's own later application too. So: not only should the first, informal application be filed as soon as practicable, the formal application should be filed as soon as practicable too.

Examination Procedure

If an examiner sees an objection to the specification or the claims (or considers the whole thing unpatentable), he writes to the applicant's patent agent stating his objection. The applicant must show that he is wrong, or alter the specification or claims, or abandon the application. (If he and the agent cannot agree, the matter will go to a Principal Examiner, and if necessary the applicant can appeal from him to the Patents Court.) This is for a British application. The position is similar in the EPO, the appeal going to a "Board of Appeal".

Grant and Revocation after Grant

If and when all objections have been overcome, the applicant must pay another fee and the patent will then be granted. Its owner may then start to sue for any infringements that have occurred since that application was published. The patent may still be revoked, however, either by a procedure in the Patents Court or in the Patent Office, if anyone can show (in effect) that it should not have been granted. (Such an attack on the patent is almost certain to be made if the patentee sues for infringement, as part of the defence to the action.). To attack a patent in the Patent Office will be much cheaper than attacking it in the court, mostly because of the different way in which the evidence is provided; but an attack in the Patent Office will often be less likely to succeed and is likely to be slower. In practice, people use the Patents Court or Patents County Court if they want revocation of a patent.

EPO Oppositions

There is one feature of the EPO system which calls for special mention: the misnamed "opposition". Within nine months of grant, anyone can "oppose" the patent in the EPO, that is to say, seek its revocation. If successful, an opposition will knock out the patent everywhere. Unfortunately, the opposition procedure (which has one tier of appeal, where, oddly, fresh arguments and evidence are common) is extraordinarily slow, leaving the fate of the patent or the scope of eventual claims uncertain for many years. (Of course, this may operate to a patentee's advantage —uncertainty often puts competitors off.)

Moreover the procedure is, at least to those used to the Anglo-Saxon system, crude and uncertain. It proceeds almost exclusively on paper with oral hearings seldom lasting more than a day. There is no real method of assessing evidence—assertion of technical fact by an advocate is common and accepted. "I discussed the case with an engineer yesterday and he said . . . " seems to do as well as a sworn statement. There is limited cross-examination and discovery. Quite often, parties are permitted to take the other by surprise at a hearing, for instance, by producing an exhibit "out of the hat." The slowness of the opposition system can have serious effects on enforceability too. In many European countries, the courts will not enforce the patent or hear revocation proceedings whilst there is an opposition pending, although there is the later advantage that considerable respect is given in those countries to a patent which has survived EPO opposition.

Here, our courts will not generally stay proceedings pending determination of an opposition, unless the final result of that opposition (on appeal) is imminent. Moreover, a patent that has survived an EPO opposition is not treated differently from any other patent by our courts, which decide the case using their own judgment on the evidence. The possibility of an EPO opposition is a factor in favour of a national application. Some companies, particularly US companies, avoid the EPO route for patents in Europe precisely because they do not trust the EPO opposition procedure. The EPO has said that it will hurry things up in urgent cases (both before grant or in oppositions). However, to a patentee wanting his patent granted or to an opponent wanting his opposition determined, the Office's sense of urgency seems rather like that of the person who thinks that *mañana* conveys too great a sense of haste.

Cost and Period of Protection

A patent granted by the British Office (in Newport) covers the whole of the UK, and proceedings upon it may be brought in the English, Scottish or Northern Irish courts as may be appropriate.

The patent is kept in force by annual renewal fees, increased from time-to-time to keep pace with inflation, for a total period of 20 years from filing. The inventor has also to pay the fees for filing, search, examination and grant already mentioned. There will also be the modest charges made by the patent agent who drafts the specifications and negotiates with the Patent Office. Foreign patenting will add very greatly to the cost.

Money can of course be saved by not paying renewal fees and letting the patent lapse, but patents that are not kept up for their full term are seldom much use: since all a patent can do is to stop other people using the invention, it will not be of value until the invention has reached the stage where other people want to use it. Few inventions are profitable quickly enough to tempt others to infringement in their first years; indeed, many inventions of importance seem seldom to be very profitable until quite late in the life of any patent covering them. Of course, it is often impossible to tell at the beginning what an invention is likely to be worth and, in doubtful cases, it will be better to take out a patent just in case; even so, the published figures suggest that many useless applications are filed.

Grant and Ownership

Inventors these days are usually employees of some company, and as a rule the company either is entitled to the patent under their service agreements or it buys them out before or soon after the application is filed. Arrangements can be made for the patent to be granted to whoever actually owns it—usually a company—even where the application is made by the actual inventor. Once a patent has been granted, it can be bought and sold much like other property, provided the disposition is made in writing and the transaction is registered at the Patent Office. The name of the current owner can usually be found from the Register, because failure to register could lose him some of his rights. The names of the applicants appear on the printed copies of the specification sold by the Patent Office or made available online.

A sale or other disposition of the patent may be effective in law if made by those whose names appear on the register of proprietors, whether or not it "really" belongs wholly or in part to someone else. If, therefore, the inventor (for example), or the promoters of a company intending to exploit the invention, wish to retain some control over a patent, it may be wise for them to be registered as part proprietors.

Patent Agents

In practice, the work of negotiating with a Patent Office (UK or EPO) is done by patent agents (also called patent attorneys), whose profession it is. They also draw up nearly all specifications and are concerned in nearly all Patent Office proceedings and so on. It is theoretically possible for an inventor to do everything himself without professional help, but if a patent is worth applying for at all, the difference made by practised drafting of the specifications and skilled negotiation with the examiner will be worth far more than a patent agent's fees. Furthermore, current application procedure, both national and international, is so complex that it is best left to experienced professionals. A good patent agent may (literally) be worth his or her weight in gold.

The Grounds on which a Patent may be Declared Invalid

These are of great practical importance. It should always be borne in mind that, while it is generally not too difficult to decide whether a patent is infringed or not, it is often less easy to decide whether a patent is valid: for example, something which looks very complex on first sight may turn out to be obvious to the skilled workers in the particular field (and vice versa). Thus, whenever there is a question of enforcing a patent by court proceedings, the question of validity may be the most important one in the case. It will be seen that while some of the grounds set out below may affect the patent as a whole (insufficiency of instructions, for instance), others affect only certain claims. Where this is so, it is possible for some of the claims to be valid (or even, to be partly valid) although others are invalid. Such a position gives rise to difficult procedural problems, but for most purposes the important question then is: is any claim that has been (or will be) infringed a valid claim? The other claims matter much less.

These are the grounds:

1. Lack of novelty

Lack of novelty means that a claim of the specification includes something that has been "made available to the public." This means that somehow the public have been able to learn what the invention is before the priority date. Most often that is by reading an openly published prior document that clearly describes something in the claim. But there are other ways—for

41

instance blurting it out in a public lecture or even to a single individual (provided it is not in confidence). Selling a product that can, without "undue difficulty" be analysed or dismantled to find out how it works will do. What is not enough is selling a product that cannot be analysed—the public then has access to the product of the invention but not the invention—the idea itself. In the past, public (and even in some cases secret) prior use of any sort was enough to invalidate. But that is no longer so. The prior use or document must "enable the public" to work the invention. Where this is so, in the jargon of patent law, the claim is said to be "anticipated" by the prior publication or prior user (the "prior art").

A couple of further points are worth noting: first it is sufficient if the prior art gives at least one member of the public a means of finding out what the invention is. It does not actually matter whether or not anyone did. Thus, in one case a patent for an invention about portable traffic lights was lost simply because the inventor tried his invention out at night at a junction, and it was shown that a skilled person could have worked out what the invention was by standing around and observing what happened —although of course no-one did stand out all night doing that (*Lux v Pike*, 1993). Nor does it matter whether the member of the public is here or abroad.

2. Obviousness

Obviousness means that the claim includes something that was obvious, at its priority date, in view of what had already been made available to the public. This ground is also called "lack of inventive step". It is one of the most important yet one of the most uncertain grounds. In principle, it is only common sense that any variant of an old idea that is more or less self-evident does not deserve a patent. The trouble is that in practice it is often very difficult to decide after the event (sometimes years after the event) what would have been obvious to the "skilled man"—an ordinary worker in the field. A lot depends on the court's feeling as to whether the invention was a good idea. Sometime the patentee wins by asking, "if it was obvious, why was it not done before?" That is particularly effective if, once the invention was made, lots of money was made from it.

3. Insufficiency

Insufficiency means that the specification does not disclose the invention clearly enough and completely enough for it to be performed by a person skilled in the art. It is possible for there to be insufficient instructions to carry some claims into effect, but sufficient for others; but, generally speaking, a specification tends to be sufficient for all claims or insufficient for all. It has now been decided that this ground can apply where the "disclosure" is not as wide as the claim—so that you cannot perform some part of the claim (*Biogen*, 1997). This is one of the ways the courts have dealt with the problem of a claim that is too wide—where the patentee has claimed more than he has really invented. The other way is to use a combination of obviousness and insufficiency in rather a tortuous way—to say that a claim that covers an obviously desirable thing is obvious unless there are sufficient instructions on all ways as to how to make it. There law here is not particularly satisfactory because it is not often easy to apply these general notions to particular cases. The trouble is that there is no explicit ground of undue width of claim (as there used to be) so the courts have had to concoct one. Likewise when a claim has no meaning at all ("ambiguous") then this ground of invalidity has been pressed into service to invalidate it (Kirin – Amgen 2004).

4. Obtaining

Obtaining means that the patent was granted to someone not entitled to it. This objection is seldom raised—not least because if an invention is stolen and patented the victim usually brings a claim for the patent (or invokes a special procedure before the Patent Office for revocation of that patent and regrant to him). Only the person who is really entitled to the invention can run this ground.

5. Not an invention

The "not an invention" ground means That the alleged invention is not the sort of thing that can be patented at all. This covers things like medical treatment and computer programs as such. As we have said, there is a lot of controversy about the latter ground. Notwithstanding all the talk, in practice it is usually possible to get some sort of a patent that in practice covers a computer program some way or another.

6. Wrongful amendment

There are two sorts of wrongful amendment: that the specification has been altered by amendment so as to disclose something not disclosed in the specification when it was first filed, or has been altered since the patent was granted to make the claims cover something they did not cover before.

Note: Inventions by Employees

Not all inventions made by employees belong to their employer: it depends on circumstances. Unless the employee's service agreement makes some special arrangement more favourable to him — an agreement less favourable to the employee is ineffective, except in relation to inventions made before 1978 — what governs the matter is whether or not it was the employee's job to make that sort of invention. If so, it belongs to the employer (just as a someone may be employed to make boots, which then belong to the employer, not the employee). If not, it belongs to the employee (even though he may have made it in his employer's time and misappropriated his employer's materials for the purpose). There is no halfway house, except by special agreement; so that if the invention does not belong to the employer, the employee can demand a royalty for its use or even refuse permission to use it. Inventions made before the employment began, or after it stopped, do not belong to the employer.

In deciding what the employee's job was, his general position is naturally crucial. An engineering draughtsman, for instance, is normally expected to improve the design he is drawing out if he can (although a radically new idea may be outside the scope of his employment even though sparked off by something connected with his work). A factory hand is not normally expected to invent at all. Directors are generally in a position where anything that might reasonably be connected with the company's business belongs to the company: by and large, a director must never profit at his company's expense. (The English agent of a foreign engineering concern has been held to be in that sort of position, too.)

Sometimes, there is a special agreement, under which an employee-inventor not merely applies for a patent jointly with his employer (which in itself means nothing) but actually owns his share of the patent. Inventors should note (a) that that sort of agreement is best put into writing, and (b) that the owner of a half-share in a patent cannot (unless the agreement specially says so) do anything with it except himself work the patent — something his employer may be able to do but he will not. (Forming a company to do it is not working the patent: the company will need a licence from both patentees.) Such agreements should be vetted by a solicitor — on both sides.

If the employer does particularly well out of a patented invention made by an employee, the employee can apply (to the court, or to the Patent Office) to be awarded a fair share of any "outstanding benefit" the employer has got from the invention: unless the rewarding of employees for that sort of invention is already covered by a collective agreement. People who were employed mainly abroad when they made their inventions cannot apply. In practice, this provision has had little effect until now. One of the problems was that the Act originally spoke of the *patent* rather than the invention being of "outstanding benefit". Thus if an employer merely saved himself some money by using the invention, he had not received any benefit from his patent. The provisions were so unsuccessful that they were amended in 2004 so that inventors can get a reward if their employer gets a benefit from the patent or the invention or both. The Act is shortly to come into force. When it does, we expect claims by inventors to become more significant.

Note: History of Patents

The English patent system, from its earliest foundations in the Middle Ages, has been based on the principle of rewarding education with monopoly. In the fourteenth and fifteenth centuries, grants of letters patent were made to encourage European skilled workers to come to England and teach industrial methods to the (largely agricultural and trading) English. Often, the grant of letters patent was conditional on the grantee providing practical training for a number of native apprentices in the working of the inventions. Until the early seventeenth century, it was very difficult to challenge these monopolies in the courts since to do so was regarded as evidencing a lack of proper respect for the sovereign's authority. The royal prerogative to grant patents was widely abused as a source of crown patronage, and the Statute of Monopolies (1623) confined the legitimate exercise of the prerogative power to grant patents to the true and first inventor in respect of the sole working or making of "any manner of new manufactures . . . which others at the tyme . . . shall not use". It also set a limit to the time for which the monopoly could be granted at 14 years. That statute said that the grant of letters patent shall be permitted provided also that "they be not contrary to the law nor mischievous to the state, by raising prices of [commodities] at home or hurt of trade, or generallie inconvenient".

It was not until the eighteenth century that the specification (*i.e.* the description of the invention) became important as providing the educational function of the patent and also in defining the scope of the monopoly claimed. Until then, the subject matter of the patent was usually described in very broad and general terms and the patentee was probably in a relatively strong position to beat off infringers (for whom the punishment could be imprisonment). During the eighteenth century it was established that the grant of the patent would be made conditional upon the patentee's filing a specification of his invention within six months of grant, which would show that the invention existed, telling the public how to work it, and showing what the claimed invention was. At the time, getting a patent was very expensive—as Dickens so well explained in his cynical (but accurate) description in *The Tale of a Poor Man's Patent* (patents have always been an expensive business—there is nothing new about that). The system whereby a potential patentee had to file a specification upon application for a patent dates from 1852. The official search to determine whether the invention had already been published was introduced in 1905.

4. EXPLOITING PATENTS

Patents Protect a Trade

The essential function of a patent is to keep others out. So, in the case of a manufacturer (or importer) it is an adjunct to a trade. The value of the patent depends on how valuable that trade is—and the mere fact that others cannot compete does not guarantee the patentee a profit or anything of the sort. Whether a patent is valuable depends upon the importance of the underlying invention and how well the patentee can exploit that invention in the market place. So in a sense a manufacturer does not exploit a patent at all—he exploits the invention, relying on the patent to keep that exploitation to himself.

The Importance of Validity

Of the patents that are challenged before the courts, some are found to be invalid. Since most lawsuits about patents cost at least £200,000 per side (and generally a lot more) and the larger part of the cost falls on the loser, this is a serious matter for owners of patent. (The owner of a patent can insure against the risk of having to sue infringers, and some do.) It does not, however, follow that patents are useless; rather this is a measure of success that patents have. It is expensive to challenge the validity of a patent even if the challenge succeeds, and it is hardly ever possible to be sure beforehand that the challenge will succeed. In the ordinary way, therefore, it is a better proposition commercially to make something unarguably outside the "claims" of the patent, than to risk an action for infringement of them. As a rule, it is only the most important patents that are attacked, and even then the attacker will try to find a design that escapes at least the more impressive claims as far as possible. The great majority of patents go through their lives in peace, with nobody really convinced that they are valid, but nobody prepared to take the risk of infringing them. Commercially, they are just as useful as if they had been valid. Thus, even an invalid patent is often valuable enough to make it worthwhile to keep on bluffing until the bitter end. There is a lot of truth in the old adage "a weak patent in strong hands is worth more than a strong patent in weak hands".

Avoiding Patents

By "designing round"

A more serious problem is that of the competitor who avoids infringement of a patent. It is much easier to say why a particular patented device is successful, and what else would be successful when a product using that device has been on the market for some time, than it was when the specification of the patent was drawn up. So the patent agent who makes out the specification must foresee what in up to 20 years' time other manufacturers are likely to want to do, and must frame his "claims" so as to include all these future activities—while at the same time excluding anything that has been published before.

In practice, what he does is to estimate which features of the new product are going to be important to its success, and make his claims cover whatever combinations of those features are not found in the earlier specifications found by the examiner at the Patent Office. If he gets it right, the patent should be valid and fairly hard to "design round". If he is wrong (or some unknown piece of "prior art" is unearthed), it will be found later on either that he has "claimed" something only trivially different from the subject of an earlier patent—in which case, the new patent will be invalid for obviousness), or that he has confined the monopoly to things having some feature that is not essential—in which case, competitors may be able to avoid infringing the patent by omitting that particular feature. Although the courts may disregard features shown not to be practically significant, this cannot be relied on to happen. Indeed, mostly the courts say that the patentee must have regarded the feature as significant, for otherwise he would not have put it into his claim. The more and better information the client gives to the patent agent, the better she can estimate. That is why it is important to get a good patent agent—one who can really understand the technology, who can have the vision to frame claims which are both wide enough and can stand up. A good working relationship with one's patent agent is a valuable asset indeed.

By making something "old"

A list of the earlier specifications considered by the Patent Office examiner when the patent was being prosecuted is published on the patent. Other possible pieces of "prior art" may be found by employing a private searcher. One way of avoiding a patent is to

48

go back to one of these earlier inventions. The owner of the later patent is then in a dilemma: if the rival product is within the "claims" of his specification, then his invention is not sufficiently different from the earlier one and his patent must be invalid. A defendant who says his product is old or an obvious development of what is old is said to be raising a "Gillette" defence, named after an old case (*Gillette v Anglo-American,* 1913). There the defendant's razor closely resembled an old razor and the judges said there was "no patentable, no inventive step" between the defendant's and the old razors.

If the owner of the patent has made a real technical advance and his specification is skilfully drawn, his product should have a sufficient commercial advantage over earlier designs and his patent will protect that advantage. If, however, as so often happens, he is only the first to interest the public in an idea and not the first to make it technically successful, then competition based on earlier designs may be very damaging. *Hallen v Brabantia* (1989) is a good example of this sort of thing. The plaintiff had been the first to put the "non-stick" material PTFE ("Teflon") onto a type of corkscrew called a "self-puller": when you go on turning, the cork rises up out of the bottle. But self-pullers were old and a Frenchman had put PTFE onto another type of corkscrew to help get the screw into the cork. It was obvious thereafter that PTFE would improve the "getting-in" of any kind of corkscrew, including self-pullers. So even though the plaintiff was the first to make PTFE self-pullers commercially attractive, he had no valid monopoly in them. No system of patents can stop competition of this sort: the commercial innovator of this kind must rely upon the commercial advantages of being first, ideally a good trade mark, and helped perhaps by patents on minor features and design rights to make it impossible for rival products to look the same as his.

As ways of avoiding patents go, this method of digging up an old design is reasonably safe and has the advantage in theory that there is no need to do any patent search to see if what is being done is safe. But it is never completely safe. If what is now made is exactly what was made (or described) before the patent, then certainly any claim that covers it must be invalid. Nearly always, though, some alteration in the old design will be needed, if only to make it suitable for production. Then a quite different question arises, whether the changes to the old design were obvious changes to make before the date of the patent. The answer may easily be that they became obvious changes to make only when the owner of the patent had shown that there was a market for something close to the old design. But if that is so, it is possible for the patent to be both valid and infringed.

Most firms will prefer not to take this risk unless the matter is of real commercial importance, so that in the ordinary way the patent will be almost as useful to its owner as if the earlier design had never been published. As we saw in Chapter 2, the value of a patent may depend greatly on its not being too important—like a chess pawn.

Licensing

The general principle

So far we have only considered patent monopolies as a means of keeping imitations off the market. There is another way of exploiting a patent: the grant of licences. If the patent is valid, the manufacture, importation, sale or use of a patented article (or of articles made by a patented process or machine) are each only lawful if the patentee gives permission for them. Such permission is what is known as a "licence". Subject to the exceptions mentioned below, a patentee can charge what he likes for the licence and make what rules he likes for its exercise. For those who do not wish (or cannot afford) to manufacture under the patent themselves, this is the normal way of making money out of a patent.

Permission to use and sell is implied where the patentee made the product himself or licensed its making, but even so the permission may be given subject to express limitations or conditions. Anyone who buys the article knowing of these conditions must either comply with them or risk being sued for infringement of the patent.

Limits on what can be done by way of licensing and exploitation

Not every sort of limitation or condition, though, is allowed. First there are the EU rules about "free circulation": once a patented article has been put on the market anywhere in the EU, by the owner of the patent or with his licence, he cannot stop its subsequent sale anywhere else in the EU. This means, in particular, that although it may be allowable to restrict a licensee to manufacturing under the patent only in one EU country, the patent cannot be used to stop the things he makes being sold throughout the EU. Even a licence to manufacture in a single country only has to comply with some complex and not very comprehensible regulations in order to satisfy the EU.

Next, there are the limits that competition law imposes on what can be done with patents (and other IP rights). Competition law has two sources, EU (for which inter-state trade must be affected) and our own. Our own (in the Competition Act 1998) now broadly follows EU law, although it is enough that trade within the UK may be affected. Very broadly, anti-competitive agreements and abuses of monopoly are caught. A good example would be where a patentee, as a condition of a licence (or the sale of a patented product) required the buyer to purchase wholly unrelated unpatented items from him. This area of the law is complex and often uncertain. Recently, the Court of Appeal has given it a boost, holding that for a really important patent, a refusal to licence on reasonable terms may amount to an abuse of monopoly and that some violations of the EU competition licensing rules may each give a defence to what would otherwise be an infringement of a valid patent (*Intel v Via*, 2002).

5. IMPORTANT INVENTIONS

Every now and then, somebody makes a really important invention. As a rule, nobody knows this has happened until too late, and it is found either that the person who made the crucial step did not bother to apply for a patent at all, or that his application was considered just as a matter of routine, so that he got the sort of patent we discussed in the last chapter: a patent that would do very well to cover some minor improvement, but will stand neither a determined challenge to its validity nor a determined attempt to escape from its "claims". In that case, the invention can be used by anyone prepared to spend a little time and money upon research and rather more upon litigation. Sometimes, though, the inventor—or the inventor's employer— knows he is on to a good thing. What should he do about it?

Where Others have Tried

If the invention is one that a lot of people have been trying to make, there may well be very little to be done about it, except get whatever patent the Patent Office will grant and hope for the sympathy of the court in due course. For in that case, the files of the Patent Office will contain dozens or hundreds of specifications dealing with the subject, and some of them may well have come too close to the right answer for there to be much left to patent. In theory, of course, the failure of many other workers to make the invention is strong evidence that it was a good and patentable invention, rather than something obvious; but in practice, the drafting of valid claims that are broad enough to give real protection for the invention may be impossible where there have been too many earlier proposals. Some big firms, especially, make a point of patenting every slight advance in research into some subjects; partly in the hope that, if one of their competitors finds the answer, they will have patents of their own important enough to bargain with, partly for the very purpose of making it difficult or impossible for competitors to get valid patents. The independent inventor, hoping to make a large fortune by research in competition with the research departments of such large firms, is for this reason almost certainly wasting his time, however brilliant the work he is doing. He would probably make more money by research in some field that is specialised enough for his success not to be a serious challenge to his bigger rivals.

An Important Invention

Let us consider then the case of a manufacturer who is in possession of an invention that he believes is important, and that is unexpected enough to offer a chance of a really valuable patent. It will have to be a valid patent, for it is sure to come under hostile scrutiny as soon as its importance is understood; and it must have "claims" that are wide in scope, so that competitors cannot escape from it except by spending large sums upon research. It follows that attention will have to be paid to legal technicalities, which means extra trouble and extra expense in applying for the patent—although they will be trifling compared with the trouble of fighting a lawsuit later on, and the expense that will be incurred even if the suit is successful.

The initial application

The first step will be the filing of an application accompanied by a specification. This will not be the ultimate specification: its real purpose is to provide priority for the invention. It will be worth giving more care than usual to the drafting of this, so as to be certain that it both includes as much detailed information as possible and foreshadows the claims that will be incorporated in the final specification. Those claims will have to be broad: they must cover not only the actual machine or process that the inventor would like to see used commercially, but also any alternative form of the invention that competitors may want to use—or that competitors may be prepared to use if compelled to do so by the need to avoid the patent. To be sure that such broad claims will hold as "priority date" the date of the original application, as much basis as possible for them must be laid in the original specification: both by indicating the general principles of operation of the invention, and by suggesting alternatives to whatever is actually described in detail in the specification. Many inventors dislike trying to think of and describe alternatives that they believe to be inferior, but it ought to be done. They should be encouraged to think of as many variants of their basic idea as possible—good, bad, and indifferent. It is perhaps a good idea to ask them to put themselves in the mind of someone trying to pinch their idea. If the alternatives later turn out to be hopelessly inferior, they can be abandoned when the final specification is drawn up.

If, as often happens, the inventor later thinks of a development of the ideas in the original preliminary application, it will be desirable to file another application, so as to get the best priority for the development. It will not get the original priority date even if it is within the general ideas disclosed in the first application. So also with any later new developments. The application on which the patent will be based will have to be filed within a year of the first application anyway.

Protection abroad

It will soon be necessary to consider patenting abroad: even a company not able to contemplate manufacturing abroad or bringing infringement actions abroad to protect an export market, may want to license foreign manufacturers and get something back that way. (Even a foreign manufacturer who is really interested mainly in "know-how" will often be unwilling to sign a satisfactory agreement, unless there are patents in his home country to hang the agreement on.)

First, Europe; the initial application can be filed here: a British application can found priority in Europe as well as a European one can. But before any application is filed that is meant to be proceeded with, a decision will have to be taken whether in Europe to seek separate national patents, or a European patent: or both. (See Ch.3; and note that if both British and European patent applications are wanted, either a single international application must be made for them — see below — or both applications must be filed on the same day; otherwise one will anticipate the other.) In the case of a really important invention where patenting costs are only a minor factor, the sensible thing to do is to go via both the national and the EPO routes. This provides the maximum flexibility downstream. You can often adjust the application that is trailing behind (almost certainly the EPO application) using the experience gained from the earlier one — though there are limits to this.

In countries outside the European system, the initial British application (or applications) can again be used to give priority. Almost all industrial countries are parties to an international convention (called the "Paris" Convention, going back to 1881 with revisions every 20 years or so) concerning IP, which allows residents of any such country to file a patent application at home, and then within a specified period (normally 12 months) to file corresponding applications in the rest of such countries "as of" the date of his home application. The normal practice is consequently to make foreign applications by means of the convention, and ignore the few small non-parties to it.

As we said in Chapter 3, it is possible to avoid the trouble and expense of preparing and filing separate applications for all countries where patents are wanted by filing an "international application" under the PCT. So the inventor must choose whether to use this route for his application rather than separate national routes.

The specification

The final specification must be filed within 12 months of the first application in any case, and unless foreign patenting is to be handled entirely by an international application will have to be ready long enough before then for specifications based on it to be filed at Patent Offices abroad within the 12-month period. Before the filing, the inventor should set to work to discover the secret of his own success and, when he has, should put the answer into a further specification.

It was explained in the previous chapter that for a patent to be fully effective, the distinguishing features of the "invention" (as listed in the claims of the specification) must all be features that play a real part in the success of the new device. The system of guessing which features matter is too risky when the patent will be important: so the specification must be drawn up by someone who knows what the vital points are.

The Patent Office examination

The applicant will not at this stage yet know whether his patent is going to be a satisfactory one. He will not know this until his invention has been compared with those in earlier specifications, and it usually pays in practice to leave the job of searching for these earlier documents to the examiners at the Patent Offices concerned. Nor can the claims of the specification receive their final form until the examiner's comments have been received. If the specification has been well drawn up, the examiner may not have any serious objection to make: he will almost certainly find something to comment upon in the wording of the specification. It does sometimes happen that his search produces nothing. This is inconvenient, since it leaves the patent agent handling the case in the dark as to what earlier documents there are. To avoid this, the draftsman will sometimes "draw a search" by including initially a broader claim than he considers himself entitled to. Further, it may be advisable to make even the most half-hearted objection by an examiner an excuse for quite large alterations in the "claims"; for the claims are being framed less with a view to satisfying the examiner than with a view to what a judge may say later on.

It may prove desirable sometimes to frame the specification in a way to which the examiner will object; examiners are not trained lawyers, and have a lot of work to get through, and naturally tend to prefer standard patent jargon and standard forms of claim to anything new. This is fine for doubtful inventions, since the incomprehensibility of the jargon makes it harder for the patentee's competitors to decide whether the claims mean anything or not, or are anticipated or not. A court less conditioned to the jargon, may take a different view of it. Besides, sooner or later new sorts of claim become desirable: claims for important biotech inventions and such like. There has to be a first of such things, and any good examiner will probably notice and question it. Finally, we should mention an amusing ploy used by one wily old patent agent when he wanted to ensure that he could have a second look at the application before it was accepted — he used to include a claim to a "Wellington Boot". The examiner would have to object to this — and thus was prevented from just accepting the application.

If necessary, disagreements with the examiner must be disposed of by obtaining a "hearing", that is, by going to the Patent Office and arguing the point out with one of the higher officials. If she in turn is not persuaded, it will be necessary to appeal to the Patents Court or the EPO Board of Appeals depending on which patenting route has been taken.

Amendment after grant

The examiner's search usually uncovers a representative collection of the published documents on which later attacks on a patent might be based, while the applicants themselves will usually know what sort of thing was made and used up to the date of the application. Sometimes, however, a publication will turn up later, which was not considered when the specification was drafted, and that seriously threatens the validity of the patent. Or it may turn out that something too close to the claims of the patent was publicly used, either in this country or abroad, before the date of the application, the applicants not knowing of it (or omitting to mention it to their patent agent). The validity of the patent can then only be secured by "amending" the specification: that is, by altering the claims so as to narrow them down until they no longer include whatever it is that has turned out to have been unpatentable. It is nearly always far better to amend as soon as the patent is thought to be invalid; amendment is easier then (for it is less likely to be opposed) and fewer problems will arise afterwards. Moreover, the patentee ought not to leave in his specification claims he knows or suspects may be invalid, and if he does so, when in due course he does apply for amendment, he may be required to explain the reasons for delay. This occurred in *Wilkinson Sword* (1975), where the explanation was accepted, and *Smith Kline & French v Evans* (1989), where it was not. In the case of a patent whose specification was drafted without especially full investigation of the invention and its potentialities for future developments, the specification is likely to be defective anyway by reason of matters not known to the draftsman, so that amendment is worth considering as soon as the patent is found to be important enough to be worth spending money on.

Amendment of the specification requires the permission of the Patent Office or, if the patent is the subject of an action pending in the court at the time, of the court. Permission to amend is not very difficult to obtain, provided the patentee moves quickly once he knows of the need to amend, and has not originally had greedily wide claims. It is not possible to widen the "claims" (so that nothing can infringe after amendment unless it infringed before) and it is not possible to add completely new matter. (So it is not possible, for instance, to cure by amendment a failure to give adequate instructions to carry out the invention, nor to add a new feature that was not mentioned in the specification and has since been found essential to the working of the invention. One may properly cut a claim down, to exclude something old or obvious, but it is dangerous (though sometimes useful) to try to include an explanation of the reasons for what has been done.) Further, amendment of the specification may make it impossible to recover damages for infringements that took place before amendment. The result is that while the power to amend is very useful, it is a poor substitute for successful drafting of a specification in the first place.

If the patent has been granted by the EPO and is being "opposed" (really made subject to a claim for revocation), then it can be amended in those proceedings. The amendment takes place "centrally", that is to say it applies in all the countries designated in the application. Apart from that, there is currently no procedure for central amendment of European patents—you have to go to each country—and each country has different (or no) rules about amendment. There are current plans to change this nonsense.

Action in the Courts: For Infringement or Revocation

The ultimate testing ground for a patent is the court. The first case in which a patent is involved is vital for that patent— there is normally just one fight about the validity and scope of a patent. Normally, such a fight is started by the patentee suing for infringement, to which a common response is a counter-claim for revocation. But the potential defendant can start things by claiming revocation—to which the patentee often responds by counter-claiming for infringement. If the patentee loses, it means either that his patent is found invalid and is revoked or that the claims of the specification are declared to be too narrow to cover the articles the defendant is making. In the former case, there is no longer any patent; in the latter, everyone in the industry now knows how to get round it. If he wins, on the other hand, his competitors will probably respect that patent in future: there are always other things to make and sell that do not involve a patent action. Furthermore, if the patent is held valid, the patentee will receive a "certificate of contested validity," which, while not forbidding others to challenge the validity of the patent or to claim they are not infringing it, will make it extra expensive for them if they lose. (The actual effect of a certificate is to entitle the patentee, if he wins another action on that patent, to ask for "solicitor and own client" instead of "standard costs" for the action. "Standard costs" are supposed to correspond to the reasonable amount it would be possible to spend in fighting the action—any doubts being resolved in favour of the paying party. It is not entirely clear what "costs as between solicitor and own client" (which is what the Act says) means—it may mean what has actually been spent or it may mean something rather less—so called "indemnity" costs. Either way, the difference, for a patent action, may be very large.)

Delayed actions

It was emphasised in Chapter 1 that, in most cases, if a patent action is going to be fought at all, the sooner it is started the better. Equally, there are cases where an action should not be started at all. For example, a patent of dubious validity may be of considerable commercial value, being respected by most competitors. If someone does pluck up enough courage to infringe it, it may be better to buy him off, with a licence at low rates (or even free of royalty) rather than risk suing. It may be better thus to buy off a whole series of competitors—a sort of game of sardines. If, on the other hand, the patent is probably valid, and infringers are not of great importance compared with those who respect the patent or pay royalties, it may be worthwhile waiting until the patent has almost expired and then cleaning up by demanding damages from infringers—rather than upsetting things by suing earlier. (In any case, where an infringer is not sued right away, consideration should be given to notifying him of the existence of the patent, to stop him pleading innocence later.) Again, suppose a competitor finds a way round the patent, and tries to patent his alternative. The immediate reaction of most businessmen is to attack his patent. Often, it is the wrong reaction. The right thing to do can be to encourage him to have his patent, to stop other rats using the same hole.

From the point of view of an intending imitator of the patented article, there is a serious risk that he may be allowed to make his imitation for several years and may then be faced with a claim for a very large sum in damages. He can bring an action before he starts manufacturing, asking the court to declare that the article he proposes to manufacture will not infringe the patent concerned. He may also ask the court to revoke the patent on the ground that it is invalid. The proceedings in either case are nearly as expensive as ordinary actions for infringement, and may be rather easier for the patentee to win, especially if there is no very precise definition of the proposed article.

Threats

A threat of proceedings for infringement of patent can be very worrying to the recipient. Naturally, a manufacturer who infringes, or the importer of an infringing article made abroad, should expect the patentee to say, "If you do not stop I shall sue you". But threats to someone's customers are another matter: they are unlikely to want to get involved, and will usually quietly stop buying his goods rather than face an action. So it is provided that anyone aggrieved by threats of an infringement action can sue for damages and for an injunction preventing further threats, "unless the defendant . . . proves that the acts in respect of which proceedings were threatened constitute or, if done, would constitute an infringement of a patent"—and the patent is not shown to be invalid. But there is this exception, that if the only threat is to sue for making or importing something (or for using a patented process) no action lies. (Taken literally, this exception does not cover a threat to sue the manufacturer or importer for selling the goods concerned; one might have expected the courts to say that Parliament cannot have meant to be as silly as that, but they did not (*Cavity Trays v RMC*, 1996). The 2004 Act, when in force, will reverse this.)

Since it is very seldom possible to be certain of proving that any particular act is an infringement of a patent, or to be sure that any claim in a patent specification will not be found invalid, this provision is a dangerous trap for unwary owners of patents. On the other hand, it is actually very difficult to get damages for unjustified threats—the problem is that it is not so much the threat as the existence of the patent action which puts people off buying the goods (*Carflow v Linwood*, 1998).

Compulsory licensing

The owner of a patent ought to make use of his invention if he can; certainly he ought not to use his patent for preventing all use of his invention. In the hope of preventing such misuse of patents, provisions of one sort or another have for many years been inserted in the Patents Acts. In particular, there have been provisions by which anyone who wants to use an invention and can show that the patents covering it are being misused in certain ways can apply to the Patent Office for a compulsory licence, enabling him to use those patents upon payment of a proper royalty. The application cannot be made for three years after the patent has been granted. Compulsory licence provisions have never proved effective, and the present ones are hardly ever used.

Patents are not, in practice, used for suppressing new ideas: the difficulty with anything really new is to get anyone to take it up. Stories about patents for everlasting lightbulbs or the like being bought by existing manufacturers to protect their existing business are apocryphal. The few applications for compulsory licences that are made are not concerned with inventions that have been suppressed, but with inventions that have already proved profitable—where the patentee wants to keep the profit to himself.

Supplementary Protection Certificates ("SPCs")

Most of the life of a patent for a medicine may be exhausted before the safety authorities give permission to market. So the patentee may have spent a small fortune yet have very little monopoly period to recover his costs and make a profit. To deal with this, there is an EC Regulation and scheme. Under this, a certificate can be obtained which extends protection for a patented medicine or agrochemical (the one actually sold, not everything covered by the patent) for up to five years from normal expiry of the patent. The amount of extension is the period between application for the patent and first permission to market anywhere in the EC less five years.

"Improvement" patents

If the invention covered by a patent proves really profitable, its owner will want to go on profiting from it after his patent expires. There is a way in which a monopoly in an important invention may be kept alive after the patent has come to an end, and that is by patenting large numbers of minor improvements to the original invention. Provided the patented improvements represent genuine development over the period during which the original patent is in force, and provided that they are patented with determination and persistence, by the time the original patent expires a would-be imitator should be faced with this situation: that the article described in the original specification is too inferior to contemporary designs to be commercially saleable, while he cannot equal the newer models without risking an action for infringement of so many of the improvement patents, that he would almost certainly lose in respect of some patent or other. Even if he were to win the action on enough of the patents to let him go on manufacturing without any fundamental change in his design, the cost of fighting and losing the action as a whole would still take much of the profit out of his venture.

For this reason, the existence of a mass of improvement patents is often a sufficient deterrent to would-be imitators. The original manufacturer's position need not deteriorate with further lapse of time: he should always be some years ahead in design so far as patentable improvements are concerned, while the longer he keeps the field to himself the greater the advantage he has in manufacturing experience. His monopoly will last until some competitor comes along with the skill needed to "design round" the more dangerous patents and the courage to fight a patent action if necessary; how long this will be will depend as usual on the importance of the market covered by the monopoly, as well as on the rate at which he continues to devise new patentable improvements. In the past, such monopolies have sometimes lasted a long time.

Where the owner of the original patent is himself the manufacturer, the patenting of improvements presents no particular difficulty. Where, however, the main patent is exploited by licensing someone else to manufacture in return for payment of a royalty on production, the patentee will find it difficult not to lose control as soon as the original patent expires. For the developments on which improvement patents can be based will be made by the manufacturer, who will also have the practical experience; the new patents will naturally belong to him and the monopoly given by them will belong to him, too. Sometimes the manufacturer can be persuaded to agree that the original patentee shall become the owner of the improvement patents, but such arrangements are mostly illegal under competition law.

It is in general very difficult for an inventor who is not actively engaged in an industry to keep any substantial control over it by means of patents. Cases do still occur from time to time of inventors making large fortunes by using their inventions to build up large manufacturing businesses, while other inventors do well enough by selling their patents to existing firms and at the same time getting important posts with those firms as consultants or designers. The inventor who makes any large sum simply by the sale or licensing of his patents seems to be very rare.

Taxation and patents

Patents are subject to special rules as to tax. As one might expect the costs of inventing and patenting an invention are normally regarded as deductible expenses when computing profits. Royalties are not allowable as business expenses of a manufacturer who pays them (so that they have to be paid out of taxed profits, if he has any profits to tax); instead, whoever pays the royalty out of taxed income should deduct tax before paying and may then keep it. (If he had no profits (*i.e.* no taxed income) to pay the royalties out of, he must deduct the tax and hand it over to the Revenue.) Furthermore, capital sums paid for patents and patent licences (but not sums paid for know-how) are treated as income of the seller spread over a six-year period; this being balanced by allowing the purchaser annual allowances on what he has paid. (This is not quite as hard on inventors as it seems; for a professional inventor must reckon the proceeds of sale of patents as income anyway. It is hard on purely amateur inventors, but they have too few votes to matter.) The position of foreign patentees needs watching here: they naturally tend to demand that a British licensee agree to pay royalties (and even more, capital sums) free of tax. There are agreements in force with most foreign countries under which a foreigner can get payment in full (in the case of royalties, the payer is compensated for the tax he would otherwise have deducted and kept); but the foreign patentee has to make the request, and licence agreements ought to be specially framed accordingly. VAT is payable on most patent-related transactions, *e.g.* royalties. On a brighter note, stamp duty on, among other things, IP transactions was abolished in 2003.

Note: Drugs, Similar Chemical Compounds, and Genetic Engineering

Problems

The effective patenting of newly invented drugs and the like presents special difficulties. The fundamental problem is this: if the drug concerned is an entirely new chemical, its discoverer will be entitled to patent it; but just because it is entirely new, he will be unable to tell what related substances will be so similar in their effects as to be just as good. If he attempts to guess what other substances will work, he may well guess hopelessly wrong; if he confines himself to those he really knows about, his competitors (who have been told by his success what sort of thing to look for) will be able to market some related substance not covered by him. The preparation and trial of any new drug is a long job, and even the biggest research laboratories can try out only a few likely compounds at a time. To a certain extent the difficulty can be overcome by the power of amendment, but this is seldom a completely satisfactory answer. The inventor's main safeguard is the cost of testing and marketing a related substance; but if the drug is profitable enough, that may be worth doing.

Even worse difficulties face the person who discovers how to prepare a substance that already exists in nature (a vitamin, for instance, or something like penicillin); for there are bound to be other ways of doing the job that he cannot cover. Further, the discoverer of a new and valuable property of an old substance must be very clever to get any sort of patent at all, even to cover the stuff as sold. What he does, for instance, is to claim "a pharmaceutical dosage form" containing the old compound. Similar dodges can be devised for other types of invention. He should be able to get a patent to cover a process of using the stuff (not, though, use in medicine); but collection of royalties or finding out about infringements may be very difficult. To deal with discoveries of new medical or veterinary uses of known compounds, the Act has a new sort of patent: a patent for the compound "for" the newly discovered use. The intention is that the owner of the patent will then be able to sue anyone who sells the stuff, knowing or intending it to be used for the new treatment.

It might be thought that such inventions were particularly valuable and need to be specially encouraged; but the law is more concerned with restricting such patents than with encouraging them. It has, in particular, only recently been decided that the discoverer of a second unexpected medical use for a compound can get any patent for that at all.

"Selection" patents

There is a special sort of invention that turns up fairly often in the field of chemistry, and leads to what are called "selection patents". When a new and valuable chemical compound is discovered—a new drug, perhaps, or a new sort of dyestuff—it will usually at once be apparent to a skilled chemist that innumerable other, closely related compounds may be as good or better. But there is usually still room for invention in making those compounds, one by one, and finding out which really are as good or better; and even more room for invention in seeing without making them all which others will be as good or better. This picking-out of the useful ones, from a large class, which is already known in general terms, is known as "selection". The courts have laid down certain rules governing patents for such inventions: in particular, the specification must explain in what way the selected ones are better than the rest: and they must really be better, and better than almost all of the others. Of course, this must be something that only an inventor could have foreseen. The rules were devised for old patents. They probably still apply, though the EPO may have relaxed them somewhat.

Genetic engineering patents

When recombinant DNA techniques were first developed in the late 1970s, it became possible to identify particular genes or the DNA codes and structures of viruses. Much speculative money went into "biotech" companies who scrambled to find these with the hope of obtaining valuable patents. By and large quite a number of such patents have been granted. One can take the view that any new information, even if obtained by routine techniques, can be the basis of a patent (as in the US where any new isolated gene stretch of DNA has been considered patentable). Or one can be stricter and require that the technique used has some novel and unexpected twist to it. Broadly, that is the position in Europe, and in either case there is now a stricter requirement that the patentee not only identifies a gene but also must say what it is for, before he can have a patent. Genetic engineering patents create great controversy, not only of a purely emotional kind ("how can you patent life?" "Such patents are monopolies over God's creation" etc.) but also of a more practical kind in that they are apt to give the patentee a total monopoly over anything to do with the gene, whether by way of research, diagnosis or even treatment. Currently, for instance, one company claims that by virtue of its patents, it alone can test for certain types of breast cancer. And of course there is no way of "designing round" this sort of patent.

Note: What Amounts to Infringement

Most of the activities that amount to infringement are what one might expect: making, selling, importing, using a patented article; working a patented process or selling, importing or using the product. But it is also an infringement to "keep" the article or product; or knowingly to supply the means for working an invention, unless what is supplied is a "staple commercial product"—and even then it is infringement if the supply is intended to induce the recipient to infringe.

On the other hand, there are general exceptions: for things done privately and not commercially (it is not at all clear what "privately" means here: probably, "privately as distinct from commercially"); for experiments with the invention; for methods of medical treatment, *e.g.* the making-up of individual medical prescriptions); for use by foreign ships and aircraft, which includes regular ferries for instance between England and Ireland (*Stena v Irish Ferries*, 2003). There is also a special provision protecting those who used or prepared to use the invention before the priority date of the patent: they may go on doing what they did or prepared to do before. (This last provision is necessary, because use of an invention only invalidates a subsequent patent for it if the use makes the invention public in the sense that the public can find out how to do it. Manufacturing processes may well not be made public or a product may be incapable of analysis.)

The infringing act must be carried out within the UK (or continental shelf—added for the oil industry). However, use within the UK is read widely by the courts, for instance an online bookmaker who had UK punters using their computers as terminals could not escape infringement by keeping his computer abroad—he was still in substance using the patented system (computer, program and terminals) within the UK (*Menashe v William Hill*, 2003).

Note: Plant Breeders' Rights

Plant breeder's rights work a bit like patents but the procedure for obtaining them is separate from the patents system. The Plant Varieties and Seeds Act 1964 is the basic legislation and there is a special Plant Varieties Office.

For a variety to be protected it must be new, distinct, uniform and stable. By "new" is meant "not previously commercialised". The Plant Varieties Office (presided over by a Controller) examines applications for plant variety rights, and will only allow them to be granted in respect of those varieties for which a special scheme has been made for the relevant genus or species to which the variety belongs. There are different periods of protection for different species (ranging from 15 to 25 years).

The plant variety right only extends to marketing of reproductive material (*e.g.* seeds, cuttings or turf, as in *Germinal v Fell*, 1992), and there are express provisions for farmers to make their own seed from their own crop and compulsory licensing to prevent abuses of monopoly. There are also special provisions governing the names of new varieties. There is a parallel Community plant variety rights scheme.

6. CROWN RIGHTS AND SECURITY

The Crown's Right to Work Patents

Any government department may use, or authorise others to use, any patented invention "for the services of the Crown". Mostly, this means for the armed forces—although some drugs for British hospitals were procured under these powers in the 1960s. The patent owner is entitled to compensation for any use by the Government in this way, but he cannot prevent that use. If the invention was one that any government department knew about (otherwise than because its owner told them about it) before the patent was applied for, this does not of itself make the patent invalid but it disentitles the owner to compensation for any Government use.

Surplus patented articles, originally made for Government use, may be freely sold—so may articles confiscated by the Customs or Excise, so may medical supplies. During a war period and for war purposes, or for national purposes during a period of emergency, or in respect of inventions concerned with atomic energy, government departments may authorise anyone to sell such articles whether originally made for Government use or not—subject to the usual rights to compensation. The Government may also have weapons and munitions made here for allies, or the UN, and sell them to the government or organisation concerned. Except in these cases, the Government has no right to authorise the sale of such articles without permission from the patent owner.

If the patent owner has licensed a firm also authorised by the Government to use an invention, the royalties fixed by the licence need not be paid so far as Government use is concerned. Such a licensee may still be liable to make some payments to the owner: guaranteed minimum royalties, for instance (*No-Nail Cases v No-Nail Boxes*, 1944). In general, however, the owner must rely on his right to demand compensation from the Crown. The amount of compensation, if it cannot be agreed, will normally be settled by referring the whole matter to the High Court. The Crown is supposed to let inventors know that it is using their patents, but it tends not to (especially but not only where military secrets are involved). One of the inventor's main problems tends to be finding out what use if any is being made of his invention. The problem is at least in part caused by the fact

67

that it is the Crown that is first supposed to decide whether it is using an invention. It will not "own up" even where it knows of the patent if it decides the scope of the patent does not cover what is being done or that the patent is invalid. Naturally, the patentee might take a different view but he does not get the chance to complain unless he finds out some other way.

There are similar provisions allowing Crown use of registered designs and design rights, although in practice this will not matter much.

One of the effects of the TRIPS agreement (see Chapter 28 below) is to limit the freedom of countries to authorise use of private intellectual property rights, although this has had only a limited impact on UK law.

Keeping Inventions Secret for Security Reasons

There are special provisions about patents containing information that relates to national security and that, if published, might be prejudicial to that security. If an application is made to patent such an invention, and if and so long as the Secretary of State (really the appropriate Service department) considers that it ought to be kept secret, the application for a patent will not be published and, though it will be examined, it will not proceed to grant. Similar provisions apply to designs (whoever heard of or even imagined a design prejudicial to national security!) and similar provisions apply to all inventions involving atomic energy, whether of military character or not. Military inventions that the armed forces think good enough to use are just the ones they will want to keep secret. So the provisions giving inventors the right to be compensated for Crown use apply in such cases as if the patent were granted in the ordinary way. In addition, the Crown can if it likes compensate the inventor for the damage the secrecy does to him.

It would, of course, be useless to keep such inventions secret here if they were published abroad. So it is made a crime for anyone resident in the UK to apply for a foreign patent if the application contains information that relates to military technology or might be prejudicial to national security, unless an application has first been filed here and six weeks have then elapsed without any direction being made that the invention should be kept secret. This is all very well in theory, but since people can apply direct to the EPO or foreign countries, it is essentially academic. The prospect of a criminal prosecution for breach of this rule is pretty remote.

7. INDUSTRIAL DESIGNS

For many years our law has included protection for industrial "designs". Originally, the general idea was to protect the artistic element in mass-produced articles (shape or applied decoration or the like). The main mechanism for protection was supposed to be by a system of designs registered at the Patent Office—like a patent for an invention. But over the years both Parliament and the courts managed to produce a convoluted system as a result of the interaction between the law of registered designs and that of ordinary copyright. The problem arose because ordinary copyright in drawings could be infringed by indirectly copying an article made from them. This is easy enough to understand where a truly artistic drawing is concerned (*e.g.* of "Popeye," *King Features Syndicate v Kleeman,* 1942), but seems odd in the case of purely mechanical items, such as an exhaust pipe. The whole business got out of hand: not only was the law complicated, it was unsafe to make things that were copies of, or based upon, really quite old articles. For instance, Lego were using (successfully until final appeal) copyright to maintain a monopoly in their system even though the basic brick was designed in the 1940s. Absurd arguments as to eye appeal or otherwise of a Lego brick were deployed in all seriousness (*Interlego v Tyco,* 1989). In the case of spare parts (exhaust pipes), it took the House of Lords to say: never mind ordinary copyright, you are allowed to make them (*Leyland v Armstrong,* 1984).

So in 1988, Parliament tried to sort things out, creating two systems for design protection, one in registered designs and a lesser system for unregistered designs right in which arose automatically without the need for registration. It was pretty complicated in detail. Now the EU has added its half-euroworth too. Pursuant to a Directive, we expanded our registered designs law so that it corresponds with the new EU design. The EU has introduced its own system of registered designs. From April 2003, it has been possible to register these at OHIM. On top of that, the EU has created an EU unregistered designs right that arises automatically. Finally, there is scope for ordinary copyright to play a part. Some designs can be registered as trade marks or protected by passing-off.

The upshot of all this is that things are pretty complicated—four different sorts of right especially for designs, or five if you include ordinary copyright, or seven if you also include

69

registered trade marks and passing-off. No-one could, or does, call it rational—but no-one seems to be in a position to simplify things either. Broadly, the position may be rather simpler than it seems—it is unsafe to copy anything that has come on the market within the last 10 years. If you do, then you are likely to fall foul of an unregistered design right. Even simple things, such a rectangular floppy case for a flat folding umbrella can be the subject of such a right (*Fulton v Totes*, 2003). The sensible thing to do, even if you have not, or your supplier has not, copied, is to check whether an article you make or import bears a resemblance to a design registered either in the UK or at OHIM. A good patent agent can organise this for you.

UK and EU Registered Designs

Almost anything visual can be the sort of design that is registrable: "the appearance of the whole or a part of a product resulting from the features of, in particular, the lines, contours, colours, shape, texture or materials of a product or its ornamentation". It is the design as applied to any product which is protected. "Product" is widely defined too, covering even such things as "graphic symbols", whatever that may mean (probably computer icons, for instance). Designs can be registered at the Patent Office if they are new (*i.e.* not the same as any design which has already been made available to the public) and have "individual character" (*i.e.* that the overall impression it produces on an informed user of the design must differ from the overall impression produced on such a user by any design which has already been made available to the public). In assessing individual character, the freedom of the designer in creating the design is taken into account.

"Made available to be public" does not have the clear, bright line, meaning it has in patent law. For the latter it is enough if one person has the prior information and is entirely free to use it—that is why blurting out your invention before you have applied for the patent can be so dangerous. Even deposit on an obscure library shelf in an obscure language will do. It makes no difference if it the inventor himself who is responsible for the disclosure. But for design law a prior disclosure is not regarded as making the disclosure "available to the public" "if it could not reasonably have become known in the normal course of business to persons carrying on business in the EU and specialising in the sector concerned". This is dreadfully vague—and particularly odd given that for infringement there is no "sector concerned". The ECJ will have its work cut out trying to make sense of this.

Moreover, a disclosure by the designer himself or with his consent does not count if he applies for registration with one year of his disclosure.

Apart from the question of novelty, there are certain other specific exclusions from registrability—components of a complex product that are not visible in normal use of the complex product, features of appearance "solely dictated by the product's technical function", and "must fit" or "must match" features of designs are the most important. Again, these are vague concepts, bound to lead to litigation. Under our old law, for instance, "appearance dictated solely by function" had to go the House of Lords (*Amp v Utilux*, 1972). The same battle will have to be fought all over again, with what result remains to be seen.

Registration gives a true monopoly so, unlike copyright or unregistered design right a defendant infringes if he makes or deals in a product having a "design which does not produce on the informed user a different overall impression" from that of the registered design, degrees of freedom of design again being taken into account. But, as always, it helps if the defendant copied. The significance of registration could be very great for a successful design. You get up to a 25-year monopoly in your design (upon paying renewal fees). For something like a classic furniture design, that could be very important. Do not ask us why registered designs get 25 years whereas patents only get 20.

Registering a design involves much less effort (and cost) than a patent. Normally, some good photographs (from all angles) of a prototype 3-D design are all that is needed. 2-D designs (*e.g.* a wallpaper or textile) would only need a sample. The biggest defect of the system is that it takes a while (about six months) for the registration to come through and in the case of some fields, such as some toys, the craze may be over before protection is obtained. This sort of design will, however, be protected by the unregistered design right. Since the designer has a year to apply from the time he first discloses his design, he may be able to discover whether his design has any value in the market before incurring the costs of registration. Typical fees for a UK design application (including a patent agent's fees) are £40: for an EU registration £500 (in both cases an agent may have to charge more if he has to prepare the drawings). It is possible in simple cases to make the application without a patent agent, but, unless the applicant makes regular applications and knows what to do, it is best to use one.

Another advantage of the design registration system is that it can be used to claim priority in other countries (the applications abroad have to be made within six months rather than a year as in the case of patents). The international protection of designs will probably grow with the increasing trans-border nature of goods and markets. At present, most other countries have design registration schemes, although the variation from country to country is quite marked, more so than in the case of patents.

The principal difference between an EU and a UK registered design is that the former gives EU-wide rights. As in the case of EU trade marks (see below), the system of enforcement is by courts designated as Community Design courts—for England and Wales these are the Patents Court and Patents County Court. Third parties are able to apply OHIM for declarations of invalidity of community design registrations. As in the case of EU trade marks, there are Boards of Appeal from which appeals can go on to the ECJ.

We can make one confident forecast—that as the new system takes effect, the uncertainty of the law and the complex and uncertain litigation system will lead to much work for lawyers and much cost for industry. Whether any of it will do any good by way of encouragement of new design we leave the reader to decide.

UK Unregistered Design Right ("UDR")

This is a British idea. It started in 1988 as a way of replacing the over-powerful protection that was given by ordinary copyright (70 years from death of author for functional designs). It only protects against copying and has a limited term as compared with a registered design. A designer is given automatically given a UDR in "any aspect of shape on configuration" (internal or external) of the whole on any part of an article. The design must be original (in the copyright sense of being the designer's own work, not copied) and must have been recorded in a design document or a physical article. There are special modifications (both as to the extent of the right and the nationality of origin) in relation to design rights in relation to the topography of semiconductor products, following our implementation of an EU directive on the subject.

There are exceptions to UDR: there is none in a method or principle of construction, or in a design which must fit some other article (*e.g.* a spare part) or must match some other article so as to form an integral whole (*e.g.* a body panel), or in a surface decoration. There is also an exception if the design is "commonplace in the design field in question"—a fuzzy notion that the courts have had some difficulty in dealing with. In

Farmers Build v Carrier (1999), the court said it should be construed narrowly and that a comparative exercise to find out how similar the design is to those of other similar articles is involved. In *Lambretta v Teddy Smith* (2004), the Court said that "design field in question" covers the sort of designs with which a notional designer of the article concerned would be familiar. Both of these explanations are a bit helpful but hardly precise—blame the legislature not the courts.

The UDR is extremely powerful and pervasive. Almost any piece of design work will give rise to one. But a UDR only lasts, at best, for 15 years from the end of the year when the design was first made. Earlier expiry occurs if the first marketing of the design takes place in the first five years of its life. Then expiry is at the end of the tenth year in which first marketing occurred. So in practice all a designer can get is 10 years from first marketing; he is unlikely to be copied before then in any event, and his protection is cut down even more because, after five years from first marketing by the designer, his rivals can obtain a compulsory licence. So there may be quite a few cases where, when the copying starts a few years after first marketing, it will be doubtful whether a case could be brought to trial before the end of the five-year period during which an injunction can be had. In such cases the crucial question will often be: can the designer obtain an interlocutory injunction meanwhile?

In practice, UDR is valuable to protect against slavish imitations early in the life of a product. So it helps in fast-changing fashion trades, such as toys and garments. It also gives initial protection to a designer who has applied for registration of his design but is still waiting for grant. UDR cannot be used as a basis for claiming priority for foreign applications. Indeed, unless a foreign country (outside the EU) recognises a similar right, their nationals are not entitled to UDRs here.

It will obviously be important to keep drawings and prototypes for future enforcement. A well-advised design-based company would have a standard procedure for this, and for ensuring that the employment records of the design employees (and assignments from outside designers) are kept.

EU UDR

This is based on the British idea—again protecting only against copying for a limited term—but only three years from when it was first made available (in the design sense) in the EU. The definition of infringement is not the same as for a British UDR, on its face at least being confined to making or dealings in products "in which the design is incorporated or to which it is applied." The British definition covers the use of any aspect of a design or part of a design", which is wide, see *Fulton v Totes* (2003). We suspect that in practice there will be little difference in scope—the ECJ is well capable of saying that the definition of infringement is of practically the same scope.

But in other respects the EU UDR is wider than a British UDR. Thus a British UDR does not extend to just the choice of colours of the panels of an old design of garment (*Lambretta v Teddy Smith*, 2003) whereas an EU UDR would do so.

Ordinary Copyright

For copyright works made after the 1988 Act, the scope for protection of industrial designs for most artifacts is limited. It is not an infringement to make a 3-D article directly or indirectly from copyright design drawings on models for a non-artistic work. However, in relation to works for surface decoration, all 2-D designs, such as fabric designs, and works which are designs for artistic works (*e.g.* drawings for a sculpture on a sculpture itself) the works may be copied in 3-D after 25 years from the first industrialisation of the work. Prior to then, it will be an infringement to copy. So, if the copyright drawing is for making an exhaust pipe then you can copy at once (subject, of courses, to UDR). But if the drawing is for a textile design or for a sculpture or is of a cartoon character then you must wait 25 years.

Use of Other Rights to Protect Designs

Some designs can be protected in other ways: for instance a design may in some cases also be a trade mark *e.g.* the back of a playing card (*US Playing Card's Appn.*, 1907) or the scheme of coloration of medicinal capsules (*Smith Kline & French*, 1976). However, the courts are careful to prevent these other forms of protection (which may be perpetual) from straying too far into the field of designs proper, so, for example, the shape of the Philips razor was not registrable as a trade mark (see later). Similarly, plaintiffs sometimes try to use a passing-off action to protect a design, but generally fail. An example of this is *British American Glass v Winton* (1962), where the plaintiff failed to protect the design of his glass animals by passing-off because he could not show that the customers cared which make of glass animal they were buying and so were not cheated.

PART III

TRADE MARKS AND UNFAIR COMPETITION

8. DIFFERENT SORTS OF PROTECTION

Passing-off

Most European countries have some sort of general rule of law forbidding unfair competition. We do not: but most of the activities that such a rule would discourage run contrary to specific rules of English law. In particular we have a rule—and this is the subject of this part of this book—forbidding the running of a business in such a way as to filch a competitor's trade by misleading conduct. The limits of this rule will be discussed in later stages; all that need be said here is that it is, in essence, a rule to protect business goodwill. It is difficult to define goodwill. Broadly, it is that characteristic of a business that renders it permanent, which distinguishes an established business from one newly formed: "the attractive force which brings in custom" as was said by the House of Lords in a late nineteenth-century attempt to define goodwill. (Someone once said that if all the Coca Cola factories in the world burnt down in one day, it is the goodwill that would enable it to get up and running again.)

In order to protect business goodwill, the law forbids any trader to conduct his trade so as to mislead customers into mistaking his goods or business for someone else's. It makes no difference whether it is other traders or the general public that are deceived, nor whether the deception is fraudulent or merely mistaken or accidental; not how it is brought about. This sort of deception is known as "passing-off"; anyone who suffers financial loss as a result of it is entitled to bring an action in the courts, claiming compensation for his loss, and asking for an injunction against continuance of the deception. Passing-off does not extend to non-deceptive encroachments upon goodwill: it is not passing-off to say honestly "my cola is as good as Coca Cola but half the price". Passing-off is a powerful and effective remedy, provided only that the plaintiff is able to prove his case.

Where the case is clear on its face, or there is any serious indication that the defendant is dishonest, no difficulty arises, so long as the plaintiff moves quickly enough. He can ask for, and will be given a temporary injunction, putting a stop to the deception until the case can be tried. That, almost always, is the end of the matter. It is settled and there is no need ever to have a full-scale trial. In cases that are less clear, the difficulty of proof may be serious. So full trials of passing-off cases are rare. It is seldom possible to find anyone who has actually been deceived and will come and swear to it in court. *Chelsea Man v Chelsea Girl* (1987), was one of those rare instances, the customers of the plaintiff coming to court out of loyalty. *Neutrogena* (1994), was another, the deceived customers having been located via various sorts of opinion poll. The case must be proved by showing that the circumstances are such that people are certain to be deceived sooner or later. This is not an easy task and much ingenuity by way of opinion polls and the like is expended on it, generally without success. The most important reason for registering trade marks is to make it unnecessary.

Passing-off and Registration of Trade Marks

The registration of a trade mark generally makes it much easier for a plaintiff to prevent the sort of "passing-off" that involves imitation of trade marks or brand names. However, this is not always so. First, registration of a trade mark is not always possible (see Chapter 11), although since the new (1994) law, it is easier than it was. Second, and partly as a result of the fact that it is now easier to register a trade mark, enforcement in some cases has become more difficult and uncertain. Nevertheless, it remains the case that traders are well advised to obtain full registration of all their trade marks, since it will generally make legal disputes over trade marks and brand names simpler and cheaper to resolve. Perhaps even more important than that, it will generally warn rivals off altogether—why look for trouble when you are considering what mark to use? Things are different once you are committed—you may feel you have to stand and fight.

Where there has been full registration of all trade marks, the sort of "passing-off" that involves imitation of trade marks or brand names can seldom occur without infringement of the trade mark registrations taking place too. Full registration of trade marks is not always easy or even possible: there are many legal pitfalls to be avoided. (Some of these are discussed later.) Where it is possible, in principle, it enables the expensive and uncertain action for passing-off to be replaced by the cheaper and more reliable action for infringement of trade mark.

Passing-off and Goodwill

In an action for passing-off, the plaintiff must in practice prove that he has extensive enough goodwill for his goods or services to be recognised by members of the public; otherwise it will hardly be possible for people to be deceived when they come across similar goods or services put out by the defendants. It follows that the law of passing-off will protect established businesses from imitation of their names or trade marks but will not provide a shield behind which a new goodwill can be built up. Registration of a trade mark, on the other hand, is normally possible before use starts at all (the exception is in the case of very descriptive marks—see later). Since registration gives almost an absolute right to stop others from using that mark or a mark like it, goodwill can be built up behind the protection given to a registered mark. That is why prudent businessmen register (or at least seek registration) before starting use.

Why People Sue for Passing-off

Why, if suing for infringement is so much easier, does anyone sue for passing-off? (Passing-off actions are the more numerous, in fact.) There are several reasons. First, many businesses do not keep their trade marks fully registered, so that resort to a passing-off action may be necessary to cover flaws in the trade mark position. Second, passing-off can occur in cases that have nothing at all to do with trade marks: by the marketing of goods whose get-up is the same (in everything but the wording on the package) as that of an old-established line, reverse passing-off (see later), celebrity endorsement and so on. Third, the fact that enforcement of registered trade marks has become more difficult and uncertain means that a claim to passing-off may be included in proceedings as a back-up in the event that the case on the trade mark infringement fails. And there is one particularly overriding reason for suing in passing-off where this is possible —judges are very apt to stop anyone who is actually doing something deceptive. The converse is also likely to be true—mere technical infringements of a registered mark do not invoke judicial sympathy in the same way and so judges are apt only to stop clear cases. That is why, for instance, Arsenal had so much trouble—see later.

Registered Trade Marks

There are now two types of registered mark enforceable in the UK, the UK national registered mark (obtained from the UK Trade Mark Registry under the provisions of the Trade Marks Act 1994) and the Community registered trade mark ("CTM") (obtained from OHIM under the provisions of the Community

Trade Mark Regulation). The CTM can also be enforced in the other EU countries. For most purposes, the law relating to UK marks and CTMs is the same. This is because the Trade Marks Act 1994 is itself based on European legislation, namely the European Trade Mark Directive. For this reason, the UK must take into account decisions of the ECJ on the Directive and the Regulation. Many of the cases referred to in the following chapters are decisions of that court. The differences in procedure relating to CTMs are dealt with in Chapter 13.

A plaintiff who sues on a UK or a Community trade mark must satisfy one of three different tests, depending on the relevant facts. Which test applies is crucial, since it will affect how easy it is for the plaintiff to win. If the mark used by the defendant is identical to the plaintiff's registered mark and is being used by the defendant for identical goods or services to those for which the plaintiff has registered his mark, then the case is straightforward. To succeed, the plaintiff only has to prove that the marks are identical and that the goods or services are identical (assuming that the plaintiff's trade mark is valid and that no relevant exception applies—these issues are discussed in Chapters 10 and 11). It is in this situation (identical mark/ identical goods or services) that it is a major advantage to the plaintiff to have a registered trade mark, since there is no need for him to prove that he has an extensive enough goodwill to be recognised by the public or that the public has been deceived, as there would be in a passing-off case.

If, on the other hand, the defendant only uses a similar mark or uses an identical mark but only for similar goods or services (or both), the test the plaintiff must meet is more onerous. He must prove that, because of the similarity of the marks or the goods or services, there is a likelihood of confusion. This is rather like the requirement to prove deception in a passing-off case and so can make the case much more complicated. The test goes further than passing-off in one respect: the plaintiff does not actually have to prove he has a goodwill—his mark is taken to be in use and to have a goodwill (*Reed Employment v Reed Elsevier*, 2004).

Finally, if the facts are that the defendant is using a sign that is identical or similar to the plaintiff's registered mark in relation to goods or services that are identical, similar or dissimilar to those for which the mark is registered, the plaintiff can still succeed in a case for infringement if he can prove two things. First, that his trade mark has a reputation (again this is very similar to the requirement in passing-off). Second, that the defendant's use of the mark, "being without due cause, takes unfair advantage of, or is detrimental to, the distinctive character or the repute of the trade mark." At the present time, what exactly the European legislators meant by this rather peculiar phrase is uncertain. It is discussed in Chapter 9. Self-evidently, this again is a considerably more onerous test for the plaintiff to meet than that for identical marks and goods/services.

Litigation Caused by Uncertainty

Where a potential plaintiff has a registered trade mark and the potential defendant uses a mark that is identical to the plaintiff's mark for goods or services identical to those for which it is registered, the case is usually clear. A complaint by the potential plaintiff will usually result in the potential defendant stopping the offending activity, which is very likely to have been inadvertent. It is relatively easy for a trader contemplating using a new mark to check the trade marks register (this can now be done with a fairly high degree of accuracy online at www.patents.gov.uk and www.ohim.eu.int) to find out whether it can be safely used or not. Having a patent or trade mark agent or solicitor do a trade mark search or, at the very least, doing one yourself online, is obviously the best way to avoid disputes.

Litigation is much more likely to arise where there is no registered trade mark and the potential plaintiff therefore relies on passing-off or where there is a registered trade mark but the potential defendant is not using an identical mark or is using an identical mark but only for similar or dissimilar goods or services. In this situation, the difficulties in proving the case are likely to mean that the outcome will not be certain for either side. Unless there is a plain case of passing-off, the uncertainties of the law caused by a failure of the legislation to address most if not all of the basic problems of trade marks, coupled with appalling drafting, further encourages litigation. "Clarification" by the ECJ, in the many cases since the new law came in, seems by and large to makes things worse.

9. TRADE MARK INFRINGEMENT

How a trade mark can be infringed is closely linked to the more philosophical question of the function of a registered trade mark, which is discussed first in this chapter. This chapter then discusses the three tests for trade mark infringement in more detail than the last. Even if one of the three tests for trade mark infringement is met, a case for trade mark infringement may still fail if either the trade mark should not have been registered (the circumstances in which this may be so are addressed in Chapter 11) or the defendant has a defence to trade mark infringement (possible defences are discussed in Chapter 10).

What a Registered Trade Mark can Stop

The registration of a trade mark gives the owner the exclusive right to use the registered mark. This exclusive right is defined negatively by rules that set out what acts others cannot do— these acts, if done without the consent of the proprietor, amount to trade mark infringement. The prime rationale behind the rules is to ensure that the registered trade mark acts as a "guarantee of origin" (a phrase in the Directive). The "guarantee" is to ensure that when a member of the public sees the registered trade mark used in relation to certain goods or services they can be sure that the goods or services in question come from the registered proprietor or someone under his control. The point is to make sure that the public is not deceived. If the public buys a can of soft drink bearing the name *Coca Cola*, they are entitled to assume that it is the famous soft drink and not an imitation made by somebody else. The infringement rules are intended to prevent this kind of imitation.

In fact, as will be seen below, the rules go further than this and prevent other kinds of imitation and even, in the case of goods imported from outside the EU, the use of marks on the genuine goods. Quite how far the law should go in protecting trade marks is a matter of extensive debate amongst lawyers and a subject not merely of academic interest. It can have a major practical effect on traders and consumers. A recent case, illustrates the point.

Arsenal v Reed (2003) was about football merchandise. In common with other top clubs, Arsenal made a great deal of money by selling merchandise bearing the club's name and badge. The name and badges were registered as trade marks for things like T-shirts, scarves and hats. All the merchandise sold by the club was labelled "official" and the club had invested a good deal of effort in trying to ensure that the public knew its merchandise was official and in attempting to prevent others from selling "unofficial" merchandise. Mr Reed was an Arsenal fan who had been selling goods bearing the Arsenal names and logos from a stall near Highbury for over 30 years. The vast majority of his merchandise was unofficial and was indicated as such by prominent signs on his stall. Arsenal sued Mr Reed for passing-off and trade mark infringement. The case in passing-off failed in the High Court because the judge found that the club had not proved that fans buying from Mr Reed would be confused into believing that the merchandise came from the club or was licensed by it. In 30 years of trading, the club could not show a single instance of confusion that had come to light.

The case on trade mark infringement turned on the question of how far the protection given by a registered trade mark should extend. Arsenal argued that since Mr Reed was using their registered trade marks in relation to goods for which those marks were registered it was a straightforward case of trade mark infringement. Mr Reed maintained that mere use of the offending sign was not sufficient to constitute trade mark infringement. In order to be an infringement, the use had to indicate trade origin. Mr Reed said, and the judge in the High Court agreed, that he was not using the Arsenal name and badge to indicate trade origin (*i.e.* to say that the goods had come from a certain source), but simply as a badge of allegiance. The public bought the goods for the Arsenal name or crest, not because they thought it was an "official" club product. The tricky legal point was whether use of a sign as a badge of allegiance should be sufficient to amount to trade mark infringement.

The judge decided that this point of law should be referred to the ECJ for a definitive ruling. Arsenal and Mr Reed duly travelled to Luxembourg to argue over the function of a trade mark before the judges there. The judgment, which was given a year-and-a-half after the reference was made (about the average time for a reference), provoked a storm of academic and judicial dispute. The court repeated the mantra that the essential function of a trade mark was to guarantee the identity of origin of the marked goods or services, but found that it was immaterial to the question of infringement that the sign was perceived as a badge of allegiance. It concluded that, in the circumstances of the case, the trade mark proprietor was entitled to prevent use of the trade mark.

As is usual following a reference, the case returned to the referring court, in this case the High Court, to allow the judge to apply the ECJ's guidance to the facts of the case. Normally, that is pretty much a formality. But here it was argued on behalf of Mr Reed that the European Court had exceeded its jurisdiction and, consequently, the conclusion it had reached should not be applied by the High Court. The excess of jurisdiction was said to arise from the fact that the ECJ is only able to give guidance on points of law, whereas in this case it appeared to have come to a conclusion on the facts and one which was contrary to the findings of fact made by the High Court, namely that the marks were just badges of allegiance. Although the judge considered it to be an unattractive outcome, he accepted Mr Reed's submission that the ECJ had gone too far and found that, despite its ruling, Mr Reed should win. This radical step, although considered to be justified by many intellectual property lawyers, was promptly stamped upon by the Court of Appeal, which held that the real basis for the ECJ's decision was that the use complained of was liable to jeopardise the guarantee of origin, and that the High Court had made no finding of fact on this point. Consequently, it was open to the ECJ to conclude that the use by Mr Reed was liable to jeopardise the guarantee of origin of Arsenal's trade marks since this was a finding of fact which was inevitable in the circumstances.

Thus the upshot for the law of trade marks is that although the essential function of the trade mark remains as a guarantee of origin, the acts which may be prevented having regard to that function have been stretched beyond deception of the public as to the origin of the goods to any use of the trade mark in the course of trade which, whilst it does not serve to indicate origin, may harm the trade mark's use by its proprietor as a guarantee of origin. The result for Mr Reed and other traders like him is that they will be prevented from selling anything other than "official" Arsenal merchandise (if they can get it), and for consumers that they will only be able to buy their shirts, scarves and the like from "official" sources.

There are two postscripts. First, just a day after the decision in the Court of Appeal in *Arsenal*, the House of Lords, in a case called *R. v Johnstone* (2003), said that for infringement there had to be trade mark use by the defendant. The context was a criminal charge under the provisions of the Trade Marks Act. The defendant dealt in bootleg CDs (*i.e.* unauthorised recordings of live performances). The registered trade mark said to be infringed was the name of the band, Bon Jovi. Mr Johnstone said he was only using the name to indicate the performers—not as a trade mark. He might have succeeded on that basis—whether the public took the use as only denoting the band or as denoting the band and a trade mark or just as a trade mark was never decided. By the time the case got to the House of Lords, Mr Johnstone had served his sentence so there was no point in a retrial. Some say this case puts the Court of Appeal decision in *Arsenal* back into the melting pot. We shall have to see—the *Arsenal* case is now settled. For more about the *Johnstone* case, see Chapter 17. The astute reader may wonder why Mr Johnstone was charged under the Trade Marks Act, rather than under the Copyright Act, for the bootleg CDs undoubtedly infringed both copyright in the music and the performers' rights. The answer is almost certainly that it is much easier to prove title to a registered trade mark (just produce the certificate of registration) than to prove title to a copyright or a performers' right. For these, the live evidence of witnesses of the creation or of the performance may be required, particularly in a criminal case.

The other postscript also shows how copyright and trade marks can overlap. When the High Court judge found against Arsenal the first time and sent the case off to Luxembourg, Arsenal decided to do something about its badge. The old one, a splendid Victorian thing with a Latin motto, was out of copyright. Arsenal commissioned a new badge—in which there would be copyright. The copyright would last for ages—70 years after the death of the author. Pirate copies could be suppressed by the use of copyright rather than trade marks. Legally the plan worked, though the fans did not like it, especially those with tattoos of the old badge.

The Tests for Trade Mark Infringement

As already outlined, there are three types of trade mark infringement.

Identical marks and identical goods/services

Cases involving the use of identical marks and identical goods or services are the most straightforward type. The plaintiff only has to prove that the mark used by the defendant is identical to his registered mark and is being used by the defendant for goods or services identical to those for which the plaintiff has registered his mark (assuming that the plaintiff's trade mark is valid and that no relevant defence applies—these issues are discussed in Chapters 10 and 11). The vast majority of cases of this type will settle unless, of course, there is some other issue at stake, such as in the *Arsenal* case. Of course, it is not always easy to say whether or not the marks and goods or services are identical.

Consider the following examples. In *British Sugar v James Robertson* (1996), the plaintiff had registered *Treat* for dessert sauces and syrups (it used the mark on a sauce for pouring onto ice cream). The defendant launched a sweet spread labelled "Robertson's Toffee Treat", which competed with jams and other spreads, particularly chocolate spread. The court had to decide whether the defendant had used an identical mark. The court found that it had, since the word "Treat" was on the Robertson's product for all to see. The judge contrasted this with the example of "theatre atmosphere", in which he said that no-one but a crossword fanatic would say that "treat" was present.

In *LTJ Diffusion v SADAS* (2002), a case referred to the ECJ from the French courts, the plaintiff's registered trade mark was *Arthur* in a fancy script; that of the defendant was *Arthur et Felicie*, in a device mark. Applying the rationale of the judge in *British Sugar*, these marks would be considered identical. However, the European Court's view was that a sign could only be identical to a registered trade mark where there was reproduction, without any modification or addition, of all the elements of the registered trade mark or where, viewed as a whole, it contained differences so insignificant they would go unnoticed by an average consumer. Whilst the European Court did not have to decide the case on the facts, it seems pretty clear that following this reasoning the marks would not have been found to be identical. Following that guide, the English Court of Appeal held that "Reed Business Information" is not identical to "Reed" alone (*Reed Employment v Reed Elsevier*, 2004).

Working out whether the goods or services are identical is usually more straightforward. On the whole, the question will be resolved by deciding whether the goods or services for which the defendant is using the sign are the same, in ordinary parlance, as the goods or services for which the plaintiff has registered the mark. Thus, in *British Sugar*, the plaintiff's argument that the defendant was using the mark on a dessert sauce or syrup, for which the plaintiff's mark was registered, on the ground that on the back of the jar the defendant said that Toffee Treat could be used with desserts failed: Toffee Treat was primarily sold as a spread and no-one would naturally call it a "dessert sauce" any more than they would call a jam a such a sauce.

The position may be more complicated with services, which are often defined in trade mark specifications much less precisely than goods. Wary of this, the courts have said that specifications of services should be read narrowly. Thus in *Avnet v Iosact* (1998), the court said that the defendant, an internet service provider, was not offering advertising and promotional services by providing customers with web pages on which they could publicise their products. And in the *Reed* case, a sophisticated internet jobs site was not "an employment agency service" because it did not actually put employers and employees in contact with each other.

Identical marks and similar goods/services or similar marks and identical goods/services

The second type of trade mark infringement case arises where the mark used by the defendant is identical to the plaintiff's registered mark, but the goods or services for which the defendant is using the mark are only similar to those for which the plaintiff has registered the mark, or the goods or services are identical but the marks are only similar. In these circumstances, the plaintiff must show that because the marks are identical and the goods/services are similar, or vice versa, there exists a likelihood of confusion or association on the part of the public. Much judicial ink has been expended over the meaning of a likelihood of confusion/association and the correct approach to this category of cases. Many of the cases discussing these issues have been decided by the ECJ (*Sabel v Puma*, 1998; *Canon v MGM*, 1999 and *Lloyd*, 2000). It has come up with the "global appreciation" test.

In a nutshell, this requires the court to take into account all relevant factors, such as the degree of similarity between the marks and the goods/services, and the distinctiveness of the registered mark, to work out whether confusion is likely. These factors are interdependent. Therefore, a lesser degree of similarity between goods or services may be offset by a greater degree of similarity between marks, and vice versa. Similarly, the more distinctive the registered trade mark (either in itself or because of the reputation it possesses on the market), the greater the risk of confusion. Conversely, the less distinctive the registered trade mark, the smaller the risk of confusion. So when *The European* newspaper sued *The European Voice* newspaper for trade mark infringement, the fact that "European" was an ordinary English word in common use, which was not in itself distinctive of the plaintiff's newspaper, militated against a finding of a likelihood of confusion (*The European v The Economist*, 1998). (The concept of distinctiveness is discussed in detail in Chapter 10.)

When it comes to assessing the similarity of the marks, they must be looked at from the point of view of the average consumer. The average consumer is assumed to look at the mark as a whole and, in particular, its distinctive or dominant components, rather than analysing its details. Although the average consumer is assumed to be reasonably well-informed, observant and circumspect, account has to be taken of the fact that a consumer rarely has a chance to make a direct comparison between the marks and is, therefore, likely to have an imperfect recollection of the registered mark. This factor was crucial in *Wagamama v City Centre Restaurants* (1995). The plaintiff ran a Japanese-style noodle restaurant under the registered mark *Wagamama*. The defendant started an Indian restaurant called *Rajamama*. The judge found that because *Wagamama* was quite meaningless to the public, being an entirely made-up word, imperfect recollection of the mark was very likely. Therefore, although seen side-by-side the marks were easily distinguishable, in normal use they would not be so seen. Moreover there was a real risk of another sort of confusion—many of those who did not mistake *Rajamama* for *Wagamama* might think that *Rajamama* was run by the same concern that ran *Wagamama* – an Indian variant of the Japanese restaurant. There was a substantial likelihood of confusion on both counts and hence passing-off.

As far as the similarity of goods/services is concerned, there are a number of things to consider when comparing the goods/services for which the defendant has used the mark and the goods/services for which the mark is registered. The most important are the uses of the goods/services; the users of the goods/services; the physical nature of the goods/services; the trade channels through which the goods/services reach the market, including in the case of goods sold in supermarkets, whether they are found on the same or different shelves, and the extent to which the goods/services compete. Thus, in *British Sugar* the fact that the products in question had different uses, were not in direct competition, were different in physical nature (the plaintiff's could be poured, the defendant's not) and were found in different places in the supermarket (the defendant's were with the jams, not the syrups), meant that the products could not be regarded as similar.

Identical or similar marks and identical, similar or dissimilar goods/services

The final category of trade mark infringement case is primarily concerned with the situation where the defendant is using a sign which is identical or similar to the plaintiff's registered mark in relation to goods or services dissimilar to those for which the mark is registered. Originally, it was assumed, at least in the UK, that this type of case was limited to dissimilar goods. However, recent decisions from the ECJ have stated that it also applies where the goods/services are identical or similar (see *Davidoff v Gofkid*, 2003, and *Adidas-Salomon v Fitnessworld*, 2003), and the statute has now been amended to apply in these cases. Whatever the nature of the goods/services, there will only be trade mark infringement if the plaintiff can show that his trade mark has a reputation and that the defendant's use of the mark, "being without due cause, takes unfair advantage of, or is detrimental to, the distinctive character or the repute of the trade mark". The effect is to give the owner of a well-known trade mark a greater degree of protection—but how much still remains rather uncertain.

The requirement that the plaintiff's mark have a reputation is akin to that in passing-off (as to which see Chapter 15). Customers must know the mark as the plaintiff's "badge". The second part of the test is more complicated: the ECJ says a public perception of "a link" will do—though what amounts to "a link" remains a mystery at present. Some examples may assist. The kinds of scenario which are likely to be caught are as follows.

Dilution

If a famous mark and, in particular, one known for exclusiveness and luxury is used for all manner of goods, its identity and value will be undermined or diluted. So use of *Chanel* or *Gucci* on plastic toys, pizzas, disposable nappies or video shops would be detrimental to the distinctive character or repute of those marks.

Tarnishing

Some goods or services are generally considered by the public to be unattractive in character. Tarnishing occurs when a mark with a reputation for something entirely different is used in connection with goods or services of this type. Classic instances of tarnishing are use of the mark *VISA* for condoms (*Sheimer's TM Appn.*, 2000), and use of the mark *Klarein* for a liquid detergent when the mark *Claeryn* was well known for Dutch gin (*Lucas Bols v Colgate-Palmolive*, 1976), a famous Benelux case. Some think that this sort of decision can go too far—in the UK for instance *Jif* lemon juice happily coexisted for many years with Jif detergent and even Jiffy condoms. (*Jif* detergent for unfathomable marketing reasons now calls itself *Cif*.)

Exploitation

This has been described as "free-riding on the coattails of a famous mark" (*Adidas-Salomon*, 2003). In that case, it was suggested that use of the *Rolls Royce* mark by a manufacturer of whisky in order to promote his brand would amount to taking advantage of the mark's distinctive character or repute. Again, to British eyes that is taking things a bit far.

But note that the detriment or unfair advantage must be real and not fanciful. See, for example, *Premier Brands v Typhoon Europe* (2000), in which the owner of the well-known mark *Typhoo* for tea, failed to prevent the defendant from using *Typhoon* for kitchen equipment. The plaintiff's argument that *Typhoon* would cause dilution and tarnishing, because of the association with the destructive power of tropical cyclones, was rejected. The fact that anyone even dared advance it shows how far things have gone.

Use

What type of use of his mark may the owner of a registered trade mark prevent? The use made by the defendant must be in the course of trade, as opposed to for private or domestic purposes. But as long as the use is in trade, a very wide variety of acts may be prevented. The most obvious uses the plaintiff will be able to stop are putting the mark on goods or their packaging, offering goods or services for sale by reference to the mark, actually selling or supplying them by reference to the mark, importing and exporting them by reference to the mark and using the mark on business papers (catalogues, invoices, headed note paper and the like) and in advertising. The use does not have to be in writing. Oral use of the mark (*e.g.* a radio or television advert) can also be prevented. However, the mark must be used "in relation to" the relevant goods or services. For instance, use of

Wet Wet Wet as part of the title of a book about the pop group called "A Sweet Little Mystery—Wet Wet Wet—The Inside Story" is use of the mark in relation to the pop group and not in relation to books, which were the goods for which the trade mark was registered (see *British Sugar*, referred to above).

Who Should be Sued for Infringement

Most prudent traders avoid the possibility of infringement by checking the Registers of trade marks in the UK and at OHIM before adopting a new mark. But if infringement does occur, an action to enforce the rights of the owner of the mark may be brought either against the person who applied the mark to the goods in the first place (or imported them, if they were marked abroad), or against anyone who has subsequently traded in them. Each subsequent trader, however, will usually have the right to bring into the action as a "third party" the person who sold the goods to him, so that in the last resort whoever marked or imported the goods will usually be liable for the whole of the damages, and if he has the money to pay them, there will often be commercial advantages in bringing the action against him only. Dealers lower down the line are less frequently sued, unless the owner of the mark cannot discover who made or imported the goods (suing the dealer may be one way of finding this out), or the dealers themselves have large stocks of falsely marked goods.

In this connection, trade marks for services are ordinarily quite different from trade marks for goods: trade marks go on goods, and stay with them as they pass from hand to hand. Marks for services are ordinarily used just by the one business that actually provides the services.

Threats

If the owner of a registered trade mark discovers that someone is carrying out activities that he believes infringe his trade mark, then one apparently obvious thing to do before suing is to write a warning letter to the potential defendant. If this course is taken (and in many cases it can be an extremely useful tactic, since it may avoid the need to issue proceedings altogether), some care must be taken. This is because the Trade Marks Act, in certain circumstances, provides a person aggrieved by unjustified threats of proceedings for infringement of a registered trade mark with a cause of action against the person who makes such threats. If successful, the person aggrieved can obtain an injunction against the continuance of the threats and damages in respect of any loss sustained by the threats, for example, if he has lost customers as a result of the threats. The relief cannot be obtained if the person who made the threats can show that the acts in respect of which proceedings were threatened do constitute a trade mark infringement.

The simplest way round the problem is to do nothing more than merely notify the potential defendant that the trade mark is registered, which does not constitute a threat. If any other type of letter is to be written, then the safest thing to do is to instruct a solicitor or trade mark agent. Sometimes the best thing to do is sue first and offer to settle at the same time—there is a difference between threatening to put the knife in and negotiating terms for its removal.

Contested Actions

The defendant in an action for infringement of trade mark can (and if he fights the case at all usually does) claim by way of defence that the registration of the mark is invalid, and ask the court to cancel it. If this happens the case is likely to be made more lengthy, complicated and expensive. If the validity of the registration is disputed and is upheld by the court, the owner of the mark may ask the court for a "certificate of validity" for the registration (just as in a patent case). In practice, the certificate acts as a warning to the trade that this particular mark is too firmly established to be safely challenged.

10. EXCEPTIONS TO TRADE MARK INFRINGEMENT

It will have been seen from the previous chapter that the owner of a registered trade mark has the potential to prevent a wide range of activities by another trader on the ground that they are an infringement of his trade mark. In order to ensure that other traders can nevertheless compete freely and fairly in the market place, trade mark law provides a number of defences to an infringement action. One possible defence is that the trade mark registration is invalid or should be cancelled (see later). This chapter deals with the specific exceptions to trade mark infringement which apply even if the mark is validly registered.

Use of Own Name or Address

Honest use (strictly "use in accordance with honest practices in industrial or commercial matters") by a person of his own name, even though that name is used in the course of trade, is not a trade mark infringement. The use will not be considered to be honest if it causes deception of customers. So in practice, save in relation to unused registered marks (where there will be no confusion), this defence is seldom of value. For instance a Mr William Asprey, could not rely on this defence in respect of his use of the name "William R. Asprey" for a shop selling luxury goods when there was evidence that customers of the plaintiff's well-known shop *Asprey* would be confused (*Asprey & Garrard v WRA*, 2002). The defence probably applies to company names as well as those of real people. The House of Lords thought so, but was not entirely sure and so asked the ECJ (*Scandecor*, 2002)—there was no answer because the case settled). It would not apply to a name newly adopted by a company. Otherwise, there would be an obvious way to avoid trade mark infringement.

"Indications of the characteristics of goods or services"

This is probably the most important exception, although the most difficult to identify in practice. This is mainly because there are a number of different types of "descriptive" use that may be covered by the exception. We use inverted commas because the exception covers uses that are not purely descriptive, in particular, use in a trade mark sense for the defendant's goods (*Premier*

Luggage, 2002 and *Gerolsteiner Brunnen v Putsch,* 2004). The latter case illustrates the point. The plaintiffs' registered mark was "Gerri" for mineral water. The defendants sold an Irish mineral water called "Kerry Spring" imported into Germany from a company called Kerry Spring Water. The German court thought that *Kerry* was so close to the registered mark that there would be confusion (only aural—and note that German courts are more apt than most to find confusion). On a reference, the ECJ held that the descriptive use defence applied even though the use had trade mark significance.

Other, more obvious cases, are where the defendant is using the plaintiff's registered trade mark as a description, rather than as a trade mark. For example, use on the label of a jar of spread of the words "Robertson's Toffee Treat" was held not to be an infringement of the plaintiff's mark *Treat,* on the ground that "Treat" was being used by the defendant descriptively, in contrast with its name as maker", *i.e.* Robertson's (*British Sugar v James Robertson,* 1996). Similarly, "spork" on a price list to describe a cross between a spoon and a fork was not an infringement of the registration of *Spork,* the term having been used generically in the trade, and the defendant's price list clearly indicating the manufacturer of the product (*Green v Regalzone,* 2002). Likewise, "Huggies will keep your baby dry" for nappies would not infringe the registered mark *Baby Dry.*

There are also cases where the defendant is using the plaintiff's registered mark to refer to the plaintiff's goods or services by way of comparison. For example, the use by Ryanair of the British Airways trade mark, *BA,* as part of the slogan "EXPENSIVE BA . . . . DS!" (*British Airways v Ryanair,* 2001). The precise circumstances in which comparative advertising will be permitted are discussed below. Next, the defendant may be using the plaintiff's registered trade mark to refer to the plaintiff's goods or services, so as to indicate some characteristic of the defendant's goods or services. For example, "These tights contain *Lycra*". Finally, the defendant may be using the plaintiff's registered trade mark to refer to the plaintiff's goods or services because he is legitimately dealing in the plaintiff's goods or services.

Spare Parts

Where a defendant needs to use the plaintiff's registered trade mark in order to indicate the intended purpose of a product or service, there is an exception to infringement. The most common examples are use by the defendant to refer to accessories and spare parts. This type of case often arises in the car industry. Thus, use of the phrase "*Ford* spares sold here" would not be an infringement. However, the use made of the trade mark must be honest. In a case where the defendant had previously been an authorised Volvo dealer, had then had the dealership revoked and started using the phrase "Independent Volvo Specialist", with the words "Independent" and "Specialist" appearing in much smaller lettering, the court found that the defendant could not take advantage of the defence. The court was clearly influenced by the fact that the defendant had previously been an authorised dealer and had written to customers in such a way as to give the misleading impression that it continued to be an authorised dealer (*Volvo v Heritage*, 2000). By way of contrast, the ECJ held that "BMW Specialist" written fairly was all right (*BMW v Deenik*, 1999). In trade marks, as in life, a lot depends not only on what you say but how you say it.

There Must be Honesty

In the case of all of the above exceptions, the defendant will only be able to take advantage of it if his use is honest. As with the defence of use of own name, the use will not be honest if it causes confusion. In the case of comparative advertising, the use will not be honest if a reasonable reader, on being given the full facts, would be likely to say that the advertisement is not honest. In this context, the court will bear in mind that the general public are used to the ways of advertisers and expect hyperbole. This means that an advertisement will probably have to be significantly misleading to be found to be dishonest for this purpose (*Cable & Wireless v BT*, 1998). The Ryanair advertisement, referred to above, compared the prices of Ryanair's midweek return with BA's return same week fare, rather than with its cheaper return fare requiring a Saturday night stay. The advertisement's small print indicated that the fares given were midweek return fares. The judge found that the average consumer would not have found the price comparison misleading because he would expect there to be some sort of conditions and the small print made that clear. Therefore, Ryanair's use of the BA mark was found to be honest comparative advertising and the trade mark infringement claim failed.

Earlier Rights

A registered trade mark cannot be used to stop someone who has used the mark continuously in a particular locality prior to the date on which the trade mark was registered or, if the trade mark was already in use at that date, prior to the date on which the trade mark owner first started using the trade mark, from using the mark in that locality. The owner of the earlier right must show that at that date his use of the mark was protected in the relevant locality by the law of passing-off. (For the requirements of a cause of action in passing-off, see Chapter 15.) Suppose the plaintiff had registered a trade mark for domestic cleaning services, but prior to the date of his application, the defendant was already using the same mark for domestic cleaning services in the London area. If the defendant could prove that it had a reputation for cleaning services in the London area at the date of the plaintiff's application such that it could have prevented the plaintiff from using the mark in the London area by relying on its rights in passing-off, the defendant will have a defence to an action for trade mark infringement.

Defendant Using his Own Registered Mark

The Trade Marks Act states that if the defendant has himself registered a trade mark, the use of that registered trade mark for the goods or services for which it is registered will not amount to an infringement of the plaintiff's registered trade mark. This defence, available under the previous Trade Marks Act, was re-introduced in the new Trade Marks Act 1994. However, this is one of the more blatant instances of the UK legislators going on a frolic of their own, since the defence has no basis in the European Trade Mark Directive from which the Act is supposed to be derived. Consequently, it is probably unsafe for a defendant to rely on it in relation to a UK mark. It does not appear in the Community Trade Mark Regulation and, therefore, does not apply to Community registered trade marks. Nor does it apply to a passing-off claim (*Inter-Lotto v Camelot*, 2003).

11. TRADE MARK REGISTRATION

Here we explain what sort of thing can be registered as a trade mark, discuss the conditions for registration to be possible and give an outline of the procedure for registration and opposition. It must not be forgotten that registration is not the be all and end all of a mark's existence. A mark which has been registered can, at a later date, be revoked or invalidated (see Chapter 12).

What Kind of Sign can be Registered?

The types of things that can be registered as trade marks were much expanded by the Trade Marks Act 1994 and the Community Trade Mark Regulation. In addition to the obvious things such as words, logos and pictures, it is now possible, in principle, to register three-dimensional shapes, *e.g.* the shape of the *Coca Cola* bottle for non-alcoholic beverages; colours, *e.g.* the colour orange Pantone 151, being the predominant colour applied to the visible surface of packaging and/or advertising and promotional materials for telephone handsets etc. (*Libertel*, 2003); combinations of colours (*Heidelberger Bauchemie*, 2004); and sounds, *e.g.* the *Direct Line* jingle or *Für Elise*, the latter held registrable by the ECJ in *Shield Mark v Memex* (2003).

The only limit is that the mark must be capable of being represented graphically and must be identified precisely. On this basis it is probably impossible to register signs consisting of smells. The ECJ decided, in relation to a "balsamically fruity scent with a slight hint of cinnamon" that the requirements of graphic representability are not satisfied by a chemical formula, by a description in written words, by the deposit of an odour sample or by a combination of those elements (*Sieckmann*, 2002). Of course, just because a sign is the type of thing capable of being registered does not mean it necessarily will be. In particular, the mark must be distinctive, not descriptive (as discussed below). Distinctiveness is likely to be much more difficult to prove in the case of exotic marks such as shapes, colours and sounds: these are far less likely to be regarded by members of the public as indicating the source of the product than conventional marks.

Registrable Marks

Since the fundamental function of a trade mark is to act as a guarantee of origin for the public, in order to be registered, the mark must serve this purpose. To ensure that this is the case, the Act and Regulation impose a series of requirements, which any mark applied for must meet. In the case of a Community trade mark, the mark applied for must meet each requirement in all parts of the Community.

The mark must be distinctive, not descriptive

Distinctiveness is a crucial concept in the law of trade marks and passing-off. A distinctive mark is one that is suitable for distinguishing the goods of one trader from those of another. The contrast is with a descriptive mark: one that describes the goods in question and is therefore generally unsuitable for distinguishing the goods of one trader from those of another, because it would be applicable to all of them. Distinctiveness and descriptiveness are not black and white concepts. In general, marks are spread along a spectrum, with completely descriptive marks at one end and completely distinctive marks at the other. Consider, for example, possible marks for camera film. "Camera Film" would be at one end of the spectrum. It is totally descriptive and would therefore be completely hopeless at performing the function of a trade mark. "High Definition" would be a bit of the way along the spectrum, but would still be a highly descriptive. "Picture Bright" would be further along, descriptive but not quite as much, and not the sort of phrase others would normally want to use. Finally, "Kodak" is at the other, distinctive, end of the spectrum (some say it was George Eastman's greatest invention—highly distinctive and meaningless in all languages). A made-up word, is ideal, from a trade mark lawyer's point of view, for distinguishing goods. But from a marketing point of view, there is a strong increasing tendency to prefer descriptive marks, since they are more likely to tell the public something about the attributes of the product or service in question.

To be registerable, a mark must reach a certain threshold of distinctiveness that can be achieved by the nature of the mark itself or by use having turned it into one relied upon by the public or a combination of the two. Quite where the threshold is is a matter of debate and some fluctuation. On the whole, the level of the threshold seems to have been decreasing of late. Much excitement (among trade mark lawyers—doubtless the rest of the world could not care less) was caused by the registration as a Community trade mark of "Baby Dry" for nappies. The decision of the ECJ (*Procter & Gamble v OHIM*, 2001) was widely criticised as applying too low a threshold, on the ground that the mark is descriptive for nappies and that other traders are likely to wish to use it descriptively. The court thought that "Baby Dry" was a "lexical invention" though no-one else did. Although a defendant using such a phrase may have a defence (as to which, see Chapter 10), the problem is that registration of descriptive marks of this sort hands a weapon to large and wealthy companies who are more likely to have the resources to pursue extensive trade mark registration and enforcement programmes against smaller, poorer traders. They may in theory have a defence, but in reality are likely to back down when threatened with a registered trade mark by a big company. Perhaps in response to the furore over its *Baby Dry* decision, the court has now visibly (but without the grace of admitting it got *Baby Dry* wrong) backed off, holding that "Doublemint" for chewing gum is too descriptive, and that the rights of other traders should be taken into account when registration is being considered apart from any defences which may exist once the mark is registered (*Wrigley's Appn.*, 2003). But the line between too descriptive and not remains wobbly as the decision allowing *SAT.2* for satellite broadcasting shows. *SAT.1 SatellitenFernsehen's Appn.*, 2004).

In addition to considering the inherent distinctiveness of the mark, that is, the capacity of the mark to distinguish goods from those of other traders in itself, a further important consideration in assessing whether a mark is registrable is any distinctiveness, which the mark has acquired through use. Whilst some marks (such as "Camera Film") could never in practice acquire distinctiveness through use, many other descriptive marks may, on being used extensively for a particular product or service, become sufficiently well known that they achieve what is known as acquired distinctiveness.

There is no hard and fast rule for assessing whether a mark is sufficiently distinctive and not too descriptive to be registrable. If the mark is already customarily used in the trade, then it will almost certainly not be registrable. Further, if other traders might legitimately wish to use the mark to describe their product or service it is likely not to be registrable, notwithstanding *Baby Dry*. Certain categories of mark are generally more difficult to register, in particular, geographical marks (*e.g.* "Chiemsee", the name of a Bavarian lake, for clothing (*Windsurfing Chiemsee v*

Huber, 1999); laudatory marks (*e.g.* "Treat" for dessert sauces and syrups, found invalid in *British Sugar v James Robertson*, 1996). Marks which are common surnames are, perhaps surprisingly to be granted on a first-come, first-served basis. A later user of the same name will have to be careful to fall within the honest use defence (see above), *Nichols TM Appn*, 2004. (*Nichols* allowed for food and drink items).

The mark must not be contrary to public policy or morality

This requirement covers a multitude of sins. In particular, a mark is likely to be refused if it would cause offence or offensive behaviour. Two examples give a flavour of the type of marks that are likely to be refused on this ground. In *Ghazilian's TM Appn.* (2002), *Tiny Penis* for clothing, footwear and headgear was refused on the basis that the mark would cause offence to "right-thinking" members of the public if used on, say, advertising bill boards or on the side of a bus. The judge stated that "correct anatomical terms for parts of genitalia should be reserved for serious use and should not be debased by use as a smutty trade mark for clothing". Thus, it appears that had the trade mark been sought for, say, condoms, it might well have been accepted unless held too descriptive. In *CDW Graphic Design's TM Appn* (2003), www.standupifyouhatemanu.com for various goods, including car bumper stickers, mugs and T-shirts, was refused on the ground that it was likely to function as a badge of antagonism and to increase the incidence of football violence or other offensive behaviour. (One of us has no comment).

The mark must not be deceptive

A mark cannot be registered if it will deceive the public, for instance, as to the nature, quality or geographical origin of the goods or services. The classic example is the *Orlwoola* for various articles, including clothing. The Court of Appeal decided that it should not remain registered since if the goods were made wholly of wool, the mark was descriptive, and if they were not made wholly of wool, it was a misdescription that was certain to deceive (*"Orlwoola"*, 1909).

The mark must not be a specially protected emblem

Certain emblems are specially protected. Thus trade marks consisting of or containing various emblems such as Royal arms, representations of the Royal crown and the Royal family, flags, national emblems of Paris Convention countries, emblems of international organisations, coats of arms and Olympic symbols are subject to special rules relating to registration.

The mark must not be applied for in bad faith

The requirement that an application must not be made in bad faith applies to UK trade marks only at the application stage, although in the case of a Community trade mark, bad faith can be relied upon as a ground for invalidity of the trade mark. In the case of UK trade marks, the requirement is of rather uncertain scope. There is considerable uncertainty as to what type of behaviour may be covered and as to how reprehensible the behaviour must be for the application to be refused (in particular, it is unclear whether subjective or objective dishonesty is required). The following types of behaviour may be regarded as exhibiting bad faith.

The applicant is not the owner of the mark

This is sometimes referred to as trade mark misappropriation or theft. It occurs when the applicant knows or ought to know that the trade mark belongs to someone else, but nevertheless proceeds to make an application for the mark in his own name. Consider, for example, *Harrison v Teton Valley* (2004). The mark applied for was "China White" for cocktails. Registration was opposed by the owners of the well-known nightclub China-white. The nightclub sold a house cocktail known by the name "Chinawhite". It had been developed by employees of the opponent, including the bar manager. The bar manager approached the applicant and told him that he was working at Chinawhite nightclub and had developed a cocktail called "Chinawhite" to be sold at the nightclub. The applicant then applied for the trade mark in his own name. This was found to fall short of the standards of acceptable commercial behaviour observed by reasonable businessmen. So it was held that the application had been made in bad faith.

The applicant has no intention of using the mark at all or for some of the goods/services applied for

An applicant for a UK trade mark must sign a form stating that the trade mark is being used by the applicant or with his or her consent in relation to the goods or services stated, or there is a *bona fide* intention that it will be so used. On this basis, it has

101

been said that if the applicant has no intention to use the mark at all, the application is made in bad faith and should be refused. Similarly, in cases where the applicant intends to use the mark but only for some of the goods or services for which it has been applied for, the mark should be refused for those goods and services for which the applicant does not intend to use the mark. For this reason, whilst it is important for a trader to make sure that he applies for a mark that will cover all the goods and services for which he may use the mark, too broad an application may well be cut down. Having said that, the legal justification for refusing or restricting the scope of a mark on the grounds of lack of intention to use is somewhat dubious since the law provides a specific ground for revocation of a mark where it has not been used for a period of five years (this is discussed in Chapter 12). For this reason, OHIM has taken the view that lack of intention to use should not, of itself, be regarded as bad faith when considering the validity of a Community trade mark (*Trillium*, 2000). Given OHIM's attitude, it seems likely that the UK Trade Mark Registry will adopt a more lenient approach to this type of case. But this spells trouble for the future—specifications much wider than the scope of use will inevitably help clog up the Registers and bring people who have no real commercial conflict into pointless trade mark disputes.

Special requirements for shape marks

As has already been explained, signs consisting of the shapes of goods are now registrable as trade marks. However, in order to ensure that a trade mark proprietor cannot thereby monopolise shapes that other traders have a legitimate interest in using, the registration of shape marks is subject to certain special restrictions. In particular, a sign cannot be registered if it consists exclusively of the shape, which results from the nature of the goods themselves, the shape of goods that is necessary to obtain a technical result, or the shape that gives substantial value to the goods. It should not be forgotten that these requirements are in addition to those that apply generally to all types of trade marks, in particular, the requirement that the mark be distinctive, not descriptive. If any mark falls foul of the special requirements for shape marks, it is very likely that it will also be insufficiently distinctive to be registered.

The case of Philips' three-headed rotary shaver illustrates how the special requirements for shape marks operate in practice (*Philips v Remington*, Court of Appeal 1999 and ECJ,

2003—note how long it took). Philips' mark actually consisted of a drawing of its three-headed rotary shaver, consisting of three circular heads with rotating blades in the shape of an equilateral triangle. In practice, everyone treated this as a registration of the shape itself. It relied on this mark to sue Remington for trade mark infringement by the sale of its three-headed rotary shaver, which also used three rotating heads forming an equilateral triangle. Remington argued that Philips' trade mark was invalid on various grounds, including that it did not comply with the special requirements for shape marks.

As to the first requirement, Remington's case was that because the shape registered resulted from the nature of a three-headed rotary shaver it should not have been registered. However, the Court of Appeal took the view that the purpose of the requirement was to exclude from registration basic shapes that should be available for use by the public at large. In this case there were other shapes of shavers and, in particular, other possible shapes for three-headed electrical shavers, therefore there was no reason to exclude this particular shape from registration. As to the second requirement, Remington argued that the essential features of the shape shown in the trade mark were designed to achieve a technical result and therefore should not be registrable. The Court of Appeal agreed, rejecting Philips' argument that because there were other ways of achieving the same technical performance (for example, using four heads not three or arranging the heads in a different configuration), the mark was valid. This point was also referred to the ECJ, who came to the same conclusion. So Philips lost. As to the third requirement, Remington's argument that the shape registered gave substantial value to the goods and, therefore, was not registrable, failed. The Court of Appeal held that there was a distinction between the second requirement which excluded functional shapes and the third requirement which excluded "aesthetic-type" shapes. Only if the shape, as a shape, had substantial value should it be excluded from registration on this ground. On the facts, the court found there was no evidence that this was the case.

Earlier Marks and Rights

In order to be registered, a mark must comply with the requirements of registrability set out above. But even if all these requirements are complied with, a mark may still fail to achieve registration because it clashes with an earlier registered trade mark or other unregistered right. Note that, in the case of a UK trade mark application, if the applicant can get the consent of the proprietor of the earlier trade mark or other earlier right, then the mark applied for can be registered. In the case of a Community trade mark application, the following grounds for refusal of an application only apply if they are raised in an opposition by the proprietor of the earlier mark or right.

Earlier trade marks

In the case of an application for a UK mark, the earlier trade marks that need to be considered are those UK trade marks, international trade marks (UK) and Community trade marks with earlier application dates and, in addition, any earlier well-known marks (international marks and well-known marks are discussed in Chapter 13). In the case of an application for a Community trade mark, the earlier trade marks that need to be considered are Community trade marks, trade marks registered in any Member State and trade marks registered under inter-national arrangements with effect in a Member State with earlier application dates and any earlier well known marks.

The question of whether or not there is sufficient similarity between one of these earlier trade marks and the mark applied for, such that the mark applied for should not be registered is assessed by a series of three tests mirroring those that apply in cases of infringement. Accordingly, if the mark applied for is identical to an earlier trade mark and the goods or services for which it is applied for are identical with those for which the earlier trade mark is protected, the mark will not be registered. If, on the other hand, the mark applied for is identical to an earlier trade mark, but the goods or services for which it is applied for are only similar to those for which the earlier trade mark is registered, or the goods or services are identical but the marks are only similar, the mark will not be registered only if, because of the similarity of the marks or the goods or services, there is a likelihood of confusion. Finally, if the mark applied for is identical or similar to the earlier trade mark and is applied for in relation to goods or services that are identical, similar or dissimilar to those for which the mark is registered, the mark will not be registered only if the earlier trade mark has a reputation and the use of the mark applied for without due cause would take unfair advantage of, or be detrimental to, the distinctive character or the repute of the earlier trade mark.

These tests have already been discussed in detail in the context of infringement. Since the same principles apply, that discussion will not be repeated here. In addition, it should be noted that where the grounds for refusal of registration exist in relation to only some of the goods or services for which the mark is applied for, the mark should be refused only in relation to those goods or services, permitting registration in respect of the other goods or services applied for.

Other earlier rights

A trade mark application may also be refused if use of the mark applied for is liable to be prevented by virtue of a law protecting an earlier unregistered mark. In the case of UK trade mark applications, the application may also be refused if use of the mark applied for is liable to be prevented by virtue of any other earlier right, *e.g.* copyright, design right etc. In the case of Community trade mark applications, other earlier rights can be relied upon as a ground of invalidity once the mark is registered, but not as a ground for opposing the application. Invalidity is discussed in Chapter 12.

As far as earlier unregistered marks are concerned, the position for a UK trade mark application is that if it can be shown that, at the date of the application, a third party could have prevented any normal and fair use of the trade mark applied for by relying on its rights in passing-off, the mark will be refused (see Chapter 12). In summary, it will have to be shown that the third party had a reputation in respect of the earlier trade mark at the date of application and that use of the trade mark applied for at that date would have resulted in members of the public being deceived into thinking that the goods or services for which the mark is applied for were the goods or services of the third party. Unlike in a standard passing-off case, the use of the mark applied for will be considered in the abstract, by reference to anything that would be considered normal and fair use of the mark, but without reference to any particular surrounding circumstances. As with earlier trade mark rights, if this ground can only be made out in respect of some of the goods or services, the mark should only be refused in respect of those goods or services. In theory, it might be possible for the mark to be limited in geographical extent, if the ground can only be made out in some parts of the UK. However, this approach could create practical problems in defining the area in question.

In the case of Community trade mark applications, the position may be rather different, because the law protecting the earlier unregistered mark could be the law of any Member State, not necessarily the English law of passing-off. In addition, there is an added requirement that the earlier unregistered mark be of more than local significance. At present, it is not entirely clear what this requirement entails. It is probably the case that use throughout a single Member State would be sufficient.

As far as other rights are concerned, the most obvious cases in which a UK trade mark would be refused registration on this basis are if a third party could prevent use of the mark applied for by relying on copyright, design right or registered design. For example, if the mark applied for consisted of a logo or device which infringed someone else's copyright, registration would be refused.

Applications and Oppositions

An application to register a UK mark must be made to the Registrar of Trade Marks. The Registrar's office is at the Patent Office, which he administers under the alternative title of Comptroller-General of Patents, Designs and Trade Marks. The office is in Newport, Wales. Applications are normally made by trade mark agents, but it appears to be increasingly common for members of the public to apply without using an agent. If possible, it is wise to employ an experienced agent to make the application since this can prevent problems with the application and registration in the long run. However, the Patent Office now has an excellent website (at www.patent.gov.uk) that offers plenty of information for those wishing to go it alone. Using the services of an agent, the costs of applying for a registration are of the order of £400, of which £200 is the official fee. If there are problems leading to significant correspondence with the Registry, the costs will be higher. The registration must be renewed (fee currently around £200) every 10 years.

Applications for Community trade marks are made to the Office for the Harmonisation of the Internal Market (OHIM) which is based in Alicante, Spain. These applications are dealt with in Chapter 13.

The classes of goods and services

Goods are divided into 34 classes for trade mark purposes, services into another eleven. Typical classes of goods are: machines and machine-tools; fuels, industrial oils and lubricants; vehicles; clothing; games and playthings; wines, spirits and liqueurs. The "service" classes are fewer and broader: *e.g.* "Advertising and Business" (such as efficiency-experts and copy-bureaux); or "Material Treatment" (such as "engraving," that could be of jewellery or of tombstones). An application may be made for goods and services in more than one class, although each class additional class requires payment of an extra fee.

The scope of the goods and services applied for is particularly important. Obviously, it is in the applicant's interest to apply for all the goods and services on which he uses or potentially wishes to use the mark (note, care should be taken to include spare parts and accessories, or ancillary services). However, it must be remembered that for a UK registration the mark could potentially be refused or cut down on the ground of bad faith (as to which, see above) or later revoked for non-use (as to which, see Chapter 12), if it is applied for goods and services in relation to which the applicant has no intention of using the mark. So far as OHIM is concerned, undue width of specification is not currently an objection (and indeed is positively welcomed). But it increases the potential for partial revocation for non-use later.

The applicant

The application should be made by the person, firm or company actually using or intending to use the mark. An agent or representative of an overseas proprietor should not apply for a mark without the authorisation of the proprietor, otherwise the proprietor can oppose the application or, if the mark is granted, can apply for a declaration of invalidity of the registration or ask for his name to be substituted as the proprietor. A mark can be applied for by two or more applicants and, in theory, each is allowed to use the mark for his own benefit, without the permission of the other. However, there is a danger that two proprietors using the mark independently could make the mark deceptive and liable to revocation (see Chapter 12).

Examination of the application

Every application is examined to see that it complies with the basic requirements as to registrability. In particular, the Registrar will consider whether the mark is for something that may be registered, whether it is distinctive, not descriptive, and that it meets all the other criteria discussed above, including considering whether there are any earlier marks that might prevent its registration. Currently, there are proposals to abandon searches for earlier, conflicting marks. It seems that OHIM will go that way it (it only searches through prior Community marks), but the UK Registry will not. A problem with a mark that has not been examined for conflict with an earlier mark is that the owner cannot, unless he has done his own search, be sure he safe.

If the Registrar or OHIM, as the case may be, considers that any of the criteria are not met then he will inform the applicant, who has a chance to respond in writing. In the UK, if the applicant so wishes, he can have a hearing. The applicant may need to file evidence in order to try to overcome any objections. Most commonly, if it is suggested that the mark is not distinctive, the applicant will need to file evidence of the use made of the mark in order to try to prove that it has acquired distinctiveness through use. A final decision of the Registrar that the mark is not registrable can be appealed to the High Court or the so-called Appointed Person (someone with experience in trade mark law, usually a Queen's Counsel or an academic). Appeals from OHIM go first to a Board of Appeals and then on to the Court of First Instance of the ECJ in Luxembourg, then on to the full court or a chamber of it. In the UK, courts are apt to uphold the decision of an experienced trade mark official—but in Europe, at least until recently, the courts in Luxembourg have not given respect to decisions below and have tended to be erratic.

In the UK, it takes around nine months to obtain a registration if all goes smoothly. In OHIM things can take a lot longer. If there are objections to be overcome, it may take longer. Hence the need to apply for registration well in advance of actual use, wherever possible.

Acceptance and publication

In the UK, if and when the Registrar has no further objection to the mark, the application will be accepted and the intention to register it will be published in *The Trade Marks Journal*. Once the application has been published, anyone who wishes to oppose the registration of the mark has three months to do so. Therefore, the mark will not be actually registered until after this period. It is usually registered about 15 weeks after publication if there is no opposition. Occasionally, even where there is no opposition, the Registrar may change his mind and refuse the application if new matters have come to her notice indicating that it was accepted in error. If this happens the applicant should be given an opportunity to respond before the final refusal.

Things are much the same at OHIM except slower.

Opposition

Anyone may oppose an application on any of the grounds for which the Registrar may refuse to register a mark (set out above). The usual reason for opposition is that the new mark is too similar to a mark the opponents are using or have registered or hope to use or register. (Once they have decided to oppose the application at all, however, opponents will naturally raise any other objections to it that they can find.) The procedure for opposition commences with the opponent filing a statement of his grounds of opposition to the mark. The applicant responds with a counter-statement. Then each side files evidence in support of their case. If the parties wish, there will then be a hearing before one of the Registrar's hearing officers to decide the matter. An appeal from the decision of the hearing officer can be made to the High Court or the Appointed Person (as described above in relation to examination).

Oppositions are often bitterly fought, not only by opponents (who have often much to lose, since the new registration might reduce the value of their existing goodwill), but also by applicants, although the goodwill in a new mark may not be worth the legal costs involved, particularly if the matter is appealed, which can involve significant legal costs.

OHIM too has an opposition procedure. It is much more paper based, and is apt to be long and drawn out. Appeals go on the same route as for appeals from a refusal by the Office, *i.e.* to a Board of Appeal, then to the Court of First Instance and finally to the European Court itself. With such a four-stage procedure, and the flood of cases, it is not surprising things take so long—yet this sort of timing is particularly inappropriate for the determination of trade mark rights where marketing people need speedy answers. Something needs to be done, but the EU thinks it has more important things to attend to, so things will have to get worse before effective action is taken.

12. REMOVAL FROM THE REGISTER

Once registered, a mark is not immune to attack. Anyone can apply for its registration to be revoked (removed from the register) or declared invalid (treated as though the registration never was). Which you get depends on the ground of attack. For instance, revocation for non-use only runs from a date set by the court, whereas proof of one of the grounds for refusal of registration normally leads to a declaration of invalidity. In practice, there is no difference between them—either way the mark is knocked out. Most such applications occur because the mark is an obstacle to another's trade mark application or because the trade mark owner has sued for trade mark infringement and the defendant says, by way of defence, that the mark should not be on the Register. For UK trade marks, applications are made to the Registrar or the High Court, although if proceedings concerning the mark are pending in court (as they will be in an infringement case), the application must be made to the court. The procedure in the case of Community trade marks is covered in Chapter 13. This chapter sets out the grounds on which a mark can be removed from the Register. Many of the grounds are the same as the grounds for refusing to register a mark which are dealt with in Chapter 11 and reference should be made to that chapter where indicated.

Grounds for Revocation

Non-use

A mark which has not been used in the UK (or in the EU, in the case of a Community trade mark) for five years can be revoked. The rationale for this rule is to reduce the number of trade marks and, hence, conflicts between them. Time only begins to run from the date when the mark is actually put on the register. Since it can take a while (about nine months for a UK mark, a couple of years for a Community mark) for an application to be processed, in practice the owner has a long time from application to put it into use. When challenged for non-use, the burden is on the trade mark owner to show he has used it within the relevant period. The use must satisfy a number of requirements. First, it must be by the owner or with his consent. So use only by a licensee will do.

110

Second, it must be in relation to the goods or services for which the trade mark is registered. If the goods or services are widely defined, it may be necessary to dig deeper into the specification to work out precisely what things the mark has been used for in order to arrive at a fair specification of goods or services having regard to the use made. For example, in *Thomson Holidays v Norwegian Cruise Lines* (2003), "Freestyle" was registered for "arrangement and booking of travel, tours and cruises; escorting travellers and arranging the escorting of travellers; providing tourist office services and booking and provision of accommodation and catering services for travellers". The mark had actually only been used by the trade mark owner for package holidays of the 18–30 variety. It sued the defendant for using *Freestyle* for cruise holidays (generally known for attracting older customers). At first instance, the judge limited the specification to exclude cruises on cruise ships on the ground that they formed a distinct category of holiday product, which differed in kind and customer from land-based holiday products, such as those offered by the trade mark owner. The Court of Appeal rejected this limitation, saying that the specification should be limited to "package holidays" since this would be how the average consumer would describe the services provided by the trade mark owner.

Obviously, the precise scope of the limitation made by the court can be crucial in a trade mark infringement case. In *Thomson Holidays*, the trade mark owner lost on infringement at first instance, when its mark was limited to exclude cruise holidays, but won on appeal, when its mark was limited to package holidays. Cruise holidays were held to be a type of package holiday. It followed that the marks and services were identical and there was infringement of the same mark/services type. So, if a mark has been on the register for more than five years, a trade mark owner cannot be sure that a widely drawn specification will enable him to prevent any use of the trade mark falling within the specification. If he has not used the mark across the whole width of the specification, it is vulnerable to being cut down. Nonetheless in the real world he is likely to gain an advantage. People do not want to get into trade mark fights, so if a person is not committed to a mark, he is likely to use another rather than become involved in a protracted non-use fight.

Third, the use must be use of the trade mark as registered or of a form of the mark differing only in elements which do not alter its distinctive character. How different can the mark actually used be from that registered before it alters its distinctive character? Some guidance can be obtained from the cases.

111

Thus, "2nd Skin" was held not to be an alteration of the distinctive character of the registered mark "Second Skin" (*Second Skin TM*, 2001). In the long-running beer wars between the US and Czech Budweisers, the Court of Appeal upheld the decision of the hearing officer in the Trade Mark Registry that use of the words "Budweiser-Budweiser-Budvar-Budweiser-Bud-bräu-Bud-" in block capitals around a circle enclosing a motif consisting of a shield with a lion on it, superimposed on a castle with towers, was use of the registered mark in a form that did not alter the distinctive character of the registered mark consisting of the words *Budweiser Budbräu* in stylised writing. However, on appeal to the High Court, the judge concluded differently. The Court of Appeal said that had there been a free choice between the hearing officer's decision and that of the judge in the High Court, it would have preferred the latter (there was no free choice because the appeal court is limited to correcting an error of principle) (*Bud and Budweiser Budbräu TMs*, 2003). The differing views expressed indicate the uncertainty where a trade mark owner uses his mark in a different form from that registered. The moral is clear: the mark should be used in the same form as registered to avoid the danger of revocation for non-use. If the owner decides to vary the mark, he should register the variant too.

Fourth, the use must be "genuine". The meaning of "genuine use" was considered by the ECJ in *Ansul v Ajax* (2003). "Minimax" was registered for fire extinguishers and associated products. The owner had stopped selling fire extinguishers, but continued to sell parts for *Minimax* fire extinguishers and to maintain, check and repair them. The European Court held that where the trade mark owner sells parts which are integral to the structure of the goods previously sold and for this purpose makes actual use of the mark, the use may be genuine. More generally, it found that genuine use entails use of the mark on the market, not just internal use by the undertaking concerned. Therefore, use of the mark must relate to goods or services already marketed or about to be marketed for which preparations by the undertaking to secure customers are under way, particularly in the form of advertising campaigns. Further, use of the mark must be real, *i.e.* warranted in the economic sector concerned to maintain or create a share in the market for the goods or services protected by the mark. Use with the motive of maintaining the registration is not "genuine" in this sense. Even a tiny amount of use (*e.g.* samples to test the market), with no intention other than trading under the mark, will do (*Laboratoires Goemar's TM*, 2004).

If the owner cannot show use of his registered trade mark, it may still be open to him to show that there are proper reasons for the non-use. If proper reasons can be shown, then the mark will not be revoked. "Proper reasons" are limited in scope. They do not include ordinary commercial delays (*Philosophy di Alberta Ferretti TM*, 2003). The owner relied upon problems with a first licensee and delays due to the time taken to develop and market a fragrance. The Court of Appeal held that such ordinary commercial delays in producing a new product did not amount to proper reasons for non-use. Again in *Cabañas Habana TM* (2000), the argument that a mark for cigars could not be used because of the US trade embargo on Cuban products was rejected because the embargo had been in force for 33 years and had become a normal condition of trade.

The mark has become a common name in the trade

If an owner, through his acts or inactivity, permits his trade mark to become the common name in trade for a product or service for which it is registered, then it is liable to be revoked. This may occur where the owner is the first on the market with a new product, the trade mark of which then becomes generally used in trade as the name of products of this type. There are numerous examples where trade marks have come to be generally used by consumers as the common name for a product. Sometimes, the mark just turns completely into the generic word: "gramophone" is an old example; "aspirin" is another (though it is still a trade mark in Germany). There are other, subtler, cases: where the public know the word is a trade mark but nonetheless use it in a generic context; "Hoover" is the classic example, "Yale" and "Biro" are others. The latter sort of case is not strong enough for revocation. Revocation is limited to cases in which the mark has become the common name *in the trade* (for which the views of consumers are relevant: *Bjornekulla v Procordia* 2004). Moreover, this must have come about due to the acts or inactivity of the owner. This means, in practice, that an owner must be careful to ensure that he polices use of his mark.

In the case of a Community trade mark, there is a specific provision that allows a trade mark owner to request that any publisher of a dictionary or the like who reproduces his mark in a way that gives the impression that it constitutes a generic name ensures that the reproduction of the trade mark in the next edition is accompanied by an indication that it is registered.

The mark is misleading

This is similar to the requirement for registration that a mark applied for must not be deceptive, as to which see Chapter 11. However, for revocation, the misleading nature of the mark must have arisen as a consequence of the use made of it by the owner or with his consent.

Partial revocation

In relation to each of the grounds for revocation, if the grounds only exist in respect of some of the goods or services for which the trade mark is registered, then the mark will be revoked only for those goods and services. See, for example, the *Thomson Holidays* case.

Grounds for Invalidity

An application for invalidity of a trade mark may be made on the ground that the mark was registered in breach of one or more of the requirements for registration. In other words, that the mark is descriptive; that it is contrary to public policy or morality; that it is deceptive; that it is a specially protected emblem; that it was applied for in bad faith; or, in the case of a shape mark, that it does not comply with the special requirements laid down for these. The difference in the case of an application for invalidity is that on the question of descriptiveness, the facts will be considered as at the date of the application for invalidity. So, if as a result of use that has been made of the mark since the date of registration, it has acquired a distinctive character, it will not be invalidated.

An application for invalidity may also be made on the ground that there are other earlier trade marks or earlier rights that should have prevented registration. In the case of a Community trade mark, an application for invalidity based on an earlier mark or right can only be made by the owner of the earlier mark or right. In the case of both UK and Community marks, if the owner of the earlier mark or right relied upon has acquiesced for a period of five years in the use of the registered trade mark, with knowledge of that use, he cannot apply for a declaration of invalidity based on that earlier mark or right. Nor can he prevent the use of the later trade mark in relation to goods or services in relation to which it has been used, based on the earlier right, except if the later mark was applied for in bad faith.

114

As with the grounds for revocation, if the grounds for invalidity exist in respect of only some of the goods or services, there may be partial revocation of the mark in relation to those goods or services only.

13. COMMUNITY MARKS, INTERNATIONAL REGISTRATION OF MARKS AND WELL KNOWN MARKS

The Community Trade Mark

The crucial difference between a UK and Community trade mark ("ctm") is that a UK trade mark provides protection for the UK only, whilst a ctm covers the whole of the EU.

Since the 1994 Act is itself based on the Trade Marks Directive, for the most part the substantive law relating to UK trade marks and ctms is the same. But the procedure for applying for and, in certain respects, litigating, a ctm is rather different. The main differences are covered here.

Applications for a Community trade mark

An application must be made in one of the official languages of the EU. In addition, a second language must be indicated, which is one of the five languages of OHIM, namely English, French, German, Italian or Spanish. The application can be filed at OHIM or the UK Trade Marks Registry. OHIM has a useful website, at www.ohim.eu.int which contains detailed information about the application procedure, among other things. Natural or legal persons not having either their domicile or their principal place of business or a real and effective industrial or commercial establishment in the EU must be professionally represented before OHIM, although an application can be filed by anyone without specialist assistance. However, as with an application for a UK trade mark and, probably more so, the assistance of an experienced representative is likely to prevent problems from arising with the making of the application and any registration subsequently acquired. The cost of an application for a ctm is significantly higher that for a UK trade mark. The cost of filing an application is currently €975 plus €200 for each class of goods or services in excess of three. The registration fee is €1100 plus €200 for each class of goods or services in excess of three (note there is no registration fee for a UK mark). The renewal fee is €2,500 every 10 years.

As with an application for a UK trade mark, a ctm must be applied for in specific classes for specific goods or services and

116

these should be carefully chosen to reflect the use which the applicant intends to make. The application should be made by the person, firm or company actually using or intending to use the mark. An agent or representative of the proprietor should not apply for registration of the mark in his own name without the proprietor's consent, otherwise the proprietor may be able to oppose the grant of the mark on this ground, apply to have the mark invalidated once registered, and oppose use by the agent or representative, if such use is not authorised.

Once the application is received, a search will be carried out for potentially conflicting Community and national trade marks and applications, the results of which are sent to the applicant. There are plans to do away with this search, which will reduce cost and time but increase uncertainty. In addition, OHIM examines the mark to see whether any of the "absolute" grounds for refusal of the mark apply, *e.g.* that the mark is not distinctive (as to which, see Chapter 11). OHIM cannot itself raise any objection based on earlier marks or rights: these must be raised by the proprietor of the earlier mark or right in opposition proceedings. The applicant will be given the opportunity to respond to any objections raised on the examination. If these are overcome, the application is published in the *Community Trade Marks Bulletin*. If they are not, and the application is refused, an applicant may appeal the refusal to the Board of Appeal. From the Board of Appeal, a further appeal lies to the ECJ.

Upon publication of the application, any person can submit observations to OHIM as to why the mark should not be registered (again based on the grounds for refusal in Chapter 11). These observations are sent to the applicant for comment. The proprietors of earlier marks or rights identified in the search will be informed of the publication of the application. They have three months from the date of publication to give notice of opposition to the registration of the mark based on their earlier marks or rights.

During any opposition procedure, both sides (the applicant and the opponent) are given the opportunity to file written observations. A decision is made on the opposition by the Opposition Division. An appeal from the Opposition Division can be made to the Board of Appeal. Again, any further appeal from the Board of Appeal lies to the ECJ. If there is no opposition, or any opposition is unsuccessful, the application will proceed to registration on payment of the appropriate fee.

Applications for revocation or invalidity

Applications for revocation or invalidity of a ctm may be made to OHIM, where they will be considered by the Cancellation Division (with appeal to the Board of Appeal and then the ECJ). In the case of applications based on earlier marks or rights, they must be made by the proprietor of the relevant earlier mark or right.

Each country has to nominate a "Community Trade Mark Court" where ctms can be litigated. The UK has nominated the High Court (Chancery Division) and the Court of Session in Scotland. Applications for revocation or invalidity may be made by way of counter-claim in those courts.

Actions for infringement

Actions for infringement of a ctm must be brought in a Community trade mark court and normally in the country where the defendant is domiciled or in which he has an establishment. In these circumstances, the court will have jurisdiction over acts of infringement in any country in the Community. An injunction will operate throughout the EU, though certain, essentially administrative functions by way of registration, have to be gone through before it can be enforced in another EU country.

"International" Registration of Trade Marks

Companies with an international business may wish to obtain trade mark protection in other countries in the world. There now exists a centralised system which simplifies the procedure for obtaining trade mark registrations in other countries. This is provided by the "Madrid Protocol", to which the UK, along with most other countries is a signatory. A detailed explanation of the ins and outs of the procedure under the Madrid Protocol is outside the scope of this book. However, in essence, what the procedure allows a trade mark applicant to do is apply for an "international registration" designating the countries in which protection is sought. The application is made through the trade mark registry of one country, but is then subject to examination in each of the countries designated. The registration obtained as a result gives the same protection as a national mark in each country.

What is not obtained by a so-called "international" registration is a true international registration—a single registration taking effect in a number of countries. A bunch of national registrations is what you get by making an "international application".

Well-known marks

Some foreign marks may be well known in the UK but not registered or even used here. Consider, for example, a recording studio situated in New York with an international reputation and clientele (as in *Pete Waterman v CBS*, 1993). Previously, whether or not such a business could bring proceedings to prevent the use of its name by a third party in the UK was somewhat uncertain. The Trade Marks Act 1994 now gives the foreign owner of a mark, which is well known in the UK the right to protection of his mark here whether or not that he carries on business or has any goodwill in the UK.

The owner must show that his mark is well known in the UK. Well known probably means something less than famous, but something more than merely having a reputation, as would be required in a passing-off case (as to which, see Chapter 15). The owner of a well-known mark can prevent the use of any mark that is identical or similar to his mark and is being used for identical or similar goods or services, if he can show that the use in question is likely to cause confusion. This is similar to the test for registered trade mark infringement which is discussed in Chapter 9. It should be noted that although use of the mark can be prevented in these circumstances by the grant of an injunction, there is no right to damages.

Whether this right really adds anything to the law of passing-off as now developed by the courts is doubtful. Since the law came in, in 1994, there has been no case where its existence made any difference; and it is difficult to think of one that might.

14. COLLECTIVE AND CERTIFICATION MARKS

Collective Marks

A collective mark is a special type of trade mark: one applied for and used by members of a trade or professional association to distinguish the goods or services of members of that association from other goods or services. The general provisions of the Trade Marks Act 1994 apply to collective marks, subject to certain qualifications. The main qualifications relating to collective marks are addressed here.

Application

The usual requirements for registration of a mark are adapted in the following way in relation to applications for registration of a collective mark. First, as already mentioned, the mark is applied for by an association and must be shown to be distinctive of the association. Second, although the mark must not be descriptive, unlike a standard trade mark application a collective mark may consist of something that designates the geographical origin of the goods or services. For example, the trade association of producers of San Daniele ham in Italy registered a mark comprising the words "Prosciutto di San Daniele Sd" for dry-cured ham from the area geographically delimited by the current boundaries of the Municipality of San Daniele del Friuli. Third, the mark must not be something that is liable to mislead the public as to the character or significance of the mark, in particular, by being taken as something other than a collective mark. Fourth, an applicant for a collective mark must file with the Trade Mark Registry regulations governing use of the mark. These regulations should include the persons authorised to use the mark, the conditions of membership of the association and, where they exist, the conditions of use of the mark. The mark will not be registered unless the regulations meet these requirements and are not contrary to public policy or accepted principles of morality. The regulations are open to inspection by members of the public and any amendments to the regulations must be accepted by the Registrar.

Infringement

The same tests for infringement apply to collective marks as to standard registered trade marks. In the case of collective marks consisting of signs or indications designating the geographical origin of the goods, the proprietor cannot prevent the use of such signs or indications by a third party where they are used in accordance with honest practices in industrial or commercial matters.

Revocation and invalidity

A collective mark may be revoked or invalidated on the same grounds as a standard registered trade mark (see Chapter 11). In addition, the mark may be revoked if it has become misleading in the way outlined above in relation to applications; if the proprietor has failed to observe or to secure the observance of the regulations governing use of the mark; or if the regulations have been amended in such a way that they no longer comply with the requirements outlined above or are contrary to public policy or to accepted principles of morality. The mark may be invalidated if it was registered in breach of the requirement that it not be misleading in the way outlined above, or the requirements outlined above relating to the regulations.

Community collective marks

A Community collective mark exists, which may be obtained from OHIM. It is very similar to a UK collective mark, but is subject to the Community Trade Mark Regulation. It takes EU-wide effect.

Certification Marks

A certification mark is unlike a trade mark (or even a collective mark) in that it does not indicate the origin of goods or services as such, but serves to indicate that the goods or services in connection with which it is used are certified by the proprietor of the mark in respect of origin, material, mode of manufacture of goods; or performance of services, quality, accuracy or other characteristics. By way of example, the British Standards Institution has registered the "kite" mark as a certification mark — goods are only permitted to carry the mark under licence from the BSI. The general provisions of the Trade Marks Act 1994 apply to certification marks, subject to certain qualifications.

121

The main qualifications relating to certification marks are addressed here.

Application

The usual requirements for registration of a mark (which are covered in Chapter 11) are adapted in the following way in relation to applications for registration of a certification mark. First, the mark must be shown to be distinguish goods or services that are certified from those that are not. Second, as with collective marks, a certification mark may consist of something that designates the geographical origin of the goods or services. Third, the applicant for a certification mark must not actually carry on business involving the supply of the goods or services of the kind certified. In other words, the applicant will generally be a trade or professional association (*e.g.* the Stilton Cheese Makers' Association). Fourth, the mark must not be something that is liable to mislead the public as to the character or significance of the mark, in particular, by being taken as something other than a certification mark. Fifth, an applicant for a certification mark must file with the Registrar regulations governing use of the mark. (An example of the sort of thing is to be found in the report of *Stilton TM*, 1967.)

Such regulations must not be contrary to public policy or morality and must comply with the following requirements. They must indicate who is authorised to use the mark, the characteristics certified by the mark, how the certifying body is to test those characteristics and to supervise use of the marks, the fees (if any) to be paid in connection with operation of the mark and the procedures for resolving disputes. As with collective marks, the regulations must be open to inspection and the Registrar must approve amendments to the regulations. Sixth, an applicant for a certification mark must be competent to certify the goods or services for which the mark is to be registered.

Infringement

The same tests for infringement apply to certification marks as to standard registered trade marks. These are covered in Chapters 9 and 10. In the case of collective marks consisting of signs or indications designating the geographical origin of the goods, the proprietor cannot prevent the use of such signs or indications by a third party where they are used in accordance with honest practices in industrial or commercial matters.

Revocation and invalidity

A collective mark may be revoked or invalidated on the same grounds as a standard registered trade mark (see Chapter 12). In addition, it may be revoked if the proprietor starts to carry on business supplying goods or services of the kind certified, if it has become misleading in the way outlined above in relation to applications, if the proprietor has failed to observe or secure the observance of the regulations governing use of the mark, if the regulations have been amended in such a way that they no longer comply with the requirements outlined above or are contrary to public policy or to accepted principles of morality or if the proprietor is no longer competent to certify the goods or services for which the mark is registered. The mark may be invalidated if it was registered in breach of the requirement that the proprietor must not carry on business supplying goods or services of the kind certified, the requirement that the mark not be misleading in the way outlined above or the requirements outlined above relating to the regulations.

Geographical Indications and Designations of Origin

We should add that there are various complicated EU regulations relating to the registration and use of geographical indications and designations of origin for agricultural products, food and wine. An explanation of this legislation is outside the scope of this book. The whole subject of "protected designations of origin" ("PDOs") has become of increasing importance not only within the EU but also internationally. Wine names, for instance, are now very well protected within the EU (the PDO system has taken over from various national law systems, for instance our own passing-off law which protected "Champagne", *Bollinger v Costa Brava Wine,* 1961). Cheese names are similarly protected — "Stilton" is the only British cheese PDO (and is a certification mark too). There are major running battles to reclaim some "stolen" names. "Feta" is a good example, made the subject of a PDO in 2002. The argument was between Greece which wanted it as a PDO and Germany, France and Holland, who did not (until recently, at least, most "Feta" cheese in Europe was not Greek). The battle is not yet over. Some names (Cheddar, for instance) are past recall. Even where PDOs are well established within the EU, there is friction with other countries (often the USA). American wine-makers, for instance, are apt to use "stolen" European names such as Chablis. These sorts of battles are often fought within the context of the WTO.

15. PASSING-OFF

A General Rule

The general rule governing passing-off is that no-one may so conduct his business so as to lead customers to mistake his goods, or his business, for the goods or business of someone else. There are lots of ways of doing this, but the heart of this wrong is telling lies to the public. If the court thinks that is going on, it is going to want to stop it—in reality this general rule is often more important than all the technical rules of the law of registered trade marks put together.

Varieties of Passing-off

Lumped together under the name "passing-off" is a considerable variety of activities, ranging from simple cases of dishonest trading—where a garage-owner is asked for a particular brand of oil, or a doctor prescribes a particular manufacturer's drug, and the customer is simply given a different and cheaper brand—to cases that are almost cases of infringement of trade mark. In these days, the simple cases are rare; the trades mentioned are unusual in that customers still expect to get something not in the manufacturer's own package. In most shops, goods pretending to be of a national brand but supplied unmarked would be immediately suspect. The majority of passing-off cases now are akin to trade mark infringement cases in that a defendant has used the trade name or other badge of the plaintiff on a product not originating from the plaintiff.

There are more sophisticated versions now and again, such as the manufacturer who declares, untruthfully, that his is the brand you find advertised on television. Or there is the practice of some large supermarket chains of getting up their "own brand" to look like the brand leader's packaging. Until 1997, a number of cases where the brand owner had tried to stop a lookalike had all failed at the interlocutory stage. The brand owners tried to prove that the public believed that they had made the goods for the supermarket; the supermarkets said they used the lookalike get-up just to show that their goods were the same sort of thing as that of the brand owner. But then *United Biscuits v Asda* (1997) went to a full hearing and the plaintiff showed (just, and with a bit of a fair wind from the judge) that the public believed that a *Penguin* biscuit lookalike called a

Puffin were made for the supermarket by him. After that trial, supermarket "lookalikes" have become rarer. There are odd cases of passing-off too, that fit no general category, but where the court feels that some kind of deceptive conduct ought to be stopped. Whenever one trader manages to benefit from another's goodwill there is likely to be at least an arguable case of passing-off.

"Badges" and Reputations

Most cases of passing-off, then, are cases where a trader without in so many words saying that his goods are someone else's nevertheless indicates this by applying to his goods some badge or sign that people have come to regard as a mark of that other's goods. In the simplest case, this badge may be an ordinary trade mark—perhaps a trade mark that for one reason or another is not registered for the goods concerned. (If it is so registered, there will be an infringement as well as passing-off.) It may be the name of a business, or of someone associated with the business. It may be a special appearance or "get-up" of the goods: a specially shaped package, for instance, such as a plastic lemon.

But all such cases have these essentials in common: the "badge," whatever it may be, must be one that has come by use to distinguish the goods of a particular trader or group of traders; and it must have been copied, whether deliberately or by accident, closely enough for people to be deceived, or at least to be confused. So the plaintiff in an action to stop the passing-off must prove two things: that the mark or other "badge" he is relying on has a sufficient reputation amongst customers; and that there is a real risk that what the defendant is doing will lead to deception or confusion of those customers. Actually, there is also a third thing the plaintiff ought to prove: that the deception causes the customers to buy the wrong brand, though this is often assumed or overlooked.

The risk of deception

Judging the risk of confusion in these cases is not unlike judging whether one of two trade marks infringes another (a matter we have already discussed). But in a passing-off action, the question is not whether any fair use of the defendant's mark or other "badge" would be likely to cause confusion, but whether what the defendant is actually doing is misleading, so that a court may have to look at all the circumstances to see whether they increase or decrease the risk. It may be important, for instance, whether and how the defendant puts his own name on his goods, and what if anything his name will mean to the customer. It may also be important to what extent the customers already know where the goods come from. A business dealing direct with manufacturers probably knows very well whom it is buying from, and is unlikely to be confused by misleading markings; it is when the goods get into shops that misleading markings really matter.

"Get-up"

It will be clear from what we have just said, that cases of passing-off by "get-up" are not very common. Very few manufacturers these days put the real emphasis of their advertising upon the mere look of their package. Even if packages did not change as often as they do, it would still be more sensible to put the real emphasis on a brand name. So the public is taught to look for the name, and they do; and are not deceived by similar packages with a different brand name or none at all.

There was a case some time ago *White, Hudson v Asian* (1965), where the court held that merely to use an orange-coloured wrapper for wrapping cough-sweets was passing-off; but it happened in Singapore, where (then) many customers could not read the names printed in European lettering on the rival wrappers. The evidence was that the plaintiff's sweets were there known and asked for simply by words meaning "red paper cough sweets." More recently, in *Reckitt & Colman v Borden* (1990), the plaintiffs, who sold lemon juice in a plastic lemon carrying a loose neck label, were able to prove that the defendant's plastic lemon, although it also carried a loose but different label, would deceive customers. The case was exceptional, however. The plaintiffs were able to prove that the customers not only did not bother to look at the label, but also that they cared about the make of lemon juice (an American judge with the improbable name of Learned Hand once put the point this way: "what moves the customers to buy?"). The plaintiffs were also able to prove actual deception by stationing solicitors behind refrigerators in supermarkets on Pancake Day, the solicitors asking people who had picked up the defendants' lemon what they thought they had. Despite some predictions to the effect that this plastic lemon case would spawn many more passing-off actions, it remains the fact that get-up cases are rare precisely because most people do read the labels on most things.

The new registered trade mark law has spawned a variety of attempts to protect by trade mark registration what cannot be protected by passing-off: for instance the three headed razor, (*Philips*, 1999 held no because they are only engineering features), the shapes and colours of washing machine tablets (*Procter & Gamble* and *Henkel*, each 2004, also no—because not distinctive) and torch shapes (*Mag*, 2004, not distinctive because public perception is not as a trademark).

Business names

Many passing-off actions have been concerned with business names, just because, in the past, these could not be registered as trade marks. Actions about business names are much like actions about trade marks. The plaintiff has to show, on the one hand, that people have come to associate the name in dispute with him, on the other that the defendant's version of it is misleadingly similar to his. In judging similarity, it is particularly important what sort of customers are concerned, and this may depend on use of the name in advertising. If the plaintiff's or defendant's name is merely used as a company name, in dealings with other companies and so on, it may remain unknown. In *HFC Bank v Midland Bank* (2000), HFC tried to stop the Midland Bank from changing its name to HSBC. It failed because it could not show that someone with whom HFC had achieved brand name recognition would be deceived by the use of HSBC.

Exceptional cases

In certain special cases, the law accepts as inevitable a certain amount of confusion, and the court will not interfere so long as the defendant does nothing dishonest and nothing to make matters worse.

Use of own name

People have a limited right to use their own name in business, even though they have a surname that is better known in the trade concerned as the name or mark of someone else. But someone who takes unfair advantage of the possession of such a name will be restrained from doing so; the books record far more cases where the courts have interfered with the use people were making of their own names than cases where the court has let them go on. An established company may claim a right to trade under its name very much as an individual may; but if a new company is formed with a name that is confusingly similar to that of some other business, the court will usually order it to change that name. There is no special right to trade under one's surname alone; nor any special right to mark one's name on goods, where the general public may see it and be misled by it. Readers needing further warning of the dangers of assuming a right to trade under one's own name may care to look at *Wright's Case* (1949) (for soap); *Parker-Knoll v Knoll International* (1962); *Dunhill v Sunoptic* (1979); and *Asprey & Garrard v WRA* (2002).

Descriptive names and marks

Those who choose to carry on business under a name that does little more than describe the business cannot complain if others do the same, and must put up with quite small differences between their trading name and other people's. Thus in a case (1946) between rival office-cleaning companies, it was held that the names "Office Cleaning Services" and "Office Cleaning Association" were not too close. In the same way, those who choose as trade marks words which virtually describe the goods should not complain if others describe their goods in similar terms: "Oven Chips" is the sort of thing which the courts will not protect (*McCain v Country Fair*, 1981). But in all these cases, the court will intervene if the defendant is dishonest. A defendant who is trying to get his goods or business mistaken for someone else's will find the court very ready to believe that he has succeeded.

Marks that the public treats as descriptions

Special difficulties arise with those very well known trade marks that the general public treats as merely the name of the article concerned. If someone goes into an ironmonger's shop and asks for a new "Yale lock", he may want one made by the Yale people themselves, but he may just mean that he wants an ordinary pin-tumbler cylinder lock without caring by whom it is made. There may be genuine confusion between him and the shop assistant as to which is meant; or a dishonest shop assistant may use the ambiguity as an excuse. As one of the *Aertex* cases (1953) illustrates, this may make it very hard for the owner of such a mark to prevent its misuse.

It may be noted that the courts have held that, on the one hand, where a former trade mark had become descriptive adding the word "genuine" to it did not make it into a trade mark again

("Genuine Staunton" for Staunton-pattern chessmen: *Jacques v Chess*, 1940) whilst on the other, use of someone else's trade mark is not made permissible by adding the word "type". A Scottish judge once described "genuine" as almost as sinister in significance as "type" (*Harris Tweed*, 1964).

Geography, the wine and "class" cases

It may be as misleading to say, untruly, that goods come from a particular area (as with "Scotch whisky" and "Swiss chocolate") as to use the wrong trade mark on them. In such cases, any trader who has a legitimate claim to use the place name concerned for his goods may sue the trader who misuses it for passing-off. (By way of example, see *Spanish Champagne* (1960), and, more recently, *Chocosuisse*, (1999).) But place names, and especially anglicised place names, may become merely descriptive of things made in a particular fashion. If so, anyone who genuinely makes his product that way may use the mark, though its use on the wrong sort of goods may still be passing-off (*Advocaat*, 1979).

There may be intermediate cases in which the meaning of a geographical term or other description may depend on context. Thus it has been held that "Champagne" necessarily connotes wine (of a particular sort) from the Champagne district of France, and that its use for similar wine made in Spain cannot be justified even if it is expressly labelled "Spanish champagne." So also with "Elderflower Champagne". "Sherry" was for some years ambiguous. Following a decision on passing-off, the position was that it could only be used alone for wine (of a particular sort) from the Xeres region of Spain, but "British sherry" was allowed because it had been used for 100 years. Now "British Sherry" is not allowed at all, Sherry having become a PDO. Many wine names now also have protection as PDOs (see last chapter).

In all these cases, the class of people who genuinely use the mark lose trade to the person who falsely uses the mark. A logical extension of the rule includes cases where the plaintiff uses some official approval mark to indicate compliance by his product with certain regulations, and the defendant falsely uses such a mark to indicate he complies too. It seems probable that the courts will support such an action as passing-off, although a case has yet to get to full trial. The nearest the trade mark system has to this sort of thing are collective and certification trade marks (see Chapter 14).

Odd and Unusual Instances

Where the plaintiff does not trade

There can be passing-off even though there is no trade or business in the ordinary sense concerned; thus the professional institutions can (and now and again, have to) sue both people who put letters after their names so as falsely to pretend to a professional qualification, and people who form societies with similar initials so as to give members something they can put after their names. There have been passing-off actions about *noms de plume* as well as about the titles to books and plays. But there has to be some sort of business connection, in a wide sense, between the plaintiff and the sort of thing the defendant is doing, so that the court can be satisfied that there is a real likelihood of the plaintiff's suffering damage to some sort of business interest if the defendant goes on with what he is doing. Thus Mr Stringfellow, the owner of a famous nightclub, failed to stop a company calling its long thin frozen chips "Stringfellows" because the court thought that he was not really suffering damage (*Stringfellow v McCain*, 1984) and the founder of a small political party called the Social Democrats could not stop the use of that title by the later, more famous, party (*Kean v McGivan*, 1982).

There have been a number of cases concerning merchandising rights in popular characters. They arise in the following way: a manufacturing organisation takes a well-known television or radio personality—real, fictional or even mythical—and exploits the popularity of the character in the advertising and selling of his goods. The question arises: can the character concerned (or in the case of fictional and mythical characters, their creators) take action to prevent such exploitation? Again, the answer turns on whether a reasonable person would think that there was any business connection between the plaintiff and the defendant. Thus, in interlocutory proceedings the court refused to restrain a builders' skip hire business from using the name of mythical television creatures (*Wombles v Wombles Skips*, 1975). In another case (*Taverner Rutledge v Trexapalm*, 1975), a lollipop manufacturer, who had taken a franchise to use "Kojak", the name of a television character associated with lollipops, found himself enjoined from using the name (pending a full trial) at the suit of a rival manufacturer who had built up a reputation selling lollipops under the name without taking a licence.

130

In the case of Teenage Mutant Ninja Turtles (*Mirage Studios v Counter-Feat,* 1991), it was held arguable that a defendant who sold T-shirts with pictures reminiscent (but not enough to infringe copyright) of the turtles was passing-off. The court said that most people expected this sort of thing to be licensed, and so "non-genuine" goods would deceive the public. What may have been overlooked, however, is that the public were probably not interested in whether or not there was a licence, what they wanted was what they got, the T-shirt with the design in question. Compare to the trademark position as in the *Arsenal* case, see Chapter 9.

A different situation may arise in an endorsement, as opposed to a merchandising, case, where the defendant uses a celebrity's name or image in connection with the promotion of his product or service. In this type of case, particularly if the celebrity in question has already previously been involved in endorsement work and the manner in which the celebrity's name or image is used gives the impression that the celebrity recommends or approves the product or service, then the public may well be misled and the celebrity would be entitled to prevent such use on the basis of passing-off. This was the case in *Irvine v Talksport* (2002), in which the defendant, a radio station, used a photograph of the well-known racing driver Eddie Irvine on the front of a brochure promoting advertising opportunities on the radio station, without his permission. The photograph had been manipulated to show Mr Irvine listening to a radio, prominently marked with the radio station's name. The judge held that a significant proportion of recipients of the brochure would have thought that Mr Irvine had endorsed or recommended the radio station.

Other odd instances

The ordinary case of passing-off concerns the sale of goods in such a way that purchasers will be deceived or confused as to whose goods they are. But there can be passing-off where the goods come from the right manufacturer: by selling secondhand goods as new, or spoilt goods as sound, or lower-priced goods as superior ones. There can be passing-off where sellers are confused as to the identity of the buyer instead of the other way round. There can be passing-off where the defendant's name cannot be objected to and it is his address that is confusing.

A single case illustrates these last two possibilities (*Pullman v Pullman,* 1919). The defendant, a former director of the family firm, many years later set up on his own, under his own name (as he was entitled to do). Then he altered the name of his house to resemble that of one of the plaintiff's factories (in itself, probably legitimate: it is not passing-off to call a private house by a name confusingly similar to that of someone else, so long as no business is involved). But he then moved his business office to his house and wrote from that address to people who had been supplying the plaintiffs with materials, offering to buy from them. That was held to be passing-off.

More recently, in *Bristol Conservatories v Conservatories Custom Built* (1989), the defendants showed photographs of conservatories to potential customers falsely claiming that they, the defendants, had built them. In fact, the photographs were of the plaintiffs' work. This was also held to be a type of passing-off (often known as "reverse" passing-off). Likewise in *Matthew Gloag v Welsh Distillers* (1998), "Welsh whisky" on bottles containing Scotch whisky was found to be, arguably, passing-off.

Suing for Passing-off

Most ordinary actions for passing-off follow one of three patterns. In the first, the plaintiff acts at once, on learning of the passing-off. He starts the action and immediately applies for an interim injunction to stop the passing-off temporarily, until the case can be brought to trial. It takes about a month for the parties to prepare written evidence from a few important witnesses and bring the case in front of a judge, who decides on the spot whether the case justifies a temporary injunction or not. By that time, both parties know enough of the strength of the other side's case to have quite a good idea of how the trial is likely to turn out, so there is generally no point in actually fighting the action any further.

In the second type of case, the plaintiff acts quickly, but either does not ask for or, perhaps, cannot obtain an interim injunction. Instead, the court may order a so-called speedy trial—that is a trial within a few months, rather than the more usual 12 to 18 months that most cases take to come to trial. The case will still require the considerable preparation involved in a full trial, as to which see below, and with less time to do it, but the advantage for both sides is that the matter will be resolved quickly and, at least in theory, before the dispute has caused significant commercial damage.

The third type of case goes like this. The plaintiff waits for months, or even years, before taking any action. It is, of course, too late to ask the court for an interim injunction or speedy trial;

it is the plaintiff's own fault that the case was not tried long ago. There is no way the parties can accurately assess each other's cases, or see how the matter looks to a judge, without taking the dispute to trial. At the trial, the plaintiffs must prove at length, by evidence from those concerned with the trade, how well known their business or their goods are and how confusing whatever the defendant is doing is. The defendant for his part produces witnesses who have never heard of the plaintiffs; witnesses who by that time have got used to the two parties having similar names or similar trade marks (or whatever the dispute is about); witnesses who are too alert to be confused by any state of affairs worth arguing over at all.

The trial will be long and expensive, because of the large number of witnesses. The outcome will be uncertain, because of the difficulty of knowing how the evidence will turn out and what the judge will think of the witnesses. Furthermore, by the time the case comes to trial, the trade and public generally have got used to having these two businesses or trade marks about and have learnt to distinguish them; so that what was passing-off when it started may have ceased to cause serious confusion by the time the case comes to trial.

The choice is left to the reader.

Note: Trade Marks and the Internet

When the internet began to be popular among corporations, the practice of "cybersquatting" sprang up. This involved registering domain names that it was thought that large corporations would want to use and would be prepared to pay for and then approaching the corporations offering to sell them for large sums, usually with a thinly veiled threat that if the corporation did not pay they would or might fall into the hands of others.

Two mechanisms have been developed to deal with this practice. The first is reliance on ordinary registered trade mark rights (and possibly passing-off). By these means Marks & Spencer (and a number of others) were able to stop a cybersquatter who had registered domain names with the words "marksandspencer" (*Marks and Spencer v One in a Million* (1998)). The advantages are that firm readily enforceable relief can be obtained and the claimant has all of the flexibility of court procedures to deploy.

The second procedure is much less expensive and can be quicker. ICANN and certain of the domestic domain-name-registration bodies (such as Nominet) have developed dispute resolution procedures by means of which it is possible to divest cybersquatters of domain names that have obviously been registered to take advantage of someone else. ICANN will (in broad terms) take action where a person has registered a domain name that is (i) identical or confusingly similar to a trademark or service mark in which the complainant has rights; and (ii) the registrant has no rights or legitimate interests in respect of the domain name; and (iii) the registrant's domain name has been registered and is being used in bad faith.

ICANN regards as bad faith the following (by way of example): (i) circumstances indicating that a person has registered or acquired the domain name primarily for the purpose of selling, renting, or otherwise transferring the domain-name registration to the complainant who is the owner of the trademark or service mark or to a competitor of that complainant, for valuable consideration in excess of documented out-of-pocket costs directly related to the domain name; or (ii) the person has registered the domain name in order to prevent the owner of the trademark or service mark from reflecting the mark in a corresponding domain name, provided that he has engaged in a pattern of such conduct; or (iii) the person has registered the domain name primarily for the purpose of disrupting the business of a competitor; or (iv) by using the domain name, the person has intentionally attempted to attract, for commercial gain, internet users to his website or other online location, by creating a likelihood of confusion with the complainant's mark as to the source, sponsorship, affiliation, or endorsement of his website or location, or of a product or service on his website or location.

Nominet's approach is similar except that it deals only with ".uk" registered domain names. Both ICANN and Nominet have helpful websites which offer comprehensive guidance to the procedure: www.icann.org and www.nic.uk

16. MALICIOUS FALSEHOOD

This chapter deals with a different sort of unfair competition, known variously as trade libel, slander of goods, slander of title, or malicious or injurious falsehood. It consists of injuring someone else's business, by making, from some "indirect or dishonest motive", a false statement to some third person. To prove dishonest motive is not always easy. Generally, the statement must be so false that the defendant cannot have believed it to be true. Real financial loss (or the real risk of it) must be shown by the plaintiff.

Because of the difficulty in proving the necessary dishonest motive, cases for slander of goods are relatively unusual. They have become even more so since the introduction of the Trade Marks Act 1994. This provides the alternative cause of action for trade mark infringement in cases where the statement made by the defendant makes use of the plaintiff's registered trade mark. In this situation, there is no need for the plaintiff to prove a dishonest motive on the part of the defendant. Cases of this type are discussed in Chapter 10. Accordingly, where a plaintiff can rely upon trade mark infringement, it will usually be a waste of time and money to include a claim of malicious falsehood (see *Cable & Wireless v BT*, 1998).

The law of malicious falsehood will still be relevant in some cases, for example, where the plaintiff does not have a registered trade mark or the defendant has not referred to the plaintiff's registered trade mark. It is best seen by considering a few examples.

Examples

De Beers v General Electric, 1975

The plaintiffs and the defendants were both manufacturers of abrasives made from diamonds. The defendants had circulated to prospective customers a pamphlet purporting to show by the results of scientific tests that the plaintiffs' products were inferior to those of the defendants. On an application by the defendants to strike the action out as disclosing no reasonable cause of action, it was held that when "puffing" of goods turns to denigration of the goods of a rival, there comes a point where this becomes actionable, and that if a reasonable person might consider than an untrue claim was being made seriously, and with malice, then the plaintiff disclosed a reasonable cause of action.

Hayward & Co. v Hayward & Sons, 1887

The defendants, having brought a passing-off action against the plaintiffs and lost, issued advertisements that made it look as if they had won. The plaintiffs brought another action, successfully, to get these advertisements stopped.

Mentmore v Fomento, 1955

The defendants had sued a third party for infringement of patent and had won; but there was an appeal from the decision to the House of Lords still on foot. The plaintiffs were (or so at least the defendants thought) infringing the same patent. The defendants' solicitor approached Selfridge's, just at a critical moment from the point of view of the Christmas trade, and indicated to the buyer that if the plaintiffs' goods were not withdrawn from sale at once, the defendants would get an injunction against the store. What he actually said was "there will be a little court job again". The defendants knew very well that, until the appeal had been decided, they would get no injunction against other infringers. The court granted an injunction to stop the defendants telling people about their successful patent action without disclosing the full facts.

Riding v Smith, 1876

The false statements concerned need not relate directly to the business. This was a case where the plaintiff's trade decreased, because of rumours that his wife, who served in his shop, had committed adultery. It was held that this was good ground for an action.

Compaq v Dell, 1992

Dell's advertisement showed pictures of computers in pairs, one of theirs and one of Compaq's. Under each was a price and the accompanying text said that the computers were "basically and essentially the same". The judge held that they were not and granted an injunction. Obviously, this sort of comparison involves a question of degree (for instance, in one pair the

Compaq computer had 50 per cent more memory). Had the difference been less marked, the defendants might have succeeded with only a slightly unfair comparison.

DSG Retail v Comet Group, 2002

The plaintiff and defendant were electrical retailers. The plaintiff began a series of promotions, the first offering discounts of 10 per cent off ticketed prices for selected goods, and the second offering to beat the defendant's price by £10 for any product over £300. The defendant retaliated by using posters at its stores stating "Today and everyday Comet prices will be lower than local competitors' . . . We even beat competitors' 10% off and £10 off weekend promotions". The judge held that, read as a whole, the public would understand the defendant's posters to mean that the defendant's ticketed prices were invariably less than the plaintiff's promotional prices. This was false, since the defendant would only charge a lower price when challenged by a customer. The judge dismissed the defendant's argument that the public would understand the statements on the posters as a mere puff and granted an injunction.

Conclusion

Enough examples have been given to show the scope of this sort of action. It must not be assumed that plaintiffs would always win such actions; traders are apt to say that other people's goods are worse than theirs, and even where such statements are demonstrably false a judge will not necessarily decide that they are dishonest. There is this further difficulty that interim injunctions are very rarely granted in these cases if the defendant intends to try at the trial to show that what he said was true. The *Compaq* case was an exception: the judge found that no jury could reasonably conclude that the statement was true. A case the other way is *Bestobell v Bigg* (1975). The defendant decorators had painted a house on the South Circular Road brown. The paint started to turn green, with hideous effect. The defendant said the paint was no good; the paint company said he had mixed and applied it wrongly. To make his point, the defendant put up a large notice for all to see saying "This house was painted with Carson's paint", clearly implying the paint was indeed no good. An interim injunction was refused because the defendant intended to justify at trial.

Litigation is always uncertain, however, and it is wisest not to do anything that can result in an action reaching a court. The safe rule is never to make disparaging statements about a rival business or its products. It should not be forgotten that if such statements hurt anybody's feelings, an expensive libel-type action may result—and these days, the feelings of limited companies are rather easily hurt.

17. THE CRIMINAL LAW

There are a variety of Acts of Parliament dealing with methods of trading that are so objectionable as to be made criminal. Most of these Acts are concerned with particular types of goods or trading, for example the Hallmarking Act 1973 and the Medicines Act 1968. It is outside the scope of this book to discuss them. This chapter deals with the specific criminal offences concerning trade marks and copyright, and the more general Trade Descriptions Act 1968.

The Trade Marks Act 1994

It is a criminal offence to make unauthorised use of a trade mark under certain circumstances. For example, if a person applies to goods or their packaging a sign identical to, or likely to be mistaken for, a registered trade mark or sells goods which bear, or the packaging of which bears such a sign or has such goods in his possession in the course of business for the purpose of selling them, an offence may be committed.

It must be shown that the defendant does the acts in question with a view to gain for himself or another, or with intent to cause loss to another, without the consent of the proprietor of the trade mark. In addition, the goods in question must be goods in respect of which the trade mark is registered or the trade mark has a reputation in the UK and the use of the sign takes unfair advantage of, or is, or would be detrimental to the distinctive character or repute of the trade mark. This is similar to one of the tests for civil trade mark infringement, which is discussed in Chapter 9. It is a defence for the defendant to show that he believed on reasonable grounds that the use of the sign in the manner in which it was used was not an infringement of the trade mark.

The House of Lords in *R. v Johnstone* (2003) recently considered this offence. We have discussed its facts (bootleg Bon Jovi CDs), and the problem of whether non-trade mark use can count as infringement, above in connection with the *Arsenal* case. Here we add the following points about the decision. It was held first that the criminal offence was no wider than the civil offence of infringement—hardly a surprising conclusion, although the criminal judge at trial got it wrong. Second, it was held that whether a sign was being used descriptively is a question of fact. Third, that a defendant would have a defence where he reasonably believed that no relevant trade mark was registered. However, the House of Lords confirmed that the burden of proof rests on the defendant to show that he honestly and reasonably believed that use of the sign was not an infringement. On this basis, it is clear that the offence is one of near absolute liability.

The Copyright, Designs and Patents Act 1988

Under the Copyright, Designs and Patents Act it is an offence for anyone, without the licence of the copyright owner, to make for sale or hire, or import (otherwise than for private or domestic use) any article that is, and that he knows, or has reason to believe, is an infringing copy of a copyright work. This provision has come into increasing play in recent years. There have been a number of private prosecutions. Some of these collapsed because of technicalities—which matter much more in the context of a criminal charge with a person's liberty at stake, than they do in a civil case where the problem is usually cured by an amendment. Also, there have been a number of public prosecutions—especially in the context of pirate videos and computer-related offences. For instance, a man was given a year in prison for supplying copyright games over the internet, *R. v Lewis* (1997). Serious collaborations to infringe can also be prosecuted for criminal conspiracy. Illicit dealings in recordings which breach rights in performances ("bootlegs") and in unauthorised decoders for satellite TV are also punishable criminally.

The Trade Descriptions Act 1968

It is a criminal offence to apply a "false trade description" to any goods, or to supply (or offer to supply) any goods to which such a "false trade description" has been applied. The words "trade description" are defined almost as widely as one can possibly imagine. They consist of

> "an indication, direct or indirect, and by whatever means given, of any of the following matters with respect to any goods or parts of goods, that is to say—(a) quantity, size or gauge; (b) method of manufacture, production, processing or reconditioning; (c) composition; (d) fitness for purpose, strength, performance, behaviour or accuracy; (e) any [other] physical characteristics; (f) testing by any person and results thereof; (g) approval by any person or conformity with a type approved by any person; (h) place or date of manufacture, production, processing or reconditioning; (i) person

by whom manufactured, produced, processed or reconditioned; (j) other history, including previous ownership or use."

A "trade description" can be applied to goods in almost any manner, including orally or in advertisements. No offence is committed unless the "trade description" is false. This ordinarily means that the public must be likely to be misled by the trade description into purchasing the goods. Thus in *Kingston v F. W. Woolworth* (1968), decided under the old law, the court held that the description "Rolled Gold" applied to a pair of cuff-links sold by the defendants for 4s. was not an offence, even though only the fronts of the cuff-links were coated with a thin layer of poor-quality gold. On the other hand, if the trade description is completely false, it probably does not matter if the public will be misled or not. Thus in *Kat v Diment* (1950), the expression "non-brewed vinegar," when applied to something that was not in fact vinegar, constituted an offence even though there was no indication that the public would be misled. Sometimes traders apply a false description and also disclaim liability. Normally this will not work. The Act has been brought into play to deal with some publishers who have the misfortune to have a best-selling author die. Attempts to put out books by a ghost-author as though they were by the dead author have been punished by magistrates.

The Act has similar provisions dealing with descriptions of services and accommodation. Thus false descriptions of holidays and holiday accommodation have been well kept down by the Act after a number of successful prosecutions. "Right on the beach" would not do for a man-made sandpit—an extreme example that really happened and was really defended. The Act also attempts to deal with unfair price tags (such as "3p off" tags on articles that in fact were never sold for the higher price). Estate agents have also been brought within the Act.

It might be thought that if the Registrar of Trade Marks were prepared to let a trade mark be registered, its use by the owner upon goods within the registration would not be an offence under the criminal law. This is not so. Therefore, whenever a trader is considering a new mark for one of his products or services, he should not only choose a mark that is registrable, but also one that will not cause him any trouble with the criminal law. It would be best for him to ensure that in use his mark could not, even remotely, be said to be a "false trade description". (Yet another reason why totally meaningless words often make the best marks.)

141

The Practical Working of the Acts

As an alternative to civil action

Although a criminal offence under either the Trade Marks Act or the Trade Descriptions Act may have been committed, civil proceedings by a trader affected by their breach are usually preferable if, as is generally the case, there is also a civil wrong. This is for a number of reasons.

First, the civil court has power to grant an injunction to restrain further acts of the type complained of and, in many cases, an injunction can be obtained very quickly; second, the award of costs in a civil court is much higher than in a criminal court; third, the procedure in a civil court is, generally speaking, much easier than in a criminal court.

Next, there is fact that IP law is apt to have tricky points —such as those which emerged in *Johnstone*. Prosecuting authorities are not experts in IP law and it has lots of little pitfalls—for instance, a series of prosecutions about "pirate films" back in the 1970s (really against a small band of collectors, including Mr Bob Monkhouse) all fell apart at the Old Bailey because of a failure to prove subsistence of copyright. The authorities have other, seemingly more pressing problems. So cases are only brought when the facts are completely clear—as soon as a problem emerges things are apt to go wrong, as they did in *Johnstone*.

It follows that in practice the criminal provisions have their main application not in the field of protecting traders against unfair competition but rather in the field of the protection of the public at large—"consumer protection". To some extent, the two overlap: thus some trading standards officers do take action against blatant pirates, such as traders in markets or car boot sales selling pirate jeans or counterfeit video tapes or DVDs.

Enforcement provisions

The Trade Marks Act and the Trade Descriptions Act make local trading standards authorities responsible for their enforcement. It is the duty of trading standards authorities (who employ inspectors) to take proceedings, and they are empowered to make test purchases, enter premises (subject to certain conditions), and seize goods for the purpose of ascertaining whether an offence has been committed. It is also possible for a private prosecution to be brought, and they are, though rarely.

Action is normally only taken by trading standards authorities on simple, plain cases where the public is in need of protection. In most cases inspectors only act if they receive a number of complaints from the public, although increasingly, in the case of counterfeits, the right owners also complain and assist in the prosecutions. There is certainly nothing to prevent anyone who feels injured by another's passing-off or infringement of a mark from reporting the matter to a local inspector: this will generally produce some result, if only a warning letter to the culprit.

Penalties

Most cases under the Trade Descriptions Act are in the Magistrates' Court where the maximum fine is £5,000. It is possible for a case to be tried by a Crown Court before a jury and there a two-year prison sentence and/or a fine could be imposed. Under the Trade Marks Act, a person found guilty in the Magistrates' Court can be imprisoned for six months and/or fined up to £5,000; a person found guilty in the Crown Court can be imprisoned for 10 years and/or fined. Oddly, the maximum penalty available under the criminal provisions of the Copyright Act are less, the maximum being two years' imprisonment. This is yet another reason why prosecuting authorities prefer to use the trade mark provisions if they can (see discussion of *Johnstone* in Chapter 9).

Part IV

Copyright

18. INTRODUCTION TO COPYRIGHT

Copyright was originally intended primarily for the protection of authors, artists and composers, and to provide a legal foundation for the innumerable transactions by which authors, artists and composers are paid for their work. Copyright and related rights have expanded far beyond their original scope in terms of the subject matter protected and the extent of protection. This chapter is concerned with the whole field of copyrights.

By 1988, copyright had been stretched so far by the courts so as to cover industrial designs for the simplest articles, giving a very long period of protection (then life of the author plus 50 years). The 1988 Act abolished copyright protection for industrial designs, replacing it with design right. Copyright only applies to stop making such articles in certain special cases—for example where the original work was a work of artistic craftsmanship. But while legislators in the UK were restricting copyright, legislators in the European Community were extending it both in time and in range by harmonising directives which are all now in force. These have had an important influence on UK copyright law. That said, the basic principles of copyright have remained largely the same for many years, and the courts regularly refer to the old cases for help with new problems.

The Nature of Copyright

The primary function of copyright law is to protect from exploitation by other people the fruits of a someone's work, labour, skill or taste. This protection is given by making it unlawful, as an "infringement of copyright," to reproduce or copy, for example, any "literary, dramatic, musical or artistic work" without the consent of the owner of the copyright in that work. It is works that are protected and not ideas; if ideas can be taken without copying a "work", the copyright owner cannot interfere. This distinction is difficult to draw, both theoretically and practically; it is discussed in some detail in Chapter 21. Here is an example. If a photograph is taken of a landscape, that photograph will be copyright: good or bad, it counts as an "artistic work." It will be an infringement of copyright (subject to exceptions dealt with in Chapter 22) if, without consent, that photograph is reproduced—either in the sense in which a newspaper would "reproduce" it by making blocks from it and using them for printing, or in the sense in which it could be said to be copied if an artist were to sit down with the photograph in front of him and make a painting out of it. But it would not be an infringement for another photographer to take a similar photograph of the same landscape: the landscape is not copyright, for the photographer did not make it (the position might be different if he had), and the second photograph, though using the idea of the first, would not be a reproduction of it.

Copyright, Reputations and Competition

Nor is it the function of copyright to protect personal or business reputations, or to prevent business or professional competition: it can sometimes be useful for such purposes, but these uses are, in a sense, accidental. Thus it is no infringement of copyright to imitate an author's literary style, or to take the title of one of his books, or, probably, even to write a book including characters he has invented—although any of these things may be unlawful for other reasons, e.g. if people are misled into thinking that the original author is responsible for the imitation. Thus also, it is normally no infringement of copyright to copy another firm's brand name or one of their advertising slogans. (Here again such acts are likely to be unlawful for reasons discussed elsewhere in this book.) It may or may not be an infringement of copyright to use a photograph of a respectable actress to adorn the cover of a disreputable magazine: it depends on who owns the copyright in that photograph, and whether it is a publicity photograph issued for general use. The actress's remedy for that sort of thing is an action for libel or (if the photograph was taken for private or domestic purposes) for infringement of her moral rights (see Chapter 25).

On the other hand, if in such a case the actress does happen to control the copyright in her photograph, an action for infringement of copyright is likely to provide the quickest and cheapest way of dealing with the matter. So also, though an advertising slogan will probably not have a copyright, a complete advertising brochure is likely to be copyright as a "literary work", while any photograph or drawing in it is likely to be copyright as an "artistic work". Such works may be trivial from an artistic or literary point of view, but they have to be very trivial before they lose protection altogether, and commercially they may have great value. A trade mark may consist of a picture, and the copyright in the picture or logo might be of great value in supplementing ordinary trade mark protection. A fake painting may well be built up largely of bits painted from genuine ones; if it is, and the genuine ones are not so old that their copyright has expired, the fake will infringe and a copyright action may offer the best way of dealing with it.

Types of Copyright Dispute

Copyright disputes (other than disputes about industrial designs) tend consequently to fall into three groups. There are the rare straightforward cases where a substantial work such as a computer program or video film has been pirated for its own sake. There are also many cases where the original work has little intrinsic value or has not been reproduced in any ordinary sense, and where copyright is invoked for ulterior reasons, usually of a commercial character. In between come those cases where the work copied is a substantial one embodying a great deal of skill or labour—a directory or a time-table or something of that sort perhaps—but nevertheless its value derives more from such things as goodwill than from the labour put into it. In cases in these last two groups, there is apt to be a lot of argument as to whether copyright law applies to the case at all.

Copyright in practice

Although reported copyright disputes tend to fall mainly into these last two groups, the practical and commercial importance of the copyright system lies elsewhere. The main function of the copyright system is to provide a legal foundation for transactions in "rights": to provide a legal sanction behind the customary arrangements by which, for instance, a composer is remunerated when some of his music is used on radio or in a film. It is very rare for such matters to give rise to litigation, and very rare for people outside the particular industry to be concerned with them or to find out much about them.

Copyright and Confidence

It is not the function of copyright to prevent betrayal of confidence, whether personal or commercial. But the conditions under which English law protects confidences as such are somewhat limited (they are discussed in Chapter 24), and copyright may be a valuable additional weapon. For instance, an ordinary business letter may be indiscreet without being confidential, and may fall into the hands of competitors without any illegality that will allow the courts to intervene. But even a business letter is a "literary work", and so copyright. There may be no way to stop a competitor into whose hands it falls from showing it to customers, but he can be stopped from making copies of it for circulation. There is sometimes a close relationship between copyright and confidence. For example, in the *Spycatcher* cases, it was suggested by the House of Lords that the Crown might have copyright in Peter Wright's book written in breach of confidence (*Att-Gen v Guardian Newspapers*, 1990).

A Short History of Copyright Law

As we have said, copyright was originally intended to protect authors, artists and composers, not industrial designers or engineers. The ancient history of copyright in books is a bit like the modern history of television broadcasting—the Crown assumed a royal prerogative of granting licences to printers. These licences were highly profitable for the King and gave him an opportunity to keep printers of seditious material in line. In the sixteenth century, decrees of the Star Chamber were used to keep printers in check. There were common law rights that gave authors (and of course the Crown, which never turned down an opportunity for profit) a limited right to share damages from book pirates.

The first real copyright act, the Statute of Anne 1709, gave authors of books the sole right and liberty of printing them for a term of 14 years. "Books and other writings" was held to include musical compositions, *Bach v Longman* (1777) and dramatic compositions *Storace v Longman* (1809). In the former case, J.C. Bach sued the publishers for reproducing harpsichord and viol di gamba sonatas. Lord Mansfield said: "A person may use the copy by playing it; but he has no right to rob the author of the profit by multiplying copies and disposing of them to his own use". This is an early instance of a recurring theme in copyright law: if something is worth copying, it is worth protecting. That principle has heavily influenced the courts and Parliament for the last 200 years.

There were further Copyright Acts in 1814, 1842, 1911 and 1956, as well as Acts dealing with specific aspects of copyright, such as the Engraving Copyright Act 1734 (the introduction of which was largely influenced by Hogarth), the Sculpture Copyright Act 1814, and the Dramatic Copyright Act 1833. The period and scope of protection was extended with each passing copyright act, since the lobbying power of persons with most to gain from extended copyright protection usually outweighed that of consumers who had most to lose from it. The current period (in the main, life of the author plus 70 years) derives from an EC Directive. The Berne Convention—one of the main international treaties on copyright—provided for a period of life of the author plus 50 years.

The current copyright Act is the Copyright, Designs and Patents Act 1988 that mainly came into force on August 1, 1989. Although the 1988 Act is long and complex, the basic principles of copyright too have remained unchanged for the last 200 years. The previous (1956) Act is still of major importance, since a large number of copyright works were created when it was in force. By and large, if a work had copyright under the 1956 Act it will keep it under the 1988 Act.

One of the original aims of the 1988 Act was to simplify copyright law. That was not realised in practice. (It is probably impossible to make a simple statutory code that deals with something as complex as creativity and its commercial exploitation.) It was also intended to serve as the law for the twenty-first century. That too has not proved possible—the 1988 Act has already been amended in several major ways including to deal with compulsory licensing of sound recordings for broadcast and to cope with the problems of reverse engineering in computer software as well as to implement the various other requirements of EC Directives. The 1988 Act has to some extent tried to take copyright law back to its roots—for protecting artistically creative people rather than industrial designs. The latter are supposed to be dealt with by design right.

Old Copyrights

As will be seen in Chapter 21, copyright lasts a very long time. There are still many works in existence that have copyright although they were created before the present Act (or even its predecessor) came into force, and to some extent it is necessary in dealing with them to refer to the old law. For most purposes, the position is that if such works are copyright at all, they are governed by the present law; they may, however, have lost copyright (or never have had it), although by present-day reckoning they are still new enough to have a copyright still in force. Such cases are not of sufficiently practical importance to justify detailed discussion of the old law in a book such as the present. It is usually sufficient to remember that if a work had copyright before August 1, 1989, its copyright continues after that date.

"Reproduction"

It has already been pointed out that the word "reproduce" as used in copyright law has rather different meanings in different contexts. This difficulty runs right through our copyright law. If we speak of one book being copied from another, this is not the same sort of "copying" as occurs when (for example) a painting is made into a plate to illustrate a book. In fact, the "copyright" in a work of literature and the "copyright" in a painting are not really quite the same sort of thing: the "copyright" in a song is again something rather different. Nor is the legal protection needed by the author or by the publisher of a novel really the same as that needed by the author of a song (who is mainly concerned to stop its being sung or recorded without payment) or by an architect (who is mainly concerned to ensure that anyone wanting a house such as he would design will employ him as architect rather than a competitor). A sculptor, on the other hand, will get his main protection from the general law of property, and his copyright is unlikely to be of great value. The Act does differentiate between different categories of "works," as we shall see, but for many purposes it lumps them all together.

19. WORKS THAT ARE THE SUBJECT OF COPYRIGHT

"Works"

Copyright extends to almost everything, published or unpublished, that can be called "a work" at all. The Copyright Act counts among the subjects of copyright: novels and other "literary works"; tables, compilations and computer programs, which count as "literary works"; lectures, addresses, speeches and sermons; plays, scripts for cinema films, dance and mime all of which count as "dramatic works" (the film itself is a work, but of a different category but may also be a dramatic work); paintings, drawings, engravings, photographs and similar things (such as photo-lithographs), sculpture, works of "artistic craftsmanship" not covered by any other head, and works of architecture—all counting as "artistic works"; music; CDs and records, tapes, perforated rolls, other devices for reproducing sounds; sound and television broadcasts and cable programmes; and the typography of books. It is of some importance to which category a work belongs since (see Chapter 22) the rights of the copyright owner depend on it. A detailed list of "works" in which copyright can exist is contained in the Note to Chapter 21.

Foreign "works"

Foreign works are protected if they come from a country (or a citizen or resident of a country) with which the United Kingdom has made a treaty to that effect. This covers practically the whole world. The foreign countries concerned likewise protect British works more or less as they protect local ones. But some countries (the USA in particular) used to require copies of the work to be marked © with the name of the copyright owner and the year of first publication.

Merit, originality, and various sorts of works

In general, works are protected regardless of merit. Thus a rather ordinary tie-on business label has been given protection as an "artistic work" (*Walker v British Picker*, 1961), as have drawings of simple machine parts (*British Northrop v Texteam*, 1974). They must be "original", in the sense of not being entirely copies of another similar work—in other words they must "originate" from their authors. So, for example, one would not get a new copyright in a tracing of an old drawing (*Interlego v Tyco*, 1989). They must also be substantial enough to deserve the name of "works", though here again (as the case just mentioned shows) the standard is not high. A ballet need not be good, but must be reduced to writing. But a play is not deprived of copyright because it is a bad play, or a painting because the artist is completely lacking in skill or taste.

Artistic craftsmanship

The term "work of artistic craftsmanship" is not quite clear. In the leading case on the subject (*Hensher v Restawile*, 1975), the members of the House of Lords expressed differing views on its interpretation, but were unanimous in holding that ephemeral, nailed-up prototypes of a three-piece suite were not works of artistic craftsmanship. The expression would include hand-decorated pottery, but a court has hesitated to say that it includes a dress. There has to be something "artistic" as well as an element of "craftsmanship". This can be important when it comes to industrial designs. When a machine part is made from drawings, there will be copyright in the drawing; but when it is made by a craftsman simply playing with a bit of metal until he gets it right, there is no copyright. Unregistered design right has a role to play in protecting works of pure craftsmanship but not *artistic* craftsmanship.

Photographs and sound-recordings

Photographs and sound-recordings are not restricted as to merit or subject matter, but like any other works they cannot be copyright unless they are "original", and this needs some consideration. In a sense, no photograph or sound recording is original: for the camera or microphone only records what is presented to it. But there is more to making a photograph and much more to making a sound recording than that, and the skill of the photographer or recording engineer will found copyright just as the skill of the artist who makes an engraving from a painting will. It is the change of form of the work and the skill involved that in these cases justifies copyright. Where there is no change of form, copyright must be justified in some other way; a mere re-photographing of a photographic print, for instance, would not give the second photograph a copyright of its own. For this, there would have to be sufficient alteration combined with the re-photographing to make the second a different "work". But it may be assumed that, in any practical case, whoever did the rephotographing could show that enough additional skill and originality was put into to give the new photograph a new copyright. So in the field of sound-recording, whilst a "mere" re-recording would give no additional copyright, in practical cases, such as transfer of a "historic" recording from old 78s on to modern disk or tape, the recording company may have done enough work improving the recording quality to make it effectively a new recording and so give it a new copyright. This is much the same problem as that of a new edition of a book: see below.

Triviality

In copyright disputes of a commercial character, the main issue in the case is sometimes whether that which has been copied embodies enough "work, labour, skill or taste" to be called an original work. It is not easy to lay down any clear rules as to this, for it is essentially a matter of opinion—of the opinion, that is to say, of whatever court tries the dispute. The opinions of judges are never very easy to forecast, for they necessarily depend a great deal on the precise circumstances of the case in which the issue concerned arises. For instance, few judges can avoid giving some weight to their opinion of the relative merits and morals of the parties to the dispute. Nevertheless, it is possible to give some idea of the probability that a particular "work" will be held to have copyright.

Different authors

The first question that arises is how much of the "work" derives from any particular author: it is only the part for which he is responsible that can be considered in deciding whether he has produced an original work. Suppose for instance that a textbook has run, as legal textbooks often do, into a large number of editions in the course of a great many years. The first edition was no doubt copyright; perhaps it still is, perhaps that copyright has lapsed. Each subsequent edition may or may not give rise to a new copyright in the whole book, depending on whether the amount of work done by the editor in producing the new edition is sufficient to be called the creation of a new work. (It does not matter for this purpose whether the new edition is edited by the original author or by someone else; the test is the same in either case.) A similar problem arises in connection with a publication

155

such as a railway timetable, which is reprinted perhaps monthly with very few alterations from one month to the next.

In connection with a textbook, this question is usually not very hard to answer, although the answer is hard to put into words; one can "feel" the difference between making minor or routine alterations in the book and making a more substantial contribution to the book as a whole. In other cases the distinction may be very hard to draw, and when this is the case, courts tend to reach illogical decisions that confuse matters still further. It has, for instance, been held that each successive monthly edition of the index to a railway timetable had a copyright of its own, although this index was merely a list of railway station names, and there were, on the average, only about 10 changes made in this list each month. Probably the true moral to be drawn from this particular case is that if a "work" in fact embodies a great deal of labour, it is unsafe to copy it in reliance upon a purely technical defence to copyright proceedings. Such an index would clearly have been copyright if it had been produced entirely afresh; the only difficulty arose from its having grown up gradually over a period of many years. It would be a surprising thing, if a work were to be refused copyright merely because it had taken years to produce, and no court would hold this to be the law if it could help it. It is, however, the law in some cases.

On the other side of the line, retracing the drawings for "Lego" bricks (adding a few manufacturing directions) has been held not to give rise to a new copyright (*Interlego v Tyco*, 1989). A learned musicologist who filled in the gaps to create a performing score of the music of a seventeenth-century composer was held entitled to copyright in the score. The court held that the process of editing undertaken by Dr Sawkins combined the scholarship and knowledge derived from a long and detailed study of the composer's music with a certain amount of artistic inventiveness. A claim against the record company, which had issued recordings of the music performed according to the claimant's score, succeeded (*Sawkins v Hyperion Records*, 2004).

"Anything worth copying is worth protecting"

One way of approaching the problem of where to draw the line between what amounts to a "work" and that which does not, is to say that anything worth copying is worthy of protection against copying. In many cases this rule is a useful guide. But the line must still be drawn somewhere, and the difficulty of drawing it tends to be most acute just in the sort of case where this rule is not applicable, in those commercial cases where something has been copied, not so much to avoid the trouble of producing something similar, as for extraneous reasons. The most that can be said with certainty is that any sort of drawing may be held to have copyright; that even a few bars of music may have copyright; at any rate if they are recognisable; and that although a single sentence (such as an advertising slogan) has never yet been held to be copyright, anything more may constitute a "literary work". (The title of a book, for example, is not copyright, and protection for it (if any) must be sought in an action for passing-off (see *Exxon*, 1982).) Merit is not necessary, but a composition that is striking—"original" in the ordinary as distinct from the copyright sense—is more likely to be protected by the courts than a commonplace composition of the same size or length. Even so, short business letters have been held copyright, notwithstanding a characteristic absence of signs of literary skill. So have advertisements in newspapers.

Compilations

It is particularly difficult to lay down rules for determining whether there is copyright in a compilation or arrangement of facts or of non-copyright material. There will clearly be copyright in such things as telephone directories, *Who's Who*, railway timetables or mathematical tables, if they are "original" in the copyright sense. Messages sent out by news agencies have been held copyright, even where literary form was not involved—as with stock-exchange prices; so have a week's radio programmes; so have the starting prices for a race (which took some skill in sorting out), but not a list of starting positions (which were merely written down as they were determined by ballot); so has an anthology of poems not themselves copyright, but not an edition of a non-copyright book shortened by cutting out about half of it. (In the last case, there were critical notes published with the new edition and these were held copyright.) Copyright has been refused to a local timetable made by selecting and rearranging entries from a larger timetable relating to a particular town, and it has been refused to a selection of seven non-copyright tables of conventional type for inclusion in a diary.

All that can be said in general is that mere industry counts less than knowledge, skill or taste in such matters; the amount of labour that goes into a particular compilation is of great importance; and that anything published in permanent form—a book, for instance—has a better chance of protection than such ephemeral productions as a notice on a notice board. The rest is a matter of how the court feels about it. In the case of the diary, for instance, the Court of Appeal decided one way, the judge who tried the case at the first instance and the House of Lords the other; a sure sign of the sort of case where anything can happen. Since the implementation of the Database Directive in 1996, there has been a different and probably stricter test for copyright protection to arise in databases. This requires that, by reason of the selection or arrangement of their contents, the database constitutes the author's own intellectual creation. It remains to be seen what difference this makes in practice in English law.

An ordinary book of non-fiction may well be copyright on two separate grounds: both from the literary skill that went into writing it, and from the skill and labour that went into selecting the facts set out in it. Historical facts, for example, are not copyright in themselves, but a selection of them can have copyright as a compilation. Here again the line is difficult to draw: a compilation of facts will have copyright, but mere ideas will not.

Copyright can Exist only in "Works"

It is worth emphasising that apart from questions of amount—of whether there is enough of a product for it to count as a "work" for copyright purposes—nothing can attract copyright unless it is the sort of thing that is called a "work". For instance, it will be an infringement of copyright to film a play without consent, but not to film a dog show or a boxing match: one is a "dramatic work", the others are not, for nobody has composed or arranged precisely what happens at them. If the promoters of such spectacles want to prevent photography, they must do it in some such way as by selling tickets only to people who agree not to take photographs. So also, a card index system is not copyright: nor is a game, though the written-out rules of the game will be, and so may any board on which it is played. Thus, the inventor of a new game may be able to prevent other people copying his board or his book of rules. A collection of five-letter code-words was held copyright as a "literary work" (skill was needed in selecting the words so as to guard against errors in transmission), but not a system for coding the wholesale prices in a catalogue: however ingenious a system, and however successful in concealing the retail profit from customers, it was a mere scheme and not a "work". The instructions for decoding the prices could have been copyright: but that copyright would not be infringed by a competitor who wrote his own instructions, quite independently.

Illegal and Immoral Works

By way of exception from the general rules, the courts will not protect a work that is illegal, immoral, indecent or similarly undeserving of protection. It is open for question whether a libellous poem can claim copyright. Inevitably, a great deal depends on the attitude of the judge trying the case. Late in 1939, for example, copyright protection was refused to a would-be humorous document entitled "The Last Will and Testament of Adolf Hitler"; while not obscene, it was, in the view of the judge, vulgar and indecent. Presumably, however, some people thought it funny, or it would not have been worth publishing, let alone worth copying too. The judge concerned was not one of them but, if he had been, the case would probably have gone the other way. Cases of this sort being rare, the limits of this exception have never been very clearly laid down. A doll that revealed what lay beneath the sporran was held entitled to registered design protection. (*Masterman's Design*, 1991).

Overlapping Copyrights

It is in general irrelevant to the question whether a work is copyright, to consider whether it is covered by some other copyright too. In the case for instance of what are called "collective works"—symposia, magazines, encyclopedias and so on—there must necessarily be a whole series of copyrights in the separate articles or stories as well as a copyright in the work as a whole: in the general plan and arrangement of the work.

Overlapping copyrights are found not only in collective works, however. In Chapter 18, it was pointed out that a painting can be a reproduction of a photograph for copyright purposes. In such a case, there will be a copyright in the painting separate from that in the original photograph. The painting is an "artistic work" in its own right, requiring skill and labour for its execution, notwithstanding that the scene depicted is taken from a photograph. In such a case, it will be unlawful to reproduce the painting unless the owners of both copyrights consent. Similar cases are common in other arts too: for instance, in a record of music, both the music itself and the recording will be copyright, unless the music is quite old. The point is important in dealing in copyright, for it will be ambiguous to refer to "the copyright in the painting", if more than one copyright exists in the painting, and an agreement using such language may have rather unexpected effects.

Translations

A translation will have copyright, independent of the work from which it is translated. The classic example of this was a case where the court had to decide upon the ownership of the copyright, if any, in a book said to have been dictated to a "medium" by the spirit of a biblical character who had died some 2000 years before. The court noted that the book was written, not in any language current in those days, but in somewhat archaic English, and decided that the translation from one language to the other must have been done by the medium —who consequently had a translator's copyright. The case is *Cummins v Bond* (1926): the full report ([1927] 1 Ch. 167) is well worth reading as itself a "literary work". It must not be supposed that the judge necessarily believed the book to have been dictated by any spirit; but a judge has to decide an ordinary civil case on such evidence as the parties choose to put before him. Since both parties accepted that the book had a ghostly origin, it was proper for the judge to decide the case on that basis.

It should be noted that the matter translated need not be anything that is capable of sustaining a copyright; the test to be applied is whether the translator has expended a substantial amount of labour, skill and knowledge upon making his translation. If he has, it will be copyright.

Other Cases

In the same way, a shorthand report of a speech has its own copyright; here it is the shorthand-writer's skill and labour from which the copyright derives. The speech will in itself probably be copyright too. So it will be also with the photograph of a painting, or painting made from a photograph; the film made from a book or play and the "book of the film"—and all similar instances. In these cases there are two copyrights (at least): one, that in the original work, covers both works; the other covers the transformed work only. So again an architect's plans will be copyright as plans—unless of course they are merely copied from other plans. If a building is built from the plans, it will attract architectural copyright that is quite distinct from the copyright in the plans. Finally, there is a copyright in the typographical arrangement of a published edition of a work, which is separate from the copyright in the work itself: see the Note to Chapter 21.

20. OWNERSHIP OF COPYRIGHT

Copyright comes into existence automatically (if it arises at all), without need for formalities or any form of application. As a person writes or paints an "original" work, so a copyright work is created. Copyright is quite unlike patents in this respect. The result is that it is possible for the question of subsistence and ownership never to arise at all, until the copyright is the subject of some dispute. It will then be necessary to work out who is the owner, with no assistance from registers or formal documents. The rules of law governing ownership are therefore important: fortunately, they are simple too.

This chapter deals with the question of who owns a copyright in the first place; what may happen to it afterwards is a different question and will be considered in Chapter 23.

The Basic Rule—Copyright Belongs to the Author

Except for the situations mentioned below, the first owner of the copyright in the work concerned is the author. The author, for this purpose, is the person who actually expends the work, labour, knowledge, skill or taste in creating the copyright work. In the case of a book for instance, the "author" of the work will be whoever composes the sentences of which it is made up. If a person dictates a book to a secretary, she will be the author—not her secretary. If, on the other hand, she merely provides the ideas, and the secretary writes the book, the secretary is the author—whether the book is published in her name or not (but see exception 1 below.) If a book is illustrated by drawings, the "author" of the drawings will be whoever drew them, notwithstanding that the idea for each illustration was taken from the book itself. There may, of course, be books where, although one person wrote the whole text, another provided and selected the material for the book and determined its arrangement to a sufficient extent to be considered a joint author of it. In general, however, the person who chooses the actual words used will be the sole author: for instance, where a "ghost" writer composes a person's autobiography, the "ghost" will be held to be the sole author even though the subject of the autobiography supplies such facts as may be included. It has even been held that the compiler of a work such as *Who's Who* is the "author" of each of the entries, although the material for the entry is supplied by the person concerned in response to a questionnaire.

In the case of a photograph, the "author", for the purpose of copyright, is the person who creates the photograph (subject to what is said below).

Where two people have made a significant and original contribution to a work that is not distinct, they may both be entitled to be joint authors. For example, in one case it was held that the composer of a violin part for "Young at Heart" was a joint author of the work.

Exception 1—Works by employees

When the author of a work is in the employment of some other person "under a contract of service or apprenticeship", and the work is made "in the course of his employment", the copyright belongs to the employer. This does not include cases where the author can be loosely said to be "employed to produce the work", but is not employed in the ordinary sense. Thus the editor or publisher who commissions a book or article gets the copyright only if the author's contract says so; the publisher who employs an author (by a "contract of service") gets the copyright automatically, just as if the person were hired to make boots there would be no need for a contract saying that the boots would belong to the owner of the factory. In the same way, the architect who is "employed" to design a house does not lose the copyright in his design to the building owner; but the architect's draughtsman, who works for a salary, will be an employee, and the copyright in the plans he is paid to draw will belong to the architect who employs him.

The exact limits of the phrase "in the course of his employment" are not very easy to define and the phrase has given rise to much litigation. For most purposes, however, it means simply that he was an employee (rather than an independent contractor) and it was part of his job to produce that work. One example is the architectural draughtsman already mentioned. On the other side of the line, there was a case where a translation had been made by a man for his employers, but in his spare time and for extra payment (as distinct from an overtime payment). It was held that the translator, not his employer, was the first owner of the copyright in the translation. (It may be that the employer could have demanded that the copyright be handed over to him; but this question did not arise, for it was not his employer that the translator was suing.) It is not quite clear to whom works of a secretly moonlighting employee belong.

Exception 2—"Commissioned works"

There *used to be* an important exception to the general rule that the author was the first owner of copyright (it has now been abolished). This related to commissioned works of certain kinds. If someone commissioned the taking of a photograph or an engraving or painting a portrait, and paid or agreed to pay for it, the commissioner would get copyright automatically in the work made in pursuance of the commission. There were quite a few cases about this—several turning on whether there was payment or an obligation to pay, since, if the sitting was free, the photographer or engraver or portraitist would own the copyright. But although this rule has been abolished, the exception still applies to works made before the Copyright, Designs and Patents Act 1988 came into force and can therefore be important, particularly for old photographs.

One case concerned the photographs for use on the Beatles' "Sgt. Pepper's Lonely Heart's Club Band" album. These photographs were taken in 1967 by Michael Cooper, a fashionable 1960s photographer. He and his assistant had taken several rolls of film of the Beatles on the famous set and of them wandering about the studio. The photographs included the one actually used for the cover and several other similar ones—"outtakes". Michael Cooper's son wanted to exploit some of these outtakes. The Beatles wanted to stop this, and one of the questions raised was who owned the copyright in them? This depended on whether they had been taken pursuant to a commission from the Beatles (or people acting for them) and whether they had paid or agreed to pay for them. The judge held that there was not enough evidence to show that there was a commission prior to the taking of the photographs, or that the person doing the commissioning had paid or agreed to pay for them. So the Beatles lost.

There are many situations in which a person commissions another person to do some creative work. Although, under the current law, the copyright belongs to the creator of the work, this can sometimes cause problems. For example, an engineering company asks an advertising consultant to design a campaign poster. Nothing is said about copyright. Who owns it? Or a managing director of a company does a drawing in her work hours and for company purposes. (She is not an employee but a director, so the first of the employees' exceptions does not apply.) Who owns the copyright in the drawing?

In strict law, in the first case, it will be the advertising consultant and in the second, it will be the managing director. But the courts are not especially comfortable with solutions like that, since they can lead to results that no-one really intended at the time. So they occasionally fudge the issue a bit. Some judges take the view that if commercial people and organisations do not make proper provision to regulate their affairs, that is tough: the courts won't spring to their aid. But others will say one of two things: either the engineering company has an implied licence to use the poster design for its campaign or, more rarely, that the company is the "equitable owner" of the copyright. That is often the result in the advertising agency line of cases. The same will apply in the second example—the company may be held to have an equitable right to the copyright. Being the equitable owner means that you have a right to have the legal title to the copyright transferred into your name. This solution is a way of getting round the problem that the Copyright Act principally gives rights to the creators of the work, but this can sometimes result in the creators holding the people for whom they do the work to ransom when this was never intended by either party at the time.

Crown Copyright

Where a work is either made by Her Majesty or by an officer or servant of the Crown in the course of his duties, the copyright belongs to the Crown. There is a separate Parliamentary copyright. The Crown does not always enforce its copyrights and allows such things as Acts of Parliament to be freely reproduced from the official editions published by the Stationery Office; but the copyright is there, and it is enforced in relation to things like Ordnance Survey maps, or directions from Ministries to local authorities. As was stated in the last chapter, copyright in these cases lasts for 50 years from commercial publication; a provision that has the merit that it is possible to find out whether the copyright in Crown works has expired without having first to find out who the author was: an almost impossible task in the case of, say, an Ordnance Survey map.

Where Authorship is not Certain

If a work appears to be signed, or to bear an author's name, the courts will assume, unless it is proved otherwise, that the person whose name or signature the work bears is the owner of the copyright in it; if not, the first publisher will be presumed to own the copyright. These are however merely rules of evidence: they do not alter rights, but sometimes make it easier for the plaintiff in a copyright action to prove his case. In particular, they make it possible to sue for infringement of the copyright in an anonymous work without disclosing the author's name.

21. WHAT IS INFRINGEMENT OF COPYRIGHT?

It was pointed out in Chapter 18 that copyright is, in essence merely a right to stop other people doing certain things (the "acts restricted by the copyright"). The definition of infringement is consequently of very great importance. The present chapter sets out to explain, just what are these activities that an owner of a copyright is entitled to stop; the rules stated in this chapter are, however, subject to certain exceptions discussed in the chapter following.

Infringement by Reproduction

First of all, copyright in a work will be infringed if the work is copied without the consent of the owner of the copyright. This is sometimes referred to as the "reproduction right". To give a simple example, consider an article in a magazine. In the ordinary course, it will have been sent in by the author (or by her literary agent): sending it in will mean that she owns the copyright and she wants it published so long as she gets the proper fee—and the only possibility of argument lies in the size of the fee. It is only when something goes wrong that a dispute about copyright can arise. Suppose she sends in illustrations with her manuscript and they are not hers to offer for publication; then each copy of the magazine "reproduces" them without the consent of the copyright owner, and that is infringement. (The person who sent the article in would usually end up paying the damages, if she has the money, but the magazine would be primarily liable for copying.) Or the whole article may be very like one that appeared earlier in some other magazine, but not quite the same. This may or may not constitute an infringement of the copyright in the earlier story according to circumstances; and it is necessary to consider in some detail, just where the line is to be drawn.

Copying

The Copyright, Designs and Patents Act 1988 uses the word "copy" in this connection. This principally involves reproducing the work concerned, or a substantial part of it, in a material form. Copying is essential to this sort of infringement. It has

167

been said often enough that six monkeys, operating typewriters at random, would sooner or later reproduce all the books in the British Museum Library; among them, works that were copyright. But there would be no infringement of the copyright, for there would be no copying: the work would have been reproduced quite accidentally, without reference to the original.

Copying need not be direct, and it need not be conscious or deliberate. All that is necessary for an infringement (so long as a substantial part of the earlier work is taken), is that the later work should somehow, through some channels, be derived from the earlier. On the other hand, this amount of copying is necessary, and must be proved: for if the copyright owner wishes to stop an infringement, she must prove to the appropriate court that infringement has taken place.

Proof of copying

The difficulty of proof is often serious. It will very seldom be possible to prove directly that copying has taken place: for only the alleged infringer knows how the work came into existence. The result is that, in practice, the only thing to do is to point to the resemblances between the two works and to say that these resemblances are too many and too close to be due to coincidence. The court can then be asked to infer that some sort of copying must have taken place. If the court accepts this argument, it will then be up to the alleged infringer to explain the resemblances away if possible. That is to say, a reasonable explanation of how those resemblances could have come into existence without any copying must be produced. Not every explanation will do, for judges are not exactly credulous people; if the explanation is that X thought the whole thing up without ever having seen or heard of the earlier work, the judge will want to see X (or hear some good reason why he cannot see X) and find out whether to believe the story or not. But if the explanation is reasonable, the copyright owner must find some other way of proving the case, and as we have said, there is usually no other way available.

An illustration of this is *Francis Day & Hunter v Bron* (1963) where the court held that although there were very great similarities between the plaintiffs' tune "In a Little Spanish Town" and the defendants' pop song, "Why", this was not enough to prove infringement where the composer of "Why" (whose story was believed) said he could not remember ever hearing the plaintiffs' tune, although he was prepared to admit that he might have heard it on the radio when he was young.

A substantial part must be copied

When it has been shown that copying has taken place, the next requirement for proving infringement is to show that the part of the one work reproduced in the other is a substantial part.

Where some part (but only a small part) part is copied exactly

While the principle "what is worth copying is worth protecting" is not always a good guide, in this case it is. Once a court is satisfied that there is a copyright work, and that the defendant in the case before it has thought it worthwhile copying out word for word some part of that work, it will be very hard to persuade that court that the part copied was not substantial. Thus, where four lines of a short poem of Kipling were reproduced in an advertisement, the court found no difficulty in holding that this was a substantial enough part of the poem for there to be infringement. As usual, however, a lot depends on how the court feels about the case. Where, for instance, the title of a short story was taken from the refrain of a popular song, and four lines from the song were printed below the title (as of course quotations often are), the court held that this was not an infringement of the copyright in the song. The line must be drawn somewhere: the owner of the copyright in the song was not really deprived of his property or of an opportunity to draw profits from his property; and regarded as a literary work, the song was not quite in the same class as a poem of Kipling.

The question of merit is rather difficult. Strictly speaking, it is not easy to see how the merit of a work should affect the matter at all. In practice, it is always easier to found a successful action for infringement of copyright upon a work that has merit than upon a work that has not. The law is never absolutely rigid, and the court will give a common-sense decision where it can. It is fortunate that this is so; but it is sometimes in consequence a little difficult to forecast what a court's decision will be in any particular case. The imponderable influence of merit (or the lack of it) in copyright actions is one of the things that make prediction difficult.

An instructive case as to what is a substantial part of a work arose from the inclusion, in a newsreel of a military parade, of a sequence taken while the band was playing the copyright march "Colonel Bogey". The sequence lasted less than a minute, and other things were happening at the same time, but the principal air of the march was clearly recognisable. This was held to amount to taking a substantial part of the march; the more so, because the soundtrack of the film could have been used by itself as a record of the march—to provide incidental music during an interval for instance. There is now a special provision excluding infringement in cases where music is merely picked up by the microphone of a newsreel camera, and not specially recorded to provide a background to the film.

Compilations

The simplest examples of compilations are, of course, works like directories, consisting of a large number of short entries without any particular literary form. Here the rule as to infringement is clear. It is a "reproduction" and so an infringement, to take the entries from one directory for use in another, even if they are independently checked against some other source of material and then completely rearranged in combination with other material. It is legitimate, however, after compiling a directory from other sources, to check it against a rival work to see that there are no mistakes or omissions. It is not so clear to what extent entries that are found to have been omitted from the new compilation may at this stage be copied into it from the old: a few may be, a substantial number may not, but exactly how many may be depends upon the circumstances of the case. In particular, it depends a great deal on whether the judge who tries the case really believes that the second work was independently compiled before the checking took place. In *Peacey v De Vries* (1921), the court believed it, but in *Blacklock v Pearson* (1915), the court obviously did not. See also Chapter 26 below on Database Right.

The same rule as for directories has been applied to a translation of a foreign play, and is probably applicable to any work considered as a collection of information. That is to say, where a work has copyright by reason of the skill and labour that went into collecting the information given in it, that copyright will not be infringed by using the work as one source among others, to supplement and correct information obtained in the main elsewhere. The copyright will, however, be infringed if any substantial part of the information set out by the work is taken as a whole, even if it is afterwards cross-checked against other sources. This is, of course, not the only test of infringement, for most works will also have copyright by reason of their literary or artistic form, and this latter copyright will be infringed if the form is taken whether the information set out is taken or not. To this question of reproduction of form we must now turn.

Where there is merely a similarity of form or general idea

In discussing this question, it must first of all be remembered that there is no copyright in ideas. Thus, an illustrated joke, for instance, will have copyright as a picture, and possibly even the words of the caption might be copyright: but the joke itself cannot be. There will consequently be no infringement if the same joke is used by someone else, differently phrased and with a different picture. In the same way it is no infringement of copyright to take the plot of a book, even in fair detail. In one case, for instance, a fairly full synopsis of the action of the opera was issued with a set of gramophone records of operatic music: this was held not to be an infringement of the libretto of the opera. Nor would the position be in any way different if that synopsis had been written up into a complete new libretto for a similar opera: for there would have been nothing common to the two works except the synopsis, and this did not infringe any copyright.

It must also be remembered that every competent worker in any field must be expected to be familiar with any important work that has gone before; and it is just the important and successful work, that everyone ought to know and that will inevitably influence works that come after it, that is likely to attract infringers. In fiction, it is indeed often the poor and unknown author whose unexpectedly brilliant work is stolen, but in real life that sort of thing seems rarely to be a commercial proposition. The inevitable influence of one work on those that follow does not involve infringement of copyright. The difficulty is to distinguish between drawing on the common stock of experience, and making improper use of other people's work. It is often difficult to work out whether a defendant has got sufficiently close to the claimant's work to infringe. The general rule now is that, if a defendant has reproduced enough for it to be clear that he has copied, that amount of reproduction will be sufficiently substantial to infringe (see *Designers Guild*, 2003). The question is whether the defendant's work incorporates a substantial part of the skill and labour expended by the designer of the claimant's work.

Judges have tried to express the way the line is to be drawn, by saying that for there to be infringement, one work must produce the "same effect" as the other, but this is not always a reliable guide. To put it slightly differently, there must be something that might make people encountering the two works in succession feel, "I have read this story—or seen this play—or heard this

171

music—before". But the mere fact that one work reminds a reader or viewer of another work is not enough—it is not an infringement of copyright to try to reproduce someone's style of writing (or composing or film-making). Some examples may help to explain how such tests work out in practice.

Example 1

Many years ago, one Austin composed a new arrangement of the music of a work that had long ago lost any copyright it had ever possessed: the "Beggar's Opera". The new arrangement was, of course, copyright; it was also a popular success. A manufacturer of gramophone records, wishing to take advantage of Austin's success, brought out a recording of extracts from the "Beggar's Opera". Since the tunes were all old, this was not in itself any infringement of Austin's copyright. But the recording went further: although the actual notes were not copied from the Austin arrangement, the tunes were "dressed up in the same way", as the judge put it. That was infringement: a record is a "reproduction". The case in fact raised in a different context the same question as the example discussed in Chapter 18, of the photographer who sees a successful photograph of a landscape and goes and takes another like it. He may photograph the same view, for there is no more copyright in a view than there was in the tunes of the "Beggar's Opera". But he must not go further and imitate to any substantial extent the tricks by which the first photographer has converted the view into a successful photograph.

The *Austin* case illustrates also the way in which the circumstances of a case influence the court's findings. The defendants there had advertised their records in a way that emphasised the relationship with Austin's successful arrangement, and in fact in this connection lay the whole reason for bringing out those records at that time at all. This made it by no means easy for the defendants to argue that they had really taken nothing from Austin: the defence was in effect merely that, as a technical legal matter, what they had done was not reproduction of a substantial part of that which was the subject of copyright. Purely technical defences are always dangerous.

If such a question arises on a comparison of two apparently independent works, the case is not prejudiced by any admissions that the one work is connected with the other, and such a defence takes on a rather different aspect. The defendant can, and does, argue that there has been no copying at all in any ordinary sense;

172

that the resemblances between the two works if not pure coincidence—any two works being indeed much more alike than perhaps their authors would admit—are the result of the sort of unconscious influence mentioned above as inevitable and legitimate; and that these resemblances are trivial, not substantial. (He may even argue that the resemblances are due to legitimate "quotation" of phrases that the hearer will be expected to recognise as coming from earlier works.) Only then does he argue that in any case, what is common to the two works is not the sort of thing that the law calls "reproduction". If there is real doubt as to the copying, the technical defence will have a much more favourable reception.

Example 2

Bauman was a photographer of high repute who took pictures for the *Picture Post* magazine. One of them was of two fighting cocks which he took in Cuba. Fussell was a painter. He saw Bauman's photograph in the *Picture Post*, cut it out, pinned it to his studio wall and from it painted a picture of two fighting cocks in the same position and attitude as the birds in the photograph. In the painting, the colouring was different, as was the general effect of the painting, which was not at all photographic. Experts were lined up on each side, including the Arts Director of the Arts Council and Professor Moyniham, a well-known painter from the Royal College of Art. The Court of Appeal judges (who were divided 2:1) spoke of the "feeling and artistic character" of the respective works. These were different and so, somewhat surprisingly, the plaintiff lost. Moral: when courts get into the realms of the "feeling and artistic character" of a work, anything can happen (*Bauman v Fussell*, 1978).

Changes in material form

A rather similar sort of question can arise where there is a change in the material form taken by a work. For instance, to take examples that have come before the courts, where it is suggested that a dress infringes a drawing of a dress, or a shop-front an architect's sketch of a shop-front. Clearly, the two cannot be identical in either case but there is still a sense in which it can be said that there can be reproduction of one work by the other. Whether there is reproduction or not in any particular case is a question on which opinions are likely to differ, with the result that it is likely to be very hard to forecast what view the judge who decides the case will take.

Other Forms of Infringement

In the case of "ordinary" literary, dramatic, musical and artistic works, reproduction (in a material form) is the primary form of infringement. For more special works there are special rules, and for "ordinary" works there are other sorts of infringement. These things are listed at the end of this chapter, and only instances will be mentioned here.

Adaptations of literary or dramatic works

It is an infringement of the copyright in a literary or dramatic work to make or reproduce an "adaptation" of it. Adaptation includes translation, and conversion into a strip-cartoon, as well as conversion of a literary into a dramatic work and vice versa. Cases about conversions and other adaptations are often very difficult, for they raise in acute form the same sort of difficulty as has already been discussed in connection with the phrase "reproduction of a substantial part of a work". Such a conversion need involve no detailed copying: a novel could be converted into a silent film, for instance (which would be "reproduction" of a dramatic adaptation, if not "reproduction" of the original work) without taking a single word—there would, indeed, be no words apart from occasional captions. This would be an infringement, if done without consent. If, instead, a sound-film were produced, it could still be an infringement, notwithstanding that the dialogue was independently written without any copying from the novel.

In the same way, it has been held in one case that a ballet infringed the copyright in a short story; there could be no question of using the same words, but the ballet nevertheless "told the same story". Simply taking the bare plot does not constitute infringement in such a case; the incidents of the story must be taken too. But it is not necessary for the two works to resemble one another to the extent needed for one novel to infringe the copyright in another novel, or one play in another play. An instructive discussion of the question of infringement of the copyright in a play by a silent film may be found in the old case: *Vane v Famous Players* (1928). We know of no case that lays down any principle as to how to decide whether a play infringes the copyright in an artistic work such as a picture;

perhaps the court would look for an actual reproduction of the picture upon the stage.

Films

It may be noted that where the making of a film infringes copyright, infringement has probably already taken place before actual photographing begins: the reproduction of, or conversion into a dramatic work of, the work whose copyright is infringed, will already have happened in the preparation of the script from which the actual film is made. The actual making of the film will be a further infringement. In the same way, there was a case where a maker of gramophone records had a right to record a song but no other rights in it. He wanted the recording to be made with orchestral accompaniment, which the published version lacked; so he had a single manuscript copy prepared of the song with a suitable accompaniment. The preparation of this manuscript was held to be an infringement of copyright: arrangement or transcription of a musical work is "adaptation" and so infringement.

Other forms of infringement

Issuing copies to the public

It will be an act of infringement to publish a work, in the sense of issuing copies of the work to the public, without consent (or to authorise issue to the public). This sort of infringement very seldom occurs alone, unless one is dealing with imported works. That is because publication is impossible unless copies of the work are in existence, and the making of the necessary copies in this country will normally itself constitute infringement. There are exceptions in respect of works which have been put on the market in the EU, but putting on the market for the first time in the UK a copyright work which has not been put on the market in the EU is an infringement.

Publishing an unpublished work

It is also impermissible to publish a previously unpublished work, without consent. This can be important, for large damages may flow from it: in particular, the author's own chance of a successful launch may be completely spoilt by an anticipatory publication.

Performing a work in public

It is an infringement of copyright to perform a work in public without consent. (The same applies to public performance of anything close enough to a work, for its reproduction to infringe copyright.) "In public" has here a rather special meaning. It refers, not to the sort of place where the performance takes place, but to the sort of audience that is present. Nor does it mean that the performance is one that anyone can attend who likes, still less that a charge must be made for admission. For this purpose, any performance is "in public" that is not restricted to members of the home circle of whoever is responsible for the performance. Guests can be present of course; there can be a very large party to see or hear the performance: but it must be a genuinely domestic affair or it will be public for copyright purposes. An amateur dramatic show by members of a Women's Institute for fellow members only; "Music While You Work" in a factory; music played so that it could be heard in the public parts of a restaurant—all these have been held to infringe copyright as "performances in public". There are certain exceptions for essentially non-profit making bodies (for the recording copyright) although these have been much limited as a result of EU legislation—see the Note below.

"Performance" for this purpose includes performance by means of a mechanical instrument: such as a cinematograph projector, a gramophone or wireless, or a television receiver, So that showing a film in public is both "causing the film to be seen in public", involving the film copyright, and a performance in public of any play or music embodied in the film; and similarly with sound recordings. Further, although artistic works cannot be "performed", it is infringement to exhibit them on television.

If a studio performance of a play is "televised" (or a studio performance of music is broadcast), and the broadcast received in the presence of such an audience so that it is "in public", this will be a performance in public of the play or music, for which whoever operates the receiving set will be responsible: he will infringe unless he obtains the necessary consent. In addition, the broadcaster has a separate copyright in the broadcast, but this copyright is not infringed unless there is a paying audience. Thus public display of a television receiver—a demonstration receiver in an ordinary shop for instance—will give rise to an infringing performance in public if what is televised is a performance of a work. A completely impromptu performance, however, will have

176

no copyright but the broadcaster's copyright, which is not infringed unless the audience pay. Thus the interposition of a wireless link, or of a cinema camera and projector, between a performance and its audience never prevents copyright from being infringed; but it may give additional possibilities of infringement.

There is a similar distinction made for recordings of sound broadcasts. It is an infringement of copyright to record a work, whether by way of recording of a broadcast or otherwise, unless the making of the record is "fair" dealing with the work for purposes of research or private study; see the next chapter. But the broadcaster's copyright in the broadcast is not infringed by a record of it made for private purposes. Since with most of the things anyone would want to perform in public—music, plays, films, sound recordings—the copyright owners want them performed, there are well-organised systems for selling the necessary licences. (See Chapter 23.)

Getting others to infringe and like cases

In accordance with ordinary rules of law, it is as much an infringement to get someone else to do an infringing act as to do it oneself. In particular, an employer is responsible for acts of infringement committed by employees "in the course of their employment".

But copyright law goes further, and makes it an infringement to "authorise" another to make a copy of a work in question. What constitutes authorisation is not always clear in practice. In essence, it involves granting or purporting to grant the right to copy. It can include commissioning another person to produce an article to an infringing design. Selling a work such as a computer program, where loading and running it on a computer involves making an electronic copy may also constitute authorising copying.

In addition, an author who offers a manuscript to a publisher to publish authorises the publisher to do so; and if the publisher sends it to a printer he authorises the printer to reproduce it. (It is usual for publishing agreements to make the author warrant to the publisher that the book infringes no copyright; but even without this warranty, the ordinary law would enable the printer to recover from the publisher, and the publisher from the author, any loss they had suffered as a result of copyright trouble.)

"Authorising" covers other things too: any case where someone who does not control a copyright accepts a royalty for its use would be authorising the use, even though the initiative came entirely from the user. With the growth of sophisticated commercial photocopying techniques, those who make available photocopying facilities, for example in libraries, should take special care to avoid being taken to authorise the use of those facilities for the purposes of infringement (*Moorhouse v University of New South Wales*, 1976). In practice, photocopying in libraries is largely now covered by special schemes).

It should be noted, however, that merely knowing that someone else is going to infringe copyright is not inducing an infringement: to sell a person a copy of a play, for instance, with a warning that it must not be publicly performed, can never be an infringement unless it is a copy of a pirated edition. What the buyer intends to do with it when she gets it is not the seller's affair. Such a sale without a warning is also probably safe, since a purchaser ought not to assume that she has any right to perform the play (with films the position is different, see Chapter 23). Similarly, to hire out records or CDs to the public who will obviously frequently use them for home taping or recording is not an infringement (*CBS v Ames*, 1981); so also the sale of high-speed tape copying machines (and therefore high-speed CD-burning machines) is not an infringement in itself, though the accompanying advertising must not go so far as to incite infringement or it may amount to inciting a crime (*Amstrad*, 1985).

In one respect, copyright law goes even further than that. It is infringement merely to permit a place of public entertainment to be used for an infringing performance, "permit" meaning merely being able to stop it and not doing so. In this case, however, if the permission was not a source of profit, it is a defence that the giver had no reason to suppose there would be an infringement. The point of this provision is that the actual performers may well not be worth suing.

Commercial dealing

Another sort of infringement, and an important one, is commercial dealing in works that infringe copyright. Generally speaking, this covers any sort of commercial dealing (including, for instance, free distribution on any appreciable scale as well as sale); but it is limited to infringing copies. A copy that was lawfully made abroad can, however, infringe here, since the copyrights in different countries are separable, making dealings with it by anyone knowing the copyright position unlawful. The provisions against dealings are, generally speaking, limited to dealings by those who know or have reason to believe that the copies are infringing copies, but an innocent dealer caught with copies in his hands can usually be made to give them up, and may be liable in damages if he cannot or will not do so.

Infringing copies may be seized by the Customs on entering the country, if the copyright owner has taken the trouble to ask them to. (The traveller who brings home a book for "private and domestic" use infringes no copyright, and the seizure provisions do not apply to her; but if she later sells the book she may infringe.)

Architectural works

Architects are, of course, entitled to copyright in their drawings for buildings. Often there are difficulties during the course of the building works and the architect does not get paid. The question then arises as to whether the architect can prevent further work on the building until payment is made. This depends on the terms of engagement, and turns on whether payment was a condition precedent to the right to use the plans or whether the architect granted the builder or plot owner a more generous licence, leaving the architect's only claim against the builder in debt. There are standard RIBA terms that govern the position (although not all architects are engaged on these terms). In general, they are quite favourable to the architect.

If it is not clear in law whether or not the architect has the copyright, in practice it may be difficult for the architect to stop construction half-way. This is because, if the architect wants an interlocutory injunction to hold the position until trial, he or she will have to show loss unquantifiable in money and give a cross-undertaking in damages. Many architects will not want to risk being held to be wrong at trial if that involves compensating the building contractor for having held up a major construction project for a number of years. One old example of architect's copyright that illustrates the problems that architects can have comes from the following case.

Example

In 1912, Heal & Son employed a firm of architects (Smith & Brewer) to design the famous Heal's building on Tottenham Court Road, London. There were no special terms concerning ownership of copyright, but at the time the possibility of a southern extension was discussed. The building was put up and in 1935 Heal's engaged a new architect (Maufe) in connection with the extension. The extension substantially reproduced the original building. Held: the defendants had infringed the plaintiff's copyright—there was no implied licence to build a similar extension. But the damages awarded were rather modest (£150) and did not represent what the original architects could have charged for employment as architects for the extension (*Meikle v Maufe*, 1941).

Note: "Works" and Period of Protection

A list of the different sorts of "work" is given below; together with the period of copyright, and the definition of infringement for each sort. Infringement is defined in terms of the "acts restricted by the copyright" for the sort of work concerned. It must be remembered that a work may incorporate more than one copyright, and the various copyrights must be considered separately (there is an exception to this, mentioned below, in connection with cinematograph films).

What was said above about dealing with infringing copies applies to all sorts of work; so does what was said about "authorising"; but "permitting a place of public entertainment to be used for an infringing purpose" is infringement only of literary, dramatic or musical copyright.

Literary and dramatic works (including written tables, compilations, computer programs)

The period of copyright is 70 years from the end of the year of death of the author or publication, whichever is later. The acts restricted by the copyright are: reproduction; publication; performance in public; broadcasting; offer for sale of records of the work; adaptation or doing of the above acts to an adaptation.

"Publication", here and below, means issuing copies of a previously unpublished work to the public (*cf.* its meaning in patent law). Including a programme in a cable programme is (here and below) equivalent to broadcasting. "Adaptation", in relation to these works, means conversion from a non-dramatic to a dramatic work or vice versa (with or without translation into another language); translation; conversion into a strip cartoon.

There are various exceptions from the definition of infringement mentioned in the next chapter; and one (not there mentioned) for recitations in public by one person of part of a work.

180

Musical works

The period of copyright, and acts restricted by it, are the same as for literary works, except that "adaptation" now means arrangement or transcription of the work. In addition to the exceptions mentioned in the next chapter, there is a provision (see Chapter 23) allowing manufacture of records of musical works for retail sale.

Artistic works

This term includes paintings, sculptures, drawings, engravings, photographs, works of architecture and other works of artistic craftsmanship. Etchings, lithographs, woodcuts, prints, etc. count as engravings unless they are "photographs", whilst "photograph" includes pictures produced by processes like photography. The term of protection is 70 years from the year of death of the author. Models of buildings, as well as buildings themselves, count as architectural works.

The acts restricted by the copyright in an artistic work are: reproduction (including reproduction of a three-dimensional work in two dimensions and—subject to the special standard mentioned previously—of a two-dimensional work in three); publication; inclusion in a television programme. There are special rules as to use of artistic works as industrial designs, discussed in Chapter 7. There are also various exceptions, discussed in the next chapter, covering the painting, photographing, etc., of sculptures permanently situated in public, of architectural works wherever situated, or of works of artistic craftsmanship that are both permanently situated in a public place and fail to qualify as artistic works under any other head. (These exceptions also cover the publication of the paintings, photographs, etc.)

Films and sound recordings

Sound recordings and films are copyright as such. The copyright in a film or sound recording belongs to whoever arranges for the making of it, usually the producer, not the cameraman or recording engineer. The term "film" is broadly defined so that (for instance) a videotape counts as a "film". Copyright in a sound recording or film expires 50 years after first release (if it is released within 50 years of being made). Or if it is not released in that time, 50 years after being made. Films and sound

181

recordings are "released" when first shown to the public or published, or broadcast or included in a cable service.

The acts restricted by the copyright in a sound recording or film are making copies of it (or, of course, of substantial parts of it); issuing copies to the public; playing or showing it in public and broadcasting it—communicating it to the public, including over the internet. It is infringement to make records from the soundtrack of the film (and to copy or sell the records) even though the pictures are not taken, and infringement to copy a substantial part of the picture matter even without the sound-track.

Typography of published books and music

There is a separate copyright in the typographical arrangement of published editions of literary, dramatic and musical works, distinct from the copyright in the works themselves. (Editions which merely reproduce the typographical arrangement of a previous edition do not count.) The copyright belongs to the publisher, and lasts for 25 years from publication. The act restricted by this copyright is making a facsimile copy. The primary function of this copyright is to protect publishers of new editions of works that are no longer copyright from pirates using up-to-date copying methods.

Broadcasts and cable programmes

Copyright subsists in broadcasts, lasting for 50 years from first broadcast; this copyright restricts both re-broadcasting of the broadcast or making films and recordings of it.

Performers' rights and recording rights

Bootlegging has long been a problem in the entertainment business. Until the Copyright, Designs and Patents Act 1988, there was a kind of legal fudge that gave performers some rights to prevent these. There were also criminal provisions. However, the effect of the fudge was to give performers rights that were too extensive and to give recording companies (who cared most about bootlegging) no real rights at all. This is what the 1988 Act tried to sort out.

In essence, the new law gives a performer a right to control the exploitation of his or her performances. It also gives a person with exclusive recording rights in connection with such a performance the right to prevent exploitation of illicit recordings (either by dealing in copies of them or by broadcasting the performance). Various criminal offences are also created.

There are certain qualifying requirements (mainly nationality or residence of the performer or the place where the performance took place). These are very liberal and the likelihood is that if the person performing could get an English copyright, he or she would be entitled to a performers' right as well.

As regards recording rights, in order to be entitled to these, a person must have an exclusive recording contract (*i.e.* a contract entitling that person, to the exclusion of all other persons including the performer, to make recordings with a view to their commercial exploitation). Similar rights to performers' rights are given—essentially to prevent exploiting illicit recordings. Performers' rights and recording rights subsist for 50 years from the year in which the performance took place.

Rental rights

Rental right arises under the Copyright, Designs and Patents Act 1988, although it is a bit different from the other copyrights. A copyright owner is, in essence, given the right to take a reasonable royalty every time a sound recording (tape, record or CD), film (including video film) or computer program is rented to the public. This is of considerable commercial importance and, to avoid abuse of monopoly, the Copyright Tribunal can set an appropriate royalty.

Public lending right

Similar to the rental right, the public lending right gives authors a right to claim a royalty every time one of their books is borrowed from a public library. The book must be registered under an appropriate scheme and the author can claim royalties that are calculated according to a complex formula, taking into account the average number of times the book is lent out. Payment is made out of central funds.

Note: Criminal Offences

As well as being civilly actionable, copyright infringement is a criminal offence. Directors of companies can be liable if the infringement was done with their consent or connivance as elderly directors of a reputable art publishing house found out to their cost when prosecuted for reproducing certain paintings in a book. Although people do not often go to prison for copyright infringement, the punishment can be severe and there are quite often stiff fines. In one case, a video pirate with no previous convictions had copied 219 video cassettes. She pleaded that she was "only trying to earn a living". The court was unmoved and, saying that it was an offence of dishonesty, gave her two nine-month suspended sentences. This is typical of the approach of the courts.

There are also provisions for Customs officials to seize infringing goods imported into the United Kingdom upon receiving suitable notice from the copyright owner.

Copy protection

Companies, particularly in the entertainment and software industries, increasingly try to ensure that their works cannot be copied by using copy-protect technology. This prevents copies from being made from (say) the CD or from a broadcast, or stops them being made in an unauthorised way. In 2003, the UK strengthened its anti-circumvention legislation by implementing an EU Directive to stop people selling (and using) devices intended to circumvent copy protection. This legislation (part of the Copyright, Designs and Patent Act) has been invoked by Sony to stop a trader selling chips that included a mechanism for circumventing games software copy protection. The chip could be fitted into a games console and tricked the console into believing that the CD or DVD being played had the necessary embedded codes. So the console could be made to play not only authentic games designed for the geographical area for which the console was intended, but also unauthorised copies and games from foreign regions. Sony obtained summary judgment (*Sony v Ball*, 2004).

22. WHAT IS NOT INFRINGEMENT?

The Owner of the Copyright Cannot Control Legitimate Copies

The copyright owner, although given large powers of control over infringement by copying and over dealings with infringing copies, has no control within a single country over legitimate copies once they have left her hands. All she can do is to ensure that such copies are not used for the purpose of other sorts of infringement. Provided she does nothing further to the work, the owner of an authorised copy can deal with it as she pleases. An ordinary business letter being copyright, the competitor who gets hold of an indiscreet letter and distributes copies of it will infringe that copyright. But provided she got hold of the letter lawfully and properly, there is nothing to stop her showing the original to customers: a more troublesome proceeding perhaps, but probably just as effective. So also, the purchaser of a painting will probably not own the copyright in it, but that only matters if he wants to copy it: he can sell or exhibit the original without troubling about copyright. It is only infringing copies of works that are dangerous in normal handling.

No formalities are needed for "consent" to the making of copies or of the performing of a work. The consent must be obtained before the acts to which it applies are done: in particular, a copy made without consent is an infringing copy, and a subsequent agreement with the owner of the copyright may not alter the fact. Further, unless the consent takes the form of a proper licence (as considered in Chapter 21), it can be withdrawn at any time. But if, at the time when a copy was made, the making had consent, then that copy is an authorised copy and the copyright owner has no more control over it.

This general rule is subject to some modification in relation to copies of works coming from outside the EU. Suppose that a copyright owner has sold copies of a copyright work in (say) the US but without giving consent for them to be re-sold in the EU. He can stop re-sale in the United Kingdom on the basis that this would constitute issue to the public of the work in question.

Specific Exceptions to the Rules for Infringement

The Copyright, Designs and Patents Act lays down a number of specific exceptions to the rules for infringement. It will be observed that several of them apply only to particular categories of "works". This limitation to particular categories is important, for a court will pay strict attention to it. Some are too special to call for discussion here; they are mentioned in the Note to the preceding chapter. Some, however, are general in application.

Fair dealing for certain purposes

First, copyright will not be infringed by any fair dealing with any literary, dramatic, musical or artistic work for purposes of non-commercial research or private study. "Fair" here means little more than that the treatment must be genuinely and reasonably for the purpose. For instance, an examination paper will be copyright; it will be an infringement for anyone to publish or copy and distribute the paper either before or after the examination concerned; but for a student to make a copy for his own purposes will not be an infringement. He will clearly be acting for the purpose of private study, and to take a single copy of such a work is probably "fair" in the sense of the Act. This, in fact, is a type of activity that the copyright law is not well adapted to prevent. On the other hand, to copy a large part of the work for private study, when the work is on sale and a copy could have been bought, probably would not be "fair", and so would be infringement. (There is a special provision, allowing works to be reproduced in the questions and answers of the actual examination.)

Similarly, fair dealing with such a work for purposes of criticism or review does not infringe. Here again, it is the dealing with the work that has to be fair—not, for instance, the criticism of it. Any extract may be published if its publication is genuinely intended to enable the reviewer to make his comments, and not to enable the reader of the review to enjoy the work concerned without buying it. Whether the whole of the work can properly be published in a review or criticism will depend upon circumstances: a whole short story could not be, but a critic of a "Penny Pool Table" was held entitled to set out the whole table in order effectively to comment upon it. But students' study notes, which reproduced substantial parts of copyright works with critical commentary, were not protected by these provisions (*Sillitoe v McGraw Hill*, 1983). A review must contain an acknowledgment of the title and author of the work.

Again, there is no infringement in fair dealing with literary, musical or dramatic works for the purpose of reporting current events, either in a newspaper or magazine or in a newsreel film or broadcast (a newspaper or magazine must state the title and author of the work). What is "fair" for this purpose is less clear. In the case cited in the last chapter, about the march "Colonel Bogey", it was decided (before fair dealing was extended to newsreel films) that what was done there would not have been fair in a newspaper—that is, it would have been an infringement for a newspaper to have said: "For the benefit of those who were unable to be present yesterday, we publish the principal air of the 'Colonel Bogey' march", and then to have printed the music.

"Criticism or review" and "reporting current events" are terms of wide and indefinite scope that should be interpreted liberally but the subjective intentions of the defendant are of limited importance in assessing whether the use of the work was for those purposes. The provision is intended to protect the role of the media in informing the public about matters of current concern to the public. The upshot is that provided the use is reasonable and is genuinely directed to the purpose of criticism or review, it is likely to be excluded from copyright protection.

An artist re-using sketches, etc.

It is not an infringement for the author of an artistic work who has parted with the copyright in it to make use again of preliminary sketches, models, etc. so long as he does not imitate the main design of the first work. That is to say, he may use details again, provided he does not actually copy them from the work whose copyright he has sold, but only separate details. It is, of course, never easy to show that an artist has infringed his own copyright, for if his style is at all individual, one picture of his is likely to be much like any other of a similar subject.

Photographs of works in public places

To paint, draw or photograph a building, or a piece of sculpture or suchlike work that is permanently displayed in public is not infringement; nor is the publication of the picture. Nor is it infringement to include such a work in a film or television broadcast. There are, of course, restrictions on photography in many public places, but they are not copyright restrictions. The pictures themselves are of course copyright, and their reproduction would need the consent of the owner of that copyright.

Incidental use

There is a rather narrow exception for incidental use of copyright works: how narrow can be seen from a case where the

Football Association sued a publisher who was producing football cards with pictures of famous footballers. They were photographed in their team strip, which bore a logo in which the FA claimed copyright. The Court of Appeal held that this was not incidental (*FA v Panini*, 2004).

Other cases

There are various provisions permitting reproduction and performance of works in the course of school lessons, and a rather limited provision permitting the publication of anthologies for school use. There are also special provisions allowing the supply by libraries of copied extracts from books and periodicals, and a provision allowing general copying, from archives, of unpublished works whose authors have been dead for more than 50 years. It is not an infringement of copyright to do any act for the purpose of parliamentary or judicial proceedings. Of course, it is also not an infringement to do an act under specific statutory authority. There are other exceptions for making certain kinds of electronic transient copies.

Time shifting

It is specifically provided that recordings made for the purpose of time shifting are not infringements. But the recording must be made "*solely* for the purpose of enabling it to be viewed or listened to at a more convenient time". So there is nothing wrong in building up a personal film library of films shown on television. There is a range of other detailed fair dealing provisions dealing with broadcast programmes and provision of subtitled copies.

Computer programs

Computer programs present a special problem. There has to be a balance between the desire of creators of programs to earn revenues and the wishes of users to make back-up copies, and the opportunity for other developers to create new programs that are compatible with existing ones. The result: it is not an infringement (for a lawful user of a program) to make necessary back-up copies. Nor is it an infringement to convert a program from a high-level language into a low-level language (*i.e.* decompile it) or copy it by doing so, provided it is necessary to decompile it to create an independent program that can be operated with the existing one and the information so obtained is not used for any other purpose. Also, it is not an infringement to do things necessary to use the program, such as correcting errors in programs unless that is specifically forbidden by contract. These exceptions derive from an EU Directive.

Parody

It is *not* usually fair dealing to make a parody of a work. There is no statutory exception for parody and the sole test is therefore: has there been a reproduction of a substantial part of the original in making the parody?

This was graphically illustrated by a case involving a label very similar to the "Schweppes" Indian tonic water label but with "Schlurppes" on it instead. It was intended as a joke for use on bubble bath. Schweppes did not find it funny. They sued. History does not relate whether the court was amused—in any event it granted Schweppes summary judgment.

Sauce for the gander

Although the courts are prepared to listen to a great deal of nonsense and hubris, they do not have infinite patience. The press often test it to the limit. Witness the following example that is indirectly related to fair dealing. In 1989, Pamella Bordes, then a minor celebrity, was on a flight from Bali to Hong Kong. Next to her for part of the journey sat a reporter from the *Daily Express*, Mr Frame. He did his journalistic best, asked many questions and made notes of what she said. When he got to Hong Kong, he wrote up the story. It was duly published, including some of Miss Bordes' choicest bons mots, in the *Daily Express* on April 3, 1989. The story was, in journalistic parlance, a sensation.

On the same day, April 3, *Today* came out. The first edition came out with a rather dull story about Miss Bordes. The second edition was much more juicy, including quotes from Miss Bordes, derived direct from the *Daily Express* piece.

The *Daily Express* sued for copyright infringement. Two days before the first hearing, a reporter on *Today* obtained an exclusive interview with Miss Marina Ogilvy and her boyfriend. During the interview, she made certain allegations against her parents and other members of the royal family. That story (together with quotations from Miss Ogilvy) was published in *Today* on Monday October 9. It was described with typical journalistic modesty (as the judge observed) as "one of the most important scoops in popular journalism in modern times". The next day, the story was carried by a number of other newspapers, among them the *Daily Star,* another paper out of the *Daily Express* stable. A large part of the *Star* piece was taken from the *Today* article. A mirror image action was launched by the proprietors of *Today.* The court held that what was sauce for the goose was sauce for the gander: since the *Daily Express* had obtained summary judgment against *Today, Today* would be given summary judgment against the *Express*, even though the *Express* had raised some possible defences of fair dealing.

The public interest—control of information and the Human Rights Act

Copyright can give the owner very great control over the information—for example it can be a very effective instrument for stopping publication of embarrassing things, and interlocutory injunctions are often available to restrain copyright infringement. The courts have not been too keen to prevent the free dissemination of information by restraining publication in advance, especially where it is material that the public should know about. Further, although the copyright statutes do not provide for it, there is a kind of public interest defence to infringement. This has been reinforced to some extent by the Human Rights Act 1998, although, in practice, human rights arguments have played very little role in copyright jurisprudence. The courts have taken the line that the Copyright Act already provides for the important exceptions.

Here are examples of how the public interest principle operates to prevent prior restraints on publication that copyright can produce.

Example 1

Dennis Nilsen was a notorious serial killer who took a series of young men back to his flat, murdered them and dismembered their corpses. He was convicted and imprisoned for life. Central Television decided to make a documentary (called "Murder in Mind") about a new way of catching serial killers such as Nilsen, known as "offender profiling". In the course of their preparations for the programme, Central became involved in making a video of an interview with Nilsen intended (at least by the Home Office) only to be used to help in teaching the police about serial killers and advancing the techniques of offender profiling. Central obtained a copy of the videotape of the interview and wanted to show a short extract from it on television as part of

190

their documentary. The Home Secretary objected, claiming copyright in the film and breach of an agreement not to use the material. The case was arguable but it was not possible to say at the interlocutory stage who was right. Central argued that it would be in the public interest for the extract to be shown since it would help to warn people of how "normal" serial killers could appear. The courts agreed that there was an issue of public interest and that Central should not be restrained by interlocutory injunction from showing the extract (*Home Secretary v Central Television*, 1993).

Example 2

In contrast, the *Daily Telegraph* was not entitled to a public-interest defence based on freedom of speech arguments when it reproduced a whole memorandum written by the then leader of the Liberal Democrats. The court held that there was no justification for the extent of the reproduction of Mr Ashdown's own words, saying that the minute was deliberately filleted in order to extract colourful passages that were most likely to add flavour to the article and thus to appeal to the readership of the newspaper. A criticism and review defence also failed (*Ashdown v Daily Telegraph*, 2002). One must read the cases with some caution. The courts are required to err on the side of permitting publication at an interim injunction stage (as in the *Central Television* case). At trial, things can look very different.

23. DEALINGS IN COPYRIGHT

The right given to an author by the Copyright Act of preventing other people from reproducing her works is of very little value in itself: for the main problem in almost every case is to get herself into a position where anyone wants to reproduce the works at all—a problem outside the scope of this book. Once it has been solved, however, a whole group of legal questions arise, not only formal problems of transfer of copyright, but various other questions as to the terms on which reproduction shall take place, what money is to be paid to the author and to the Inland Revenue, and so on. It is with questions of this type that the present chapter is concerned.

Formal Problems

On transfers of copyright

Copyright can be freely transferred, either as a whole or for a particular field: thus the film rights in a novel, for instance, or the performing rights in a play, can be transferred separately from the right of printing and publishing. Copyright can be carved up pretty much as the parties please. The copyright in any country outside the United Kingdom can—so far as English law is concerned—be dealt with separately from the United Kingdom rights. But the transfer must be in writing; and a transfer is not the same as an agreement to transfer.

Consider for instance the common case of a book or article commissioned by a publisher for a lump sum, on the terms that the publisher is to get the copyright. Perhaps there is a written agreement to that effect. Even so, however, the agreement will not then and there transfer the copyright: for it will be entered into before the work is created, and so there will be no copyright then in existence for it to transfer. If the agreement purports to assign the copyright, and there is nothing else wrong, and the agreement is signed on behalf of the prospective owner of the copyright, the effect will be that the copyright belongs to the publisher when it comes into existence. If not, the position will be that the author owns the copyright, but he has agreed that the publisher shall have it. Some publishers do, some do not, demand an actual assignment in such cases, though all could do so if they wished. For most purposes, the position is of course the same as if the copyright had been transferred; but if any sort of dispute arises, the difference will become important.

If the copyright is infringed, for instance, and the publisher wishes to sue the infringer, either the publisher must get a written assignment of the copyright, together with the right to sue for past infringements, or the action will have to be brought in the author's name, though the publisher must pay for it and will be entitled to any damages that may be recovered. Or again, suppose that there is a dispute as to who is going to have the copyright, and the author (thinking herself entitled to do so, or even acting dishonestly) sends to a second publisher who knows nothing of the agreement with the first, the second sale will be effective: the author as actual owner of the copyright could validly sell it, and the only remedy of the first publisher is to sue her for breaking her contract. (If the second publisher knew of the agreement, or even if circumstances were such that he ought to have found out about it, then he will be bound by it.)

This distinction between selling and agreeing to sell runs right through the English law of property; confusing as it is, there are many problems that cannot be understood unless it is borne in mind. In connection with the sale of a house, or something like that, few people forget that until the house has been formally conveyed to its new owner it is not hers; but with intangible property like copyright, this is not so easy to remember. There is a reported case, for instance, of the reconstruction of a company, where the old company's assets included a copyright of great value that was never actually transferred to the new company; the omission being discovered only after the old company had been dissolved. The difficulty could be, and was, overcome with the aid of the High Court; but that sort of thing costs time and money. Few companies would wind themselves up without, for instance, handing over the land on which their factory was built.

Foreign formalities

Where foreign copyrights are concerned, any transfer must conform to the legal requirements of the country concerned. Some countries demand more and some less in the way of formalities when property is transferred, and although an assignment valid by English law will usually suffice if it is made in England, it is seldom wise to rely on this. In some countries, copyright protection may involve certain formalities, and failure register may involve inconvenience. In countries like America, which have legislation regulating monopolies (as well as having copyright laws differing in some respects from ours) it is always unwise to try to do without local advice. Of course, those who are much involved in copyright matters (film companies and music publishers, for instance) have rule-of-thumb methods for handling foreign copyright problems that seem usually to work well enough.

On licensing

An owner of copyright who does not want to transfer it outright may license it: that is to say, may grant to someone else the right to do acts that would normally infringe that copyright. Again, the licence should be in writing; and here also there is a distinction that must be watched—that between a licence and a mere consent to the doing of certain acts. There is never any infringement involved in reproducing a copyright work if the owner of the copyright consents; but a true licence carries with it a right of property in a way that a mere consent does not. Thus, a true licence can give rights enforceable against the owner himself (in case he should change his mind) or against anyone to whom he sells the copyright, whilst an exclusive licensee can sue infringers. A mere consent on the other hand can be withdrawn by the copyright owner, or overridden by a sale of the copyright, leaving the other party with nothing except (possibly) a right to sue for breach of contract. Licences require no special formalities in English law.

Contracts Relating to Copyrights

Apart from the points already mentioned in this chapter, dealings in copyright are entirely a matter for contract—that is to say, those concerned may make what rules they please. What has happened in relation to any particular copyright must consequently be deduced from such agreements, formal or informal, as the parties have made; this may be a matter of very great difficulty. It should in particular be assumed that any agreement drawn up by business people will prove difficult for lawyers (including judges) to sort out; for lawyers and business people have quite different ideas both as to the way they use language and as to the sort of things that agreements ought to provide for. It is, however, possible to lay down a few general rules as to what the position is likely to be if the parties have said nothing definite to the contrary.

Implied terms

In all cases it has to be remembered that the law is very chary of reading into agreements terms that the parties have not actually stated. The rule is: such terms will only be implied if the agreement cannot be effective without them, so that there can be no doubt that if when the contract was made, the parties had been asked whether this was what they wanted, they would both have said "Yes, of course". For example, if there is a sale of a copyright work of art, such as a picture, the copyright will not be transferred with the work unless the parties agree that it shall. This is obvious in the case of a work with many copies, like a coloured print; it is not so obvious in the case of something like a painting of which only the original exists. But if the parties are silent as to the copyright, the law will not assume that they meant to transfer it unless it is clear that this must have been so. In the case, say, of a sale of a painting to a maker of Christmas cards, if both parties knew that he meant to make a Christmas card of it, it will be clear that they must have meant that he should have some right to reproduce the painting; but even then, it does not necessarily follow that he must have the ownership of the copyright rather than a licence to reproduce. In any event, unless there is something in writing, he will get merely a contractual right to have the copyright assigned to him or a licence granted to him, as the case may be.

Where works are made to order

Works made to order present a special problem (see Chapter 20). It will often be clear (if not expressly stated) that the parties meant the copyright to be transferred to the person giving the order; a term in their agreement to that effect will then be implied. For instance, where a publisher commissions a book for a lump sum payment, even if nothing is said about copyright it will normally be assumed that the publisher is meant to have it. The author is not an employee, so as to make the publisher the first owner of the copyright: this is shown by the fact that the publisher cannot tell her how to write the book but must take it as the author thinks it should be written. Nevertheless, for a lump sum payment the publisher presumably expected to get the whole thing, copyright and all. (But remember that there will only be an agreement to transfer the copyright to the publisher, not an actual transfer, unless a signed agreement says it is a transfer.) On the other hand, if payment is to be by royalty, there will be no reason to suppose that the publisher is necessarily to have more than a licence to publish; and in the case of an architectural work for instance, even if specially commissioned, the only term as to copyright that will be implied into the contract is a licence to the architect's client to erect the buildings contracted for in accordance with the drawings. The architect will therefore keep his copyright.

A clear case the other way was of a man who was commissioned to do the choreography for a ballet: clearly the copyright must have been intended to be transferred to the man who commissioned the work, for without that copyright he would not have a complete ballet. More recently, Robin Ray was asked by Classic FM to compile a list of suitable works for playing on its radio station in the UK. When Classic FM sought to use the list for other purposes, Ray sued saying that there was no licence to do so. Classic FM argued that they were licensed—and, indeed that they owned the copyright—but these arguments were rejected. The court held that they did not enjoy a licence to do with the compilation more than was contemplated at the time (*Ray v Classic FM* (1998)).

Where a publisher agrees to publish an author's work

There are cases, however, where it is clear that the parties must have intended to provide for quite a number of matters they have said nothing about. For instance, an author may send the manuscript of a book to a publisher and the publisher agree to publish it, and nothing else is said at all. In that case the law will imply, grudgingly, the bare minimum of terms to complete the contract. The publisher has a licence to publish an edition of the book, but that is all: the author of course keeps the ownership of the copyright. The publisher must pay the author a reasonable royalty: not necessarily the royalty he usually pays, rather the sort of royalty an ordinary publisher would normally pay for that sort of book. The publisher must publish an edition of the book, of reasonable size having regard to all the circumstances, within a reasonable time. A reasonable time for publishing a book in these days will be many months, and there would certainly be no obligation upon the publisher to hurry unduly; but he must not deliberately delay. He must not, for instance, as a publisher once did, deliberately delay publication so as to enable a rival to scoop the Christmas market with a book on the same subject—in return, of course, for a share of the profits on his rival's book. Finally, he is not entitled to publish the book under someone else's name as author: the position would however be different if he had bought the copyright outright, then he could probably deal with the work as he pleased, subject to any moral rights (see Chapter 25).

In the same way, if a manuscript is sent to the editor of a periodical, the editor may publish it, and must pay at reasonable rates. His usual rates will normally do, and will certainly do if the author has taken them before: but a periodical that frequently pays unusually low rates should tell new authors about them before publication, or it may find that the court considers them unreasonable. The editor of a periodical is not entitled to publish in book form manuscripts sent to him for periodical publication, without the author's consent.

Bequests of copyright works

In one case, the Copyright Act itself creates a presumption that copyright goes with the property in the actual work: where an artistic work, or the manuscript of a literary, musical or dramatic work, is bequeathed by a will that does not mention the copyright. (Of course, this only applies so far as the testator owned the copyright when he died.)

Sales of part of a copyright

The same sort of considerations arise when a copyright is partially sold; but here the position tends to be clearer, for the parties must have said something about what they intend shall happen; and all the lawyers have to decide is what the parties' words mean. (The answer may surprise the parties, but that often happens to those who are insufficiently explicit in the first place.) Thus the sale of the performing rights in a play or a song will not pass the right to make films or records of the work, unless there is some special reason why the parties must have meant this to be so; but it will pass the right to prevent any film or record of the work being shown or played in public. This will be vital in the case of a play to be made into a film, which is almost certainly intended for public exhibition (unless perhaps it is meant solely for export to a country where, either there is no copyright, or the performing right has not been sold); but it will be less important to the maker of a record. CDs and records as normally sold are in fact not licensed for a public performance, and every UK record at least bears a notice to that effect.

Collective licensing—the PRS and PPL

What actually happens with musical copyrights is that the performing rights in published music are handed over to a licensing and royalty collection body called the Performing Right Society (PRS). The broadcasting, performing and diffusion rights in sound recordings go likewise to a collecting body called Phonographic Performance Ltd (PPL), set up by the recording companies. In the case of films including previously published music, the film company buys a licence to include the music in the film (there are standard arrangements for this), but does not have authority to license public performance of it. The cinema has a standard Performing Right Society licence that covers that.

The film distributor, in effect, warrants that an exhibitor will have no copyright trouble, provided his cinemas have Performing Right Society licences (that is to say, the film company is expected to look after performing rights in any book or play the film is made from, but not performing rights in music except music specially written for the film). The actual agreements used in the film industry tend to be rather incomprehensible, but custom has established what they are supposed to mean.

People wanting to use records, tapes or CDs for public performance (*e.g.* for use in village halls) go to the two societies and obtain standard licences: one covering the copyright in music, one covering that in the recording. There is a Copyright Tribunal with power to see that the standard licences are not unreasonable.

It should be noted that the control of licensing by the Copyright Tribunal is of great importance, especially in the entertainment industry where collective licensing bodies are commonplace. In 1988, the Monopolies and Mergers Commission (as it was then called) said that collective licensing bodies were by their nature monopolistic and "it is widely accepted that appropriate controls are needed to ensure that they do not abuse their market power". There have been such controls for some time—prior to the 1988 Act there was the Performing Right Tribunal, which exercised similar powers. The 1988 Act changed its name and widened its jurisdiction considerably. As well as setting terms for collective licensing schemes, the tribunal can, for example, determine royalties for the rental right, grant certain consents on behalf of performers in certain circumstances, and settle the terms of licences of right, if the Competition Commission determines that the copyright owner is engaging in anti-competitive practices contrary to the public interest.

Where the ownership of the manuscript and copyright is in different hands

A case similar to overlapping copyrights arises where the owner of an unpublished manuscript does not own the copyright in it. He cannot publish it without the copyright owner's consent, but then the copyright owner cannot get at the manuscript without his consent: so that again an intending publisher must come to terms with both.

Publishing agreements

Two odd points relating to publishing agreements deserve mention. Such agreements often contain a clause requiring the author to offer her next book (or next so many books) to the same publisher. This is a perfectly legitimate clause for a contract to contain, and can be enforced: a court will grant an injunction not only to prevent the author disposing of those books elsewhere, but also to prevent another publisher, who took those books, although he knew about the agreement, from publishing them. On the other hand, an agreement to write a number of further books would not be enforceable by injunction: injunctions are not given to compel the performance of personal services.

The second point is more difficult. Suppose the author, not being under any obligation to offer her next book to the same publisher, writes another on the same subject and offers it to a second publisher, who publishes it and so spoils the market for the first: has the first publisher any remedy? Or suppose the publisher puts out a second book on the same subject at the same time, and so spoils the first author's sales: has the author any remedy? The answer will, of course, depend on what the' publishing agreement says, and since the publisher will very likely have drawn it up, it will probably protect him against the author but not the author against him. If the agreement is altogether silent on the subject, it seems fairly clear that in an ordinary case the author would have no remedy; probably the publisher would have none either, but this is not quite so clear.

Literary agents

It is usual for established authors at least to employ literary
agents to place their books and deal with the various forms of
copyright arising from them. Here again, the rights of the author
and his agent as against each other are what they have agreed
them to be when the agent took the job. It should be remembered, however, that as against the outside world, the agent's
powers to deal on behalf of his principal will in effect be those
that such agents usually have. The author can, if she likes and
the agent is willing, make special terms and place special
restrictions on the agent's authority; but the special terms and
restrictions will have no effect against third parties who do not
know of them.

Manuscripts sent for advice

It is not unusual for authors who are not established to send
their works to their more successful colleagues for comment,
advice, and assistance in placing with publishers or producers.
The rights of the author in such a case are clear. The person she
sends her manuscript to must not of course publish it (though he
may be expected to show it to one or two colleagues), nor may
he copy from it: but he is under no obligation to take any
particular care of it, and if it gets lost or damaged the author
should not complain.

Taxation and Authors

The question of tax upon author's earnings, important as it is,
can be dealt with here only very briefly. The position is broadly
this: any author who makes a business or profession of writing
or composing, or anyone who makes a business of dealing in
copyrights, must pay income tax on the whole profits of that
business, whether they are received in the form of royalties or of
lump-sum payments. Those who do not make a business of it,
like casual authors or people who happen to have come into
possession of an odd copyright, must pay income tax on receipts
if they are income but not if they are capital. It does not
necessarily follow that royalties are income, although they
usually are; still less does it follow that lump-sum payments are
capital. The test is more or less this: was there a valuable asset,
and has it been converted into money (in which case the
proceeds of conversion will be capital), or has it been used as a

source of profit—as an income-bearing investment, so to speak?
If it has, that profit will be income.

A sale of an existing copyright, by someone who has never
written a book before, whether for a single payment or annual
payments, may be capital, and not taxable by income tax; on the
other hand, a royalty of so much a copy on the sales of a book
is almost certainly income, even if it is paid as a lump sum when
the agreement is made. If a work is commissioned, the payment
is almost certain to be received as income whatever form it takes:
for essentially it is payment for services, not the sale of any asset.
It will be seen that the author of a really successful work will find
some difficulty in arranging her affairs so as to avoid paying out
in one or two years of extremely high income, most of what she
gets for it. However, such an author can, to a reasonable extent,
"spread" out (for tax purposes) payments she receives, over a
longer period.

24. CONFIDENCE AND PRIVACY

The present chapter deals with a matter to some extent akin to copyright: not the right to stop others from reproducing a work as such, but to stop them making use of the information contained in it. This is a job that the ownership of copyright will seldom do. Thus, it will be recalled that a purchaser of a book is entitled to read it and let anyone else read it, and even to recite bits of it in public to anyone who will listen. No limitation by way of limited licence can be imposed by the owner of the copyright if the copy is an authorised copy. Even if the copy is not authorised, all the copyright owner can do is to insist upon the handing over of the book to him—what he cannot do by virtue of his ownership of the copyright is to prevent readers of the book making use of what they learnt by reading it.

The sort of problems dealt with in this chapter generally, although not always, arise in commercial matters: with the inventor who shows the invention to others before patents have been granted or even (inventors are not always cautious people) before he has applied for patents at all; the manufacturer who supplies manufacturing drawings and specifications to a sub-contractor; the merchant who gives the names and addresses of customers to the manufacturer so that they can be supplied direct. In all cases of this sort, what the person who supplied the information really wants is to stop the recipient of the information from using it except for the purpose for which it was given. A mere right to stop the recipient from making copies, which is given by copyright, is useful but is not enough.

Rights to privacy

Privacy issues do not always arise in a commercial context. The most well-known cases concern celebrities. There have been a number of actions, usually brought by famous people, to stop the press from disclosing things about them that they would either prefer the world not to know or would prefer to disclose in particular way. These actions have been given additional impetus by the "right to private life" provisions incorporated into English law by the Human Rights Act 1998. This chapter looks first at the traditional law of confidence and then at the developing law of privacy.

The Action for Breach of Confidence

The general rule

The right needed by a supplier of confidential information is given by the law, but only in certain circumstances and subject to certain exceptions. The general rule has been put in the following way, namely, that a recipient of confidential information may not use that information without the consent of the person he got it from (*Saltman Engineering v Campbell Engineering*, 1948). Another way in which the rule has been expressed is that a plaintiff who sues for breach of confidence must show three things: first, that the information has the necessary quality of confidence about it; second, that the information was imparted in circumstances importing an obligation of confidence; and third, that there was an unauthorised use made of that information (*Coco v Clark*, 1969). The judge who decided the latter case thought that it was possible that the plaintiff would also have to show that he was personally prejudiced by the unauthorised use of the information, but did not decide the point.

When is information confidential?

Circumstances giving rise to a relationship of confidence

These can be shortly stated: a person can be prevented from misusing information given to him if, when he receives it, he has agreed, expressly or impliedly, to treat it as confidential. This does not mean that there has to be a formal agreement, although, of course, having such an agreement helps to make the position clear to everyone (which is why the cases that are fought are mostly concerned with situations where the parties did not make it clear that their relationship was confidential from the outset).

What the judges do in cases where there is no express agreement is to look at all the circumstances surrounding the relationship between the parties. If it appears that the parties cannot have intended the information to be given freely, then it was given in confidence. A lot may depend upon how the judge feels about the way the defendant behaved. If information is given for a particular purpose, it is easily inferred that the parties intended the information to be used only for that purpose. A few examples from cases, some of them quite old but that are still regularly referred to, will make the point clearer.

Example 1

In *Seager v Copydex* (1967), an inventor had discussed an invention of his with the defendant company with a view to their taking it up. In the course of the discussion, he mentioned the idea behind another invention he had in mind. Although the company did not take up the first invention, they later came out with a version of the second, even using the name that the inventor had given it. The Court of Appeal thought the defendant must have taken the inventor's idea, albeit subconsciously, and that the relationship between the parties must have been confidential since the inventor could not be supposed to have been giving the information freely; it was given merely for the purpose of interesting the defendant in his ideas.

Example 2

Again, in *Ackroyds v Islington Plastics* (1962), the defendants had been under contract to manufacture plastic "swizzle sticks" (things for getting those nasty bubbles out of champagne) for the plaintiffs. The plaintiffs had supplied the defendants for this purpose with information and with a special tool. It was held that the defendants could not use either the information or the tool for the purpose of manufacturing swizzle sticks for themselves: both had been handed over only for the purpose of helping them manufacture for the plaintiffs.

Example 3

Another example shows that the law of confidence, although mostly finding its application in the commercial field, is perfectly general. In *Argyll v Argyll* (1965), the then Duchess of Argyll sued to prevent the Duke from supplying to a Sunday newspaper (and to prevent the Sunday newspaper from publishing) what the Duke had said to her in confidence during their marriage, which had ended in divorce a little earlier. The judge said that the marriage relationship was in its nature confidential, and that the obligations of confidence continued after the marriage had ended. See also the "privacy" cases, below.

Example 4

Similarly in *Fraser v Thames TV* (1982), three actresses had given to a television company, the idea of a soap opera relating the adventures of an all-girl rock band. They contemplated that they would take the starring roles, but the TV company stole the idea and had to pay heavy damages for breach of confidence.

Example 5

The interlocutory injunctions against publication of the "Spy-catcher" diaries in the United Kingdom were based on breach of confidence by Peter Wright, although the House of Lords said that the crown may also be entitled to copyright in them (*Att-Gen v Guardian Newspapers*, 1990).

The effect of marking things "confidential"

We have said that the test of confidentiality is the express or implied intention of the parties. It follows that marking a document "confidential" will not necessarily make it so, if the person who receives it does not know, and has no reason to expect, that it is to be confidential. If you see a book advertised for sale and send in the money and get a copy of the book back, the book is already yours before you unpack it or look at it. It may turn out to be highly confidential and labelled so, but that makes no difference: you did not agree not to disclose its contents when you offered to buy it and you need not agree now. On the other hand, if the book is stated in the advertisement to be confidential, only for your personal use, then in replying to the advertisement you agree to keep it as confidential and must keep to your contract — even if on investigation the book turns out to be something you could buy at any bookstall or — as in one decided case — an explanation of a system for betting on horse races according to the phases of the moon.

Confidence and contract

Where parties are in a contractual relationship they often provide for obligations of confidence in express terms. Thus, normally, no scientist will be employed by the research department of a company unless she agrees to keep the company information secret even after she leaves the company. But even where there is no such express obligation, the relationship between the parties may of its nature give rise to obligations of confidence: as in the "swizzle sticks" case mentioned above, or in *Robb v Green* (1895), where an ex-employee was restrained from using a list of his old employer's customers for his own benefit. The point is that the law of confidence exists apart from the law of contract but, when obligations of confidence exist, there is usually some contractual relationship between the parties.

What happens where the information becomes public knowledge?

Suppose that by the time the action comes to trial the information concerned has been either wholly or partly made available to the public—what then?

At first sight, it would seem absurd that a defendant should be under any restriction in using information that is public knowledge. But things are not so simple: a defendant may obtain a considerable advantage from information which, when it was supplied to him, was confidential but which has now become public knowledge—one judge expressed this sort of situation vividly by saying that such a defendant was using the information as a "springboard for activities detrimental to the plaintiff".

At present, the law upon this subject is not clear. On the one hand it has been held that someone who lets all the information be disclosed by publication of his patent specification can no longer prevent ex-employees from revealing that information. On the other hand it is also clear that the courts are willing to give some relief to a plaintiff who shows that the defendant has obtained an unfair advantage by using the plaintiff's confidential information as a "springboard" even when the information has later become public. The courts say that in such cases, although it is true that the information was available from public sources, the defendant did not get it from them, but got it from the "tainted source" of the plaintiff's confidential disclosure to him. Once a defendant is under the suspicion that he has used a "tainted source", he may find himself in difficulty. It may then be no use his saying "Look, I know I had dealings with the plaintiff in the past which were confidential, but I developed this machine by myself and here are my plans to prove it". The court may still feel he got the idea from the plaintiff and find a breach of confidence. *Seager v Copydex* is just such a case.

Another example is afforded by the manufacturer who has a list of the customers of the merchant for whom he makes goods. In the sort of field where this point is most likely to arise, it may be that anyone could compile a pretty good list of customers and potential customers from trade directories and the like. Nevertheless, let such a manufacturer once show a disposition to take unfair advantage of his position and he may find himself forbidden to approach those customers at all. In some recent cases, judges have taken a middle course—granting an injunction to last long enough to destroy the head start gained by the defendant's breach of confidence.

The difficulties in this concept of the "springboard" case are well described in the judgment in *Coco v Clark*.

Remedies

The remedies for a breach of confidence are much the same as those granted for the infringement of the other rights discussed in this book (see Chapter 1). Thus injunctions can be, and often are, awarded, together with damages or accounts of profits. In some cases, the court will not award an injunction but will award damages only. This occurred in *Seager v Copydex* where, since the information was, at the time of the action, publicly known and the plaintiff's information was only a part of the information being used by the defendants, an injunction was thought to be inappropriate and damages enough to compensate the plaintiff. In fact there followed a dispute as to the way in which damages should be calculated and the matter had to go to the Court of Appeal again upon this question (*Seager v Copydex*, 1969). The court held that damages should be paid upon the market value of the information, which depended upon how important it was: whether, for example, it was inventive enough to support a patent, or was merely the sort of information that could have been supplied by any expert.

Interlocutory injunctions

If the plaintiff acts quickly enough, he will, in a suitable case, be granted an interim injunction: where the information concerned is not yet public, for instance, to preserve the status quo while the case is fought. But in "springboard" cases it seems that the courts are unwilling to grant such injunctions, partly because the questions of fact as to exactly how much of the information used by the defendant was taken from the plaintiff and how much the defendants got for themselves are too difficult to resolve without hearing all the evidence, and partly because, in such cases, the plaintiff may in the end, if he wins, receive only damages. *Coco v Clark* (1969) is an example of such a refusal. (But note that the judge, whilst refusing the interlocutory injunction, thought that the defendants ought, pending the trial, to pay a potential royalty into a bank account so that if the plaintiff eventually won the action, he would be safeguarded, and an undertaking to this effect was given to the court.)

Suing third parties

If the owner of the information is able to act before it has been disclosed to any third party, then an injunction preventing disclosure should be all he needs to protect it. If it has already been passed on to a third party, an injunction will not be much good unless it binds the third party too. Anyone who receives information that he knows (or ought to know) reached him through a breach of confidence, has a duty not to use or disclose it, and the court will, in a proper case, grant an injunction to enforce that duty. Thus in the *Argyll* case mentioned above, not only the Duke was placed under an injunction but also the Sunday newspaper that was going to print the information. There was a similar result in *Spycatcher*.

The exact limits to the circumstances in which third parties can be sued are not yet fully worked out because there have not been many cases on the subject. However, the law is probably that, where someone pays for the information in good faith, he cannot be stopped from using it. It would be different if he acted in bad faith (for example, where a company has bought information from someone it knew to be an industrial spy or an employee of another company), and it may be different if he does not pay for it.

Problems of proof

From what has been said, it might be thought that the law gave enough protection to confidential information to make disclosure of it perfectly safe. Any such idea would be entirely wrong. As always, neither the general law nor even a carefully drawn contract is any real protection against dishonesty. The function of these things—of a proper contract especially—is to make it clear, amongst honest parties to a transaction, just what they may and may not do.

If a would-be plaintiff does come up against a rogue, then she will find it difficult to prove her case. The burden will lie on her to show she gave the rogue confidential information in circumstances giving rise to a bond of confidence and that the rogue is using such information. In some cases, the would-be plaintiff will not even know that the rogue is using the information. For example, suppose a company learns from an employee of another company that a particular line of research has been tried and found useless. This will save the first company from trying that line, but the company from whom the information was "taken" will have very little chance of proving that the other company acted in breach of confidence. When it comes to information passed on to third parties, the problems of proof grow even harder.

Where the action will not lie

"No confidence in iniquity"

Since the action for breach of confidence is founded originally upon what is fair—it is a creature of equity—the courts will not grant a remedy if the information that the defendant threatens to reveal or use is something that ought not, in conscience, to be protected. There are many examples in the cases. Here are some:

Example 1

In *Initial Towel Services v Putterill* (1967), the plaintiffs failed to obtain interlocutory injunctions against an ex-employee and a daily newspaper when the ex-employee alleged that the information he was giving to the newspaper showed that the plaintiffs had been a party to a secret arrangement to keep prices up, contrary to the Restrictive Trade Practices Act.

Example 2

In *X v Y* (1988), the court refused permission to disclose the diagnosis with AIDS of two doctors who were continuing to practice in the light of the interest in preserving the confidentiality of medical records.

Example 3

In *Re: A company* (1989), the court permitted the disclosure of a financial management company's allegedly irregular affairs to the regulatory authorities saying that it would be contrary to the public interest if employees were inhibited from placing before the regulatory authority possible breaches of the regulatory system or fiscal irregularities.

Example 4

The court permitted a campaigning organisation to disclose information concerning the welfare of research laboratory animals to relevant regulatory authorities, but not the press. (*Imutran v Uncaged Campaigns* (2001)).

Public policy

There are some cases where, as a matter of public policy, agreements for confidence will not be enforced. The most important of these is in relation to skilled employees who leave their firm and propose to enter employment in the same field, perhaps with a rival manufacturer. The court will enforce covenants preventing the ex-employee from working for the competitor, provided that the covenant is not too broad in terms of the geographical area to which it extends and the time for which it operates. The court goes further, and, whether or not there is a covenant in restraint of trade in his contract of employment, will prevent an employee or ex-employee from disclosing the industrial or commercial secrets of his employer. What the court will not do, however, is to prevent him from using the general skill and knowledge (as opposed to confidential information), which he has acquired by reason of his employment. Obviously, the distinction between these two is a hard one to draw in some cases, but it must be drawn, for otherwise skilled employees would never be able to change their jobs. So important do the courts regard the ability of a skilled person to do his or her job that even an express agreement seeking to bind the employee not to use such general knowledge will be held invalid—although that does not mean that the employee will be free to disclose company secrets.

The position of directors deserves special mention: any information obtained by a director by virtue of her office is, in effect, held on trust for the company, and must only be used for the purposes of the company. Since the directors are responsible for the conduct of the business of the company, it is seldom open to them to say that they were not told and did not realise that the information acquired was confidential.

The duty of confidence must be owed to the claimant

In *Fraser v Evans* (1969), the claimant sought to restrain by interlocutory injunction publication in a newspaper of parts of a confidential report he had prepared for the Greek Government. It was held that although the report was confidential and although the copyright belonged to the claimant, he could not succeed. He failed as to infringement of copyright since it appeared very likely that, at the trial, a defence of fair dealing (see Chapter 22) would succeed; and he failed as to breach of confidence because the report belonged to the Greek Government and not to him. Only the person to whom the duty of confidence is owed can sue to enforce it.

Sales of "Know-How"

It is not uncommon, in these days, for know-how to be treated as an article of commerce—to be sold outright, like any other property, or to be handed over on terms like those of a patent licence. Even an actual patent licence may often turn out, in reality, to be largely a dealing in know-how—it is often the know-how that is worth the money, rather than the more or less dubious monopoly given by any patent. This sort of transaction presents no very great difficulty in the ordinary case where both parties are honest. The agreements governing such transactions deal in detail with the degree of "confidence" to be attached to the information handed over, and especially with the position after the agreement comes to an end. This sort of transaction is rather outside the scope of the present chapter, which is more concerned with cases in which there is no express agreement laying down conditions as to confidence.

The Need for Agreements

It is always better to have questions of confidence properly covered by agreement than to leave them to implications of the general law. Consider once again the case of a manufacturer trying out an invention. Everything may go well, in which case there will be no difficulty. But suppose the inventor's ideas turn out in the end to be more or less unworkable. The manufacturer may then drop the whole scheme; but suppose that in the course of finding out that the invention will not work he finds out what is wrong, and so becomes able to make something that will work. What is to be the position then? The manufacturer, especially if he has paid for the right to have first go at the invention, will feel that he has taken from the inventor nothing he has not paid for, that the new ideas are his own and that he owes the inventor nothing. The inventor will probably feel that the manufacturer is either merely being difficult, or merely making undesirable alterations in the original scheme so as to get out of paying a proper royalty. If a fight is to be avoided, there ought to be an agreement that will make it clear exactly what the manufacturer is entitled to keep if he rejects the original

211

invention, and just exactly when a royalty or purchase price is in the end to be payable.

Difficult Cases

Of course, there are difficulties no agreement can provide against; especially as neither inventors nor manufacturers are always as sensible and co-operative as they might be. For instance, if a manufacturer can be interested at all in an invention put up to him, the reason is likely to be that the problem it sets out to solve is one he knew of and had even been dabbling at himself. His reaction to seeing an outsider's proposal is likely to be that he rejects it but is encouraged to go back to his own ideas and make them work—perhaps with a bit of help from the alternative proposals that the outside inventor has put to him. Inevitably, in most such cases, the inventor will be convinced that the manufacturer has "really" stolen his invention, and the manufacturer will be convinced that he has merely pursued (as he "really" always meant to) his own previous line of development. They will never agree on the facts, and may have to ask a court to decide between them. If a proper agreement is made between them, before the invention is disclosed, this should serve to limit the range of the dispute, and so will save time, costs, and some bitterness, if nothing else; but even so a dispute may be inevitable. It is worth examining in some detail the factors that make disputes so difficult to avoid in many matters of confidence.

The instance just given suggests one factor: that much information seems very much more valuable to the person giving it than to the person listening. Another factor is well illustrated by the case suggested earlier, of a merchant who lets suppliers know the names of his customers. The real trouble here is that the merchant's position is inherently risky; sooner or later, it will pay his suppliers or his customers to cut him out, and what seems to them an ordinary change in business procedure will look to him like dirty work. He will look on a list of customers or suppliers as something of great value, since to him it is; but to others, such a list is worth precisely what it would cost to pay a person to compile it from business directories.

So often what really matters is not some trade secret, but just trade habits that nobody bothers to alter. The same thing can happen with industrial know-how: the difference between making something well and making it badly can be a matter of secret knowledge, but is more often a matter of skilled management and skilled labour. If a good person gets a job somewhere else at higher pay, and her new employer's products jump ahead in quality, it is easy to assume that some secret has gone with her; but the odds are that secrets played very little part in the matter. So one gets a sort of typical case, where the defendant has been rather careless over the plaintiff's confidence, not thinking it mattered much; and the plaintiff is over-suspicious, not realising that any competent person in the defendant's position could do the job without anybody's secrets. Both parties are sure they are 90 per cent in the right: and the result can easily be litigation, whose outcome will be anyone's guess. There are people who deliberately set out to steal their employer's secrets, but most litigation in this field, as in any other, is between people who just did not think enough.

Of course, a lot of litigation about commercial confidentiality is pursued to nip in the bud any potential competition from ex-employees. Thus, a lot of plaintiffs have succeeded in doing a great deal of damage to (quite honest) ex-employee defendants by getting things like search orders against them (see Chapter 2). For many years, the courts were concerned about dishonest defendants walking off with their ex-employer's secrets. Some judges would hand out the most draconian orders (originally intended to deal with crooked video pirates) almost on the nod. There was increasing concern about over-aggressive claimants using the courts to put these defendants engaged in lawful competition out of business. This is important, since the costs of litigation are such that clearing one's name and getting an unjustified order discharged is often a serious drain on a new business's resources. Nowadays, the grant of search and seizure orders is very carefully controlled, and it is a costly business for a claimant to obtain and enforce one. They are in consequence much less used in cases of this kind than they used to be.

Privacy and the Press

One of the first things that one learns as a law student is that there is in England no "right of privacy" as such. While that remains strictly true, the courts, have developed remedies for cases where the press reveals or threatens to reveal information about individuals which they would prefer to keep private. More recently the Human Rights Act, which incorporates the Convention on Human Rights, has been a spur to this development. This provides that "Everyone has the right to respect for his private and family life . . . ". Using the Human Rights Act as a spur, the courts have developed an approach which amounts to a law of privacy in all but name.

The "ordinary citizen" and the "celebrity"

That said, to some degree, English law treats the "ordinary citizen" differently from the "celebrity" when it comes to the law of privacy. Those in the public eye have to expect and accept greater scrutiny. In some of the cases, there are also shades of the maxim—"if you live by the press you shall die by the press". In particular, if someone actively presents a false picture to the public about matters that would ordinarily be private, the courts recognise that the press is entitled to expose the truth to the public. This was illustrated in a recent case in which a tabloid newspaper ran a story about the supermodel, Naomi Campbell, attending a Narcotics Anonymous sessions. She had previous made a point of saying (falsely) that she did not use drugs. Her lawyers, therefore, did not even try to argue that the press was not allowed to report the fact of her drug dependency and the fact that she was seeking treatment, given that she had specifically given publicity to the very question of whether she took drugs. The case went to the House of Lords, which said (by a majority) that the newspaper had gone too far in publishing details including photographs of her at the door of the Narcotics Anonymous meeting (*Campbell v MGN*, 2004). However, an ordinary citizen who had not sought to reveal details of his or her private life would probably be entitled to protection in respect of matters of this kind.

How much can the story be fleshed out?

Newspapers obvious want to print not only the bare facts of an embarrassing story but to give it added colour or credibility by, for example, adding photographs of the activity in question. Assume that publishing the facts is legitimate, how far can they go in illustrating the story? The answer is, unfortunately, not clear.

On the one hand, there is some judicial sympathy for the newspaper editor who has to make quick decisions that may not always look so good when pored over in great detail in court. It is said that unless there is reasonable latitude, the freedom of the press would be unduly curtailed. However, the majority in the House of Lords in the *Campbell* case adopted a rather stricter approach, involving consideration of whether publication of the ancillary material was necessary and whether it was likely to be harmful. The line between what is permissible embellishment of a factual story and what goes too far is not easy to draw. In general, the courts have tended to disapprove of the publication of photographs where the bare story would suffice to put the information before the public (see, *e.g.* the *Campbell* case and the *Theakston* case, referred to below).

Some examples

The origin of the right to protect personal confidences in English law is probably *Prince Albert v Strange* (1849), where the defendant publisher had got hold of private etchings by Prince Albert of the royal family at home. An injunction was granted restraining publication of a catalogue containing descriptions of the etchings. Some other recent examples illustrate the boundaries of the cause of action.

Example 1

Michael Douglas and Catharine Zeta Jones successfully sued *Hello!* magazine, which published photographs of their wedding that had been clandestinely obtained. The couple had entered into an exclusive deal with a rival magazine, *OK!*, giving that magazine exclusive picture rights for a substantial sum. *OK!* were also claimants in the action and they received the lion's share of the substantial damages awarded against *Hello!* (*Douglas v Hello*, 2003).

Example 2

A prominent footballer sued a newspaper to restrain it from publishing details of his extra-marital affairs. He lost. The Court of Appeal recognised that a public figure was entitled to have his privacy protected, but that such a person must expect and accept that his or her actions will be more closely scrutinised by the media (*A v B plc*, 2002).

Example 3

A well-known presenter of youth television programmes sued to prevent the publication of a story about sexual activity with prostitutes accompanied by photographs. The court permitted publication of the story but not the photographs, observing that photographs had a particularly intrusive nature and that the courts were generally willing to prevent publication of them (*Theakston v MGN*, 2002).

Note: A Brief Excursion into a Dry Debate

A debate has smouldered in the pages of academic journals for about a hundred years concerning the legal nature of confidential information. It is one thing to say that the law will prevent people from taking the fruits of breaches of confidence, it is quite another to work out (as a matter of legal theory) why such protection should exist in the first place. After all, there must be some basis for creating a liability. There are (essentially) three views.

The first (and probably the most ancient) is property based. This holds that confidential information is a kind of property just like any other that can be transferred and is protected by an action in essence similar to conversion of goods or trespass. But, confidential information does not have at least one important incident of other personal property—you are not guilty of theft if you steal it (see, *e.g. Oxford v Moss* (1978), a student "stealing" an examination paper).

The second is the contractualist view. This holds that confidential information is protected because of a kind of contract, express or implied. But purely contractualist theories of legal liability are out of favour at present. In any event, this theory does not really make room for the notion of stopping a third party, who has got hold of the information from the impartee, from using or disclosing it.

The third is a rather more nebulous approach based on the enforcement of equitable obligations of confidence. This is the approach that is currently dominant. Thus, there is said to be an obligation of confidence based on "good faith"—it is said that the conscience of the defendant is touched. Although the courts may not be able to define precisely when the principles will be invoked, they know a case for their application when they see one.

In practice, the inability clearly to articulate a basis or framework for protection is not as serious as it might be in other cases. There are usually so many other uncertainties of fact and law in confidential information cases (such as whether the information has the necessary quality of confidence about it) that adding a little disquiet about the basis for granting relief does not make too much difference.

The important underlying point that this debate highlights is that monopolies protected in virtue of the "proprietorship" of, or control over confidential information are only regulated by the courts (subject to the general principles of the Human Rights Act)—obligations of "good faith" are rather powerful and flexible legal instruments in the hands of judges. Now and again, senior judges remark that unless something is done by Parliament to provide for a law of privacy, the courts must step in.

25. MORAL RIGHTS

Moral rights have nothing to do with morals. They are special rights conferred by the Copyright, Designs and Patents Act 1988 and are intended to give creative people a sense of artistic control over their copyright works. The name comes from the French ("droit moral")—the French and Germans have traditionally been much more interested in these kinds of rights. The main moral rights are unlike a lot of the rest of intellectual property: they are about creativity and art, and above all, reputations not economics—so the orthodox theory goes anyway.

Artists and writers are often (and rightly) concerned about two things: fame and the "artistic integrity" of their works. Of course, both of these can be of commercial importance too; fame is usually swiftly followed by profit. Much of the popular appeal of intellectual property is derived from images of the starving (balding and bearded?) inventor in a garret, or impecunious artists eking out a living in a bare paint-splashed studio. Moral rights are inspired by a slightly different popular image: the artist whose creative genius goes unrecognised while his or her works are sold on every street corner; or the writer whose creative abilities are brought into disrepute by distasteful alteration. They are principally concerned with protecting the reputation of the artist or author.

There are four kinds of moral right. First there is *the right to be identified as the author* of a work. Second, there is *the right to object to derogatory treatment* of a work. Third, there is the *right not to have works falsely attributed to you*. Finally, and in a slightly different class, there is a *right to privacy of certain kinds of photographs and films*.

Right to be Identified as the Author

The right to be identified as the author applies to literary, dramatic, musical or artistic works and films. There are certain exceptions, such as computer programs. It is sometimes called the "paternity right," probably also from the French (it may be thought that this is a physiologically and psychologically implausible term, as well as being sexist).

An author (or director in the case of a film) has the right to be identified as such, broadly speaking, whenever the work in question is exposed to the public. So in the case of a literary work, for example, whenever the work is published commercially, the author can insist that his or her name appears as the author. Or in the case of a film, when, for example, it is shown in public, broadcast or included in a cable programme service, the director can insist that he or she is credited. Architects can insist that they are identified on the buildings they have designed.

But before anyone can insist on such identification, they have to assert their right. This can be done in various ways—either by a simple written document, signed by the author or the director or upon an assignment of copyright (say when an author hands over the copyright in a manuscript to a publisher). Nowadays, one commonly sees at the beginning of books (see this one) a recognition of the assertion by the author of their rights to be identified as the author. If the right is infringed, a person has the right to claim damages and an injunction.

Right to Object to Derogatory Treatment

This is the most troublesome of the moral rights. The Copyright, Designs and Patents Act 1988 says that a treatment is derogatory "if it amounts to distortion or mutilation of the work or is otherwise prejudicial to the honour or reputation of the author or director". There is no real guidance as to what this means. The florid terminology "honour or reputation" sounds like something out of another age and it will be interesting to see what the courts make of it. Suppose, for example, a book publisher crops a photograph to make it fit the page or colours a black and white sketch, the better to appeal to popular taste. Is that derogatory? More importantly, who should have the final say as to what is derogatory, the artist, or should one look to what "ordinary members of the public" would think, or the judge hearing the case?

Since the law is intended to protect the reputation of the artist or author, it is not an infringement if the author or director is not identified or has not previously been identified with the work or if there is sufficient disclaimer. There is no general right to prevent mutilation—the right is mainly there to prevent people thinking that the artist was responsible for it. Also, for example, making an adaptation or arrangement cannot *per se* amount to derogatory treatment—it must actually affect the author's honour or reputation.

This moral right does not apply to works made for reporting current events or in relation to the publication in newspapers of works made for that purpose. Nor does it apply to works where copyright is owned by someone's employer (when the person has made the work in the course of her employment pursuant to a contract of service). There are some other exceptions.

As with the right to be identified as the author, the right to object to derogatory treatment is infringed, essentially, by people who put the mutilated or distorted work before the public. So, the right is infringed, for example, by someone who publishes commercially a derogatory treatment of a work or issues copies to the public. In the case of a film, it would be infringed by someone who showed the film in public, broadcast it or included it in a cable programme service.

The right to object to derogatory treatment is also infringed (essentially) by people who deal in works that have been subjected to derogatory treatment knowing or having reason to believe that they have been subjected to derogatory treatment.

There are certain other exceptions—for example, the BBC can chop works around with impunity in order "to avoid the inclusion in a programme broadcast by them of anything which offends against good taste or decency or which is likely to encourage or incite to crime or to lead to disorder or be offensive to public feeling".

False Attribution of Authorship

The law of defamation is there to prevent people saying untrue and unfortunate things about people. This law is there to prevent other people thinking that you have said or done damaging things. Few things are as likely to bring a reputable author into disrepute, as it being said "So and so wrote X" where X is some especially unmeritorious work. This right gives a person the right not to have a literary, dramatic, musical or artistic work falsely attributed to him or her as author. It gives a similar right to directors, in relation to films.

Again, it is an infringement to put a work before the public in or on which there is a false attribution (for example, by exhibiting it if it is an artistic work or by issuing copies to the public, if it is a literary work). It is also infringed by someone who deals in works on which there is a false attribution knowing or having reason to believe that there is an attribution thereon and it is false. There are various other restricted acts.

The right does not only protect authors and directors. It is potentially valuable in the hands of interviewees of news-papers.

Examples

The *News of the World* published an article with the headline "How My Love For The Saint Went Sour By Dorothy Squires talking to Weston Taylor". (The Saint was a well known TV series with the main hero played by Roger Moore.) Dorothy Squires sued for libel and for false attribution of authorship. The jury awarded her £4,300 for the libel and an extra £100 for false attribution of authorship. The Court of Appeal agreed. Lord Denning said, with characteristic pithiness "The article purports to be written by Dorothy Squires. It says 'By Dorothy Squires'. That was untrue. She did not write it." She won. (*Moore v News of the World*, 1972).

Alan Clark, a colourful conservative MP, also relied on this provision to stop a spoof of his diaries written by a satirist which appeared in the *Evening Standard*. Many readers thought it was the real thing. He had not written it, and he won as well (*Clark v Associated Newspapers*, 1988).

Right to Privacy of Certain Photographs and Films

If, for private and domestic purposes, a person commissions a photograph or the making of a film, if copyright subsists in the resulting work, he or she has the right not to have copies of it issued to the public, the work exhibited or shown in public or the work broadcast or included in a cable programme service. So commissioned wedding photographs should be safe to some extent from media exposure.

Duration of Moral Rights and Waiver

Moral rights last so long as copyright subsists in the work except that the right to object to derogatory treatment lasts for 20 years after a person's death. They can be disposed of by will. A person can waive any of the moral right by an instrument signed in writing and people who commission works often insist that authors waive all their moral rights.

26. DATABASE RIGHT

English law has long recognised that copyright exists in collections of information (compilations) including rather mundane information such as timetables (see Chapter 19 above). But the right was restricted to preventing copying of the whole or a substantial part of the compilation, not to prevent use of the data at all. Not all EU countries provided copyright protection to compilations and, in 1996 the European Community decided to harmonise the law in this area by way of the Database Directive, which has been incorporated into UK law by statutory instrument.

The result of the directive is a new kind of intellectual property right, database right. It provides rights in certain circumstances to prevent the extraction or re-utilisation of data in a qualifying database. The main purpose of the right is to give protection to the large (increasingly online) collections of data where the value resides in having a large amount of information gathered together in an organised way.

However, the Database Directive is an example of how not to legislate, since the law on its face covers much more than what one would ordinarily think of as a database. Indeed, one thing one notices immediately about the directive is the vagueness of drafting. It contains many more recitals (the preambles setting the context) than substantive provisions, many of them the fruit of special interest groups getting some helpful text into the directive to be used later on in persuading the courts that the substantive provisions should mean one thing rather than another.

The substantive provisions are themselves a recipe for litigation. The degree of uncertainty inherent in the law is illustrated by the fact that in the only English case on the subject, the Court of Appeal referred 11 questions to the European Court of Justice to tell the court what the law meant (*British Horseracing Board v William Hill*, 2002). The ECJ gave its judgement in November 2004. To the suprise — and relief— of many it limited the kinds of things which would attract database rights.

What is a Database?

According to the directive (in practice, no-one refers to the UK implementing legislation), a database means a collection of independent works data or other materials that are arranged in a systematic or methodical way and are individually accessible by electronic or other means. This definition is very wide and covers (potentially) ordinary telephone directories, even collections of journal articles that have been subject to an editorial process to arrange them in some systematic or methodical way. The definition is not limited to an "electronic" database. The form of the database is immaterial.

Subsistence of database right

In order for database right to subsist, the maker of the database must be a qualifying person (including a qualifying individual corporation, partnership etc.). In broad terms, to qualify, the maker must be an individual who is a national of, or is habitually resident within an EEA state or a body corporate incorporated under the law of an EEA state based in the EEA or having operations linked with an EEA state on an ongoing basis. The result is that makers of databases outside the EEA do not qualify. In particular, US makers of databases will not have database right protection. In the US, there is no similar protection for databases and there is accordingly no possibility of reciprocity.

Substantial investment in "obtaining, verifying or presenting the contents of the database"

As well as being made by a qualifying individual, there must have been a substantial investment in the obtaining, verifying or presenting the contents of the database. This includes any kind of investment—such as financial, human or technical resources and is judged both qualitatively and quantitatively. Although one might have thought that this requirement would operate as a practical limitation on the scope of database rights, restricting them to major investments in commercial databases, this has not proved to be the case. The ECJ has held that this requirement imposes an important limitation on the otherwise broad scope of the right. The UK High Court and Court of Appeal had held that even the creation of fixture lists for horseracing involved sufficient relevant investment for the result to qualify for database right (*British Horseracing Board v. William Hill*, 2002). However, the ECJ did not follow this line. It held, instead, that the presentation of a fixture list is closely linked to the creation of the data which makes up the list. It does not require the investment independent of the investment in the creation of its constituent data. The selection, for organising horse racing, of the horses admitted to run in the race relates to the creation of the data, which make up the lists and not an investment in obtaining the contents of the database. The upshot is that neither the obtaining, nor the verification nor the presentation of the contents of a racing (or other) fixture lists involves the kind of investment which justifies protection by the database right (*British Horseracing Board v. William Hill, Fixtures Marketing v. Oy Veikkaus*, 2004).

How Long does Database Right Last and how can it be traded?

Database right lasts for 15 years from the end of the calendar year in which the database was completed, or if made available to the public, from the end of the calendar year in which it was made available to the public. However, if a database is updated regularly, the 15-year period begins to run again if the new (or revised) database would be considered to be a substantial new investment.

Database rights may be sold (by assignment, for example) and may be licensed. There are certain provisions that enable the terms of general schemes established by database right owners to be subject to the control of the Copyright Tribunal.

The Types of Protection for Databases

Database right

The principal form of protection for databases is now database right. It is quite independent of any copyright that may exist in either the database (see below), or in any of the individual works in the database.

Database right provides for certain prohibited acts. These are of two kinds: extraction or re-utilisation of the whole or a substantial part of the contents of the database. Extraction is the temporary or permanent transfer of the contents to another medium. Re-utilisation is defined in the directive as "Any form of making available to the public all or a substantial part of the contents of the database by the distribution of copies by renting, by on-line or other forms of transmission". The terms "extraction" and "re-utilisation" have been given a broad interpretation by the courts in the UK and the ECJ (*British Horseracing Board v William Hill*, 2004).

"Substantial part" is considered both qualitatively and quantitatively. Repeated and systematic extraction of insubstantial parts of the contents of a database may amount to the extraction or re-utilisation of a substantial part where they imply acts, which conflict with the normal exploitation of the database or unreasonably prejudice the legitimate interests of the maker of the database. In copyright law, it is an open question as to whether taking small but regular helpings each of which is insufficient to infringe in itself can constitute infringement in the aggregate. The Database Directive makes it clear that it is possible for this to constitute infringement. Although the test in the directive is not specially clear, it is likely that it will be given a rather commercial interpretation by the courts. Tiny amounts, which even in aggregate would not ordinarily attract a licence fee (for example), would be unlikely to count as sufficiently substantial for there to be infringement.

Additional copyright protection for databases

Somewhat confusingly, databases are also entitled to copyright protection if they satisfy the requirement of originality. For a database, this is the requirement that the database be such that by reason of the selection or arrangement of its contents, it constitutes the author's own intellectual creation. What this means in practice has yet to be worked out by the courts. However, it probably means that copyright protection will be conferred where there is a genuine (not automatic or completely obvious) selection of the materials to be included in a database, *i.e.* there has been a genuine editorial process of selection.

Exceptions to database right protection

There are rather complex exceptions to protection for "lawful users" and there are some of the same limitations as exist for copyright protection (*e.g.* Parliamentary and judicial proceedings and the like). There are not, however, the exceptions for criticism or review or for reporting current events and the education and research exceptions are narrower than for copyright protection.

Actions for Infringement of Database Right

Actions for infringement of database right are very similar to copyright infringement claims. All of the usual remedies are available (such as an injunction, damages, accounts of profits). Additional damages may be claimed in the case of flagrant infringements. Exclusive licensees may sue.

27. THE EUROPEAN COMMUNITY—FREE MOVEMENT AND COMPETITION

The Influence of European Community Law

European Community (EC) law has had a very great influence on intellectual property. This influence has been greatest in two areas. First, much of modern intellectual property law has been harmonised in the European Community, generally leading to a greater extent of protection, new rights (such as the database right) and more limited exceptions. Second (and working in the opposite direction), EC rules on free movement and on competition have had considerable influence in reducing the things that proprietors can do with intellectual property rights —particular as regards partitioning Community countries from one another.

EC legislation

As to EC legislation, the Community has been enormously active. This is only to be expected. By 1776, copyright and patents were sufficiently important commercially to warrant mention in the United States Constitution as matters about which the Federal Congress could legislate (US Constitution: Art.1, s.8(8)). Over the years, intellectual property has become more and more of an international matter and in the EC too, as regards new legislation, it has substantially become a "federal" question rather than a Member States' question.

There is nothing specifically about the EC's power to regulate intellectual property in the Treaty of Rome, but that has not stopped the legislative programme. As part of the move to create and develop a single market, the EC has passed a fair amount of legislation in the field of intellectual property that is intended to harmonise the law between Member States. The whole of UK trade mark law is based on a Community Directive (and the Community Trade Mark derives from a Community Regulation). The EC has passed directives on patents (such as the Biotech Patents Directive) and two directives granting supplementary protection certificates to compensate for delay in obtaining marketing authorisation. It has been most active in copyright, with legislation on rental and lending rights, com-

226

puter software, copyright term of protection and (most generally) copyright in the information society.

EC directives set out what the Member States have to introduce by way of legislation, but give Member States some leeway in how that is to be done. A deadline is set for passing suitable legislation and Member States have to introduce something that complies by the deadline. If a Member State fails to introduce conforming legislation by the deadline, there are several consequences. First, if the provisions of the directive are precise and unconditional, a person can rely on these provisions against administrative authorities of the state (and certain other organs of the state, but not against other private citizens), even though there is no national legislation implementing the directive. This is the doctrine of "direct effect" developed by the European Court of Justice over 20 years ago as an instance of the supremacy of EC law (*Marleasing*, 1990). Second, if there is a manifest and grave disregard of Community law obligations, a person injured thereby may, under specified conditions, be able to claim damages from the state for failure to implement the directive.

Free movement of goods and competition

As to free movement and competition, there is a fundamental conflict that the European Court of Justice has sought to resolve. Intellectual property rights are territorial (for example, a United Kingdom patent only gives a person the right to prevent competitors dealing in the product in the United Kingdom). They are also "anti-competitive" (for example, a valid registered trade mark gives the proprietor the exclusive right to use the trade mark in the United Kingdom on the goods for which it is registered). A patent involves the state authorising a person to exclude competition. Aspects of EC law on the other hand point in the opposite direction—the EC Treaty is set against both territorial rights and has policies designed to be pro-competition. It outlaws restrictions on the freedom of movement of goods across national boundaries, and there are specific provisions directed against anti-competitive abuses of market power and restrictive agreements.

There are also United Kingdom laws that mitigate the anti-competitive effects of intellectual property. These are of lesser importance in practice than European Community law. That said, the UK Competition Act 1998 followed the approach of the EC Treaty to competition regulation—with the exception that the provisions or acts in question need not have community-wide effects ("an effect on trade between member states"). The laws are very similar in what they prevent. How are these two approaches to be reconciled? Two aspects need to be considered.

Free Movement—Articles 28 and 30

Arts. 28 and 30 of the Treaty of Rome provide for the free movement of goods. (The Articles of the Treaty were renumbered and the old cases refer to Articles 30 and 36 instead of 28 and 30).

Art.28 says that quantitative restrictions on imports and measures having equivalent effect are to be prohibited. But Art.30 allows for prohibitions or restrictions for the protection of industrial and commercial property provided that they are not a means of arbitrary discrimination or disguised restriction of trade between Member States. The European Court of Justice has worked out special principles that aim to reconcile the free movement of goods with the territoriality of intellectual property rights.

The fundamental rules

First, although the Treaty does not affect the existence of an intellectual property right, there are circumstances in which its exercise can be prohibited. Second, Art.30 permits exceptions to the free movement of goods only to the extent to which those exceptions are necessary to safeguard the rights that constitute the specific subject matter of the type of intellectual property in question. Third, the right-holder's rights are exhausted when the goods are put into circulation by her (or with her consent), anywhere within the Common Market.

As will be seen, these principles only give guidance at the most abstract level. The effect of them is best illustrated by a few examples.

Example 1 (patents)

Sterling Drug held patents for a urinary infection drug in both the United Kingdom and the Netherlands. They sold the drug cheaply in the United Kingdom, but it was very expensive in the Netherlands. Centrafarm bought some of the drug in the United Kingdom and shipped it to the Netherlands. They sold it there at a handsome profit. Held: there was nothing that Sterling Drug could do about this. The rights were exhausted by putting the drug into circulation for the first time in the United Kingdom (*Centrafarm v Sterling Drug*, 1974). (Note, the result would be the same if the patentee first sold into a country where there was no patent protection. Note also, there are special rules governing the manner in which repackaging of parallel imports must be undertaken which have still to be finally resolved by the ECJ over 30 years after the Treaty came into force in the UK: see for details *Glaxo v Dowelhurst* (2004).)

Example 2 (same with trade marks)

Metro bought "Polydor" marked records in France (where they were cheap) and sold them in Germany (where they were expensive). Held: there was nothing that the trade mark proprietor could do to stop this (*Deutsche Grammophon v Metro*, 1971).

Example 3 (unconnected parties)

Terranova, who had the mark "Terranova" registered in Germany, tried to prevent Terrapin (an unconnected company) from importing building materials into Germany bearing the "Terrapin" mark. Held: Terranova could do so, provided that the mark did not act as an arbitrary means of discrimination or a disguised restriction on trade between Member States (*Terrapin v Terranova*, 1976). Note that the court said that a national court's finding of confusing similarity was not a matter for EU free movement law, even though, fairly obviously, the two were not in fact confusingly similar.

Competition—Articles 81 and 82

There are two important provisions of the Treaty dealing with competition, Arts. 81 and 82. They are designed to ensure that there is competition "sans frontières" in Europe so that in order to come within either Article, it must be shown that the agreement or conduct complained of has an "effect on trade between Members States" of the EC. These, too, were renumbered. Art.81 was formerly Art.85. Art.82 was formerly Art.86.

Art.81

Art.81 prohibits agreements that have as their object or effect the prevention, restriction or distortion of competition within the Common Market. It is of general application, although there are some specific examples given in the Article of agreements that would normally be caught such as price-fixing, or market-sharing agreements.

In the field of intellectual property, Community law is especially concerned about the following practices under Art.81: tying (for example, a patentee insisting that a licensee of a process purchase all raw materials for operating the process from the patentee); charging royalties on non-patented products; obliging a licensee to disclose all the new technical information he learns to the patentee.

Block exemptions

In order to provide some measure of certainty and predictability, the EC has enacted a series of Regulations that grant clearance to certain kinds of agreements including I.P. agreements. These are very useful. If people tailor their agreements to fit the block exemptions, they will normally be safe. Although an agreement that falls within one of the block exemption Regulations will ordinarily be regarded as satisfying the competition rules, there are no complete guarantees. The Technology Transfer Regulation of which a new version came into force in 2004 has a set of complex rules setting out what can and what cannot be done in (mainly technical—patents, know-how etc.) intellectual property licensing agreements.

Art.82

Art.82 prohibits abuses of dominant position. Being in a dominant position consists of possessing significant market power, and ordinarily it will be judged by the size of market share. A market share of greater than 40 per cent, with the other competitors having much smaller shares is one rule of thumb that is often used. There are often disputes over what the relevant market is. Possession of an intellectual property right (such as a patent) can put a person into a dominant position, but does not necessarily do so. It depends on a range of factors such as whether there are competing products and the extent to which the proprietor of the patent can act independently of other competitors and consumers. Whether a person is abusing a dominant position must be judged individually in each case.

Examples of conduct that may constitute abuse are charging

excessive prices for products protected by a patent, or refusing to licence except upon restrictive terms.

Enforcing the EC Competition Rules

The European Commission

The European Commission is the administrative institution of the EC. It is split into a number of Directorates General (commonly called "DGs"), each responsible for a particular area of law or policy. One of the most powerful DGs deals with competition policy. Under the competition rules of the Treaty, a person who is the victim of an anti-competitive agreement or an abuse of dominant position can make a complaint to the Commission. If there is a *prima facie* case, the Commission will open formal proceedings. A team of (mainly) lawyers and economists is assigned to the case and it conducts an investigation. There are extensive powers to investigate and compel persons to produce documents. The Commission also investigates of its own initiative and can conduct "dawn raids" on companies throughout the Community suspected of anti-competitive practices, taking away incriminating documents.

If the Commission considers that there has been a violation of EC competition law, it sends the undertaking concerned a document outlining the case against it. The person is entitled to an oral hearing and to put their case with witnesses. Then, if the Commission finds that a person has infringed the competition provisions of the Treaty, it can order the person concerned to stop. It can also order the payment of fines of up to 10 per cent of turnover of the undertaking concerned. Some recent fines have run into tens of millions of pounds.

In practice, a large number of cases are settled informally. The parties will agree (for example) to remove offending terms from an agreement or stop offending practices. The Commission will then send an informal letter confirming that they are no longer interested in the case.

One advantage for complainants before the Commission is that they do not have to pay their opponent's costs if they lose—unlike in the United Kingdom courts. The Commission takes charge of the proceedings and is primarily responsible for pursuing it. Fending off a Commission investigation can be a very costly and inconvenient business, so a threat of a complaint to the Commission is often enough to have some effect. If the parties are dissatisfied with a Commission decision, they can appeal it to the Court of First Instance, and ultimately to the European Court of Justice.

The United Kingdom Courts—"Euro-defences"

The competition rules are also directly effective in the national courts. The Commission, overburdened with work, and seeking to give effect to a principle of subsidiarity, has been encouraging national courts to apply the competition provisions for quite some time, rather than leaving it to the Commission to pursue complaints. Litigation in this area is a growing field. In May 2004, this culminated in the national courts receiving much greater powers to apply the competition rules to decentralise competition enforcement and to make it more effective throughout the Community. An additional advantage of proceeding in the national court is that if the court finds that there has been a violation of Community law, it can award damages to the victim and an injunction to stop future infringements of the rules.

There was a time when defendants (especially defendants to patent and copyright cases) used to raise so-called "Euro-defences" (a claim that for the plaintiff to enforce his rights against the defendant would be contrary to the EC Treaty and particularly Arts 81 and 82). For example, in a series of cases it was said that a patentee who had licensed his patent to others was unjustly (and anti-competitively) discriminating against the defendant in refusing to license the patent to him. Or it was said that a copyright owner was using the copyright to obtain an unjust monopoly in another field (see *Magill* (1991)—television companies trying to enforce copyright in television listings).

These kinds of defences are less commonly advanced than they used to be. There is no English case in which such a defence has actually succeeded and many were struck out as unarguable. It may be though, that the EC rules were therefore of no value but this is probably not so. The most important impact of them has been in requiring proprietors to ensure that their commercial agreements conformed to Community rules. It should be borne in mind in any event that since the whole purpose of a patent is to confer a monopoly rights, complaining that the patentee is exercising that monopoly right is bound to face difficulties. It used to be said among intellectual property practitioners that Euro-defences were the last defence of the pirate and the courts looked on them with some scepticism. Although acknowledging that some such defences have merit, the dominant view was: "Whatever else it is, the Treaty of Rome is not intended to be a pirate's charter" (*British Leyland v TI*, 1979). However, recently, when many thought that the Euro-defence was dead, the Court of Appeal allowed such a defence to go to trial in a patent action by Intel against a rival chip-maker, Via, which involved, among other things, a fundamental challenge to Intel's licensing policy. The case settled some time afterwards (*Intel v Via*, 2002).

28. SOME ASPECTS OF THE INTERNATIONAL LAW OF INTELLECTUAL PROPERTY

Private international law is the branch of law that deals with (amongst other things) what country claims may be brought for what matters. It is a vast subject in its own right. We will look at just a few aspects of the private international law of intellectual property, a topic of ever increasing importance. At the end of this section, there is a brief mention of some of the public international law aspects of the intellectual property.

Private International Law

Foreign intellectual property rights

Issues of the subsistence of a intellectual property right can usually only be decided in the courts of the country whose laws confer the right, and the courts of other countries have no right to judge these. This is best illustrated by four examples.

Example 1

A young architect thought that a rather more famous architect had taken his designs for a building in Holland and built a building according to those designs in Rotterdam. Making a copy of a work outside the United Kingdom is not an infringement of UK copyright, but the ambitious young architect wanted to sue in the English courts rather than in the Dutch courts. Could he claim for infringement of Dutch copyright in the English courts? For some years, it was thought that foreign copyright claims were "non-justiciable" in the English courts (see comparative example, below). However, the Netherlands and the UK are both parties to the Brussels Convention, which provides for jurisdiction in the EU countries. The court held that he was able to bring his claim for infringement of Dutch copyright law before the English court under the Brussels Convention (*Pearce v Ove Arup*, 1999).

Comparative example 2

In 1984, a company called Tyburn Productions produced a television film called "The Masks of Death" from a script original in every respect except that it featured Sherlock Holmes and Dr Watson. It tried to distribute the film in the United States, and received an angry letter from the only surviving child of Sir Arthur Conan Doyle, a Lady Jean Bromet. She claimed copyright in the characters her father had created. Tyburn appeased her by the payment of a substantial sum of money and an undertaking to delay distribution. Some time later, Tyburn wanted to produce another film—"The Abbott's Cry"—again an original script but also based on the Sherlock Holmes character. Making the film would involve them in substantial production costs and they wanted to be sure that they could distribute it in the United States before incurring too much expense. A mere assertion by Lady Bromet of her copyright would have seriously affected distribution, so they tried to clear the matter up in advance. It was not possible to force Lady Bromet to sue them so that their rights could be tested, nor could they sue for a declaration in the United States. So they tried to enlist the help of the English courts. The court held that the question whether Lady Bromet was entitled to copyright under United States law was not something an English court could decide. It was not justiciable in England. (*Tyburn Productions v Doyle*, 1990.)

Historical example 3

For many years, an ancient order of clever Carthusian monks brewed a delicious liqueur at the monastery of La Grande Chartreuse in France. The liqueur was brewed according to a secret process, jealously guarded. As well as being enormously devout, the monks were evidently shrewd businessmen, and the head of the order, the procurator, one Abbé Rey, ensured that "Chartreuse" trade marks were registered in various countries, including France and the United Kingdom. Tragedy befell the order when, in 1901, the French Government passed a law that declared illegal all unlicensed religious associations failing to obtain authorisation from the State. The monks applied for authorisation, but the French Government (which probably thought the Carthusians had had it too good for too long) refused and the order was dissolved. The monks were forcibly expelled from France and all their property, including their trade marks, was confiscated and sold. But one thing not even the French Government could take away from them was their secret process. That the monks carried with them into their Spanish exile where, not too far from the French border, they cocked a snook at the French Government, and set up in business again.

The monks were as devout as ever and the liqueur was as delicious as ever.

The inevitable happened. The liquidator, Monsieur Lecouturier, purported to grant the right to sell Chartreuse liqueur to another (who did not have the secret). Trade mark war broke out. The monks sought to prevent the liquidator, and those claiming under him, from importing liqueur marked "Chartreuse" into England, relying on their English trade marks. At first, they succeeded. But then the liquidator "by a contrivance which it is difficult to reconcile with the actual truth" (as the House of Lords charitably put it) somehow got the English trade marks transferred to him, alleging that he was the assignee of the Abbé Rey. The liquidator then tried the reverse trick and managed to prevent the monks from importing their Chartreuse into England.

The House of Lords was evidently outraged. Lord Shaw said: "I do not see anything conferring upon the liquidator of the property of the Carthusian Order a right to strip that order of their possessions in all parts of the world". It was held that the property in question (the English trade mark) was situated in England and must therefore be regulated according to the laws of England. The French transfer did not confer title to the English marks on the liquidator and the monks won (*Rey v Lecouturier*, 1910).

Patents example 4

Under the Brussels Convention (which regulates jurisdiction and judgments in the EU), there are special rules relating to claims for the infringement and validity of registered intellectual property rights. Such claims are subject to the exclusive jurisdiction of the courts of the country of registration or deposition. Thus actions concerning the validity of an English patent must be brought in the English courts.

There is, however, no such express rule in the Convention concerning infringement actions. This gives rise to the prospect of suing a defendant (usually a company) in the courts of the defendants' domicile in respect of infringement of patents in a number of different countries. For example, a claimant may choose to sue a defendant based in France in respect of alleged acts of infringement undertaken in England, France and Germany. But since validity is subject to exclusive jurisdiction of the relevant local courts, what if the defendant says by way of defence that the patents are all invalid?

The English courts have taken the practical view that infringement and validity are so bound up together that they should be tried together. Accordingly, if validity is raised as a defence, the whole case (infringement and validity) has to be tried in the country of registration of the patent (*Coin Controls v Suzo* (1997), *Fort Dodge v Akzo Nobel* (1998)). Other European countries have taken a rather different view. There is currently a case before the ECJ that may rule definitively on what is the right approach (*Gat v Luk*, 2004).

Of course, one cannot sue in any country for infringement if no acts have been done in the jurisdiction of the country conferring the right that constitutes infringement. So, for example, one cannot sue for infringement of an English trade mark in respect of any acts done in Ireland.

Foreigners generally entitled to claim United Kingdom intellectual property rights

Most foreigners are entitled to many of the copyrights in the United Kingdom pursuant to various mutual recognition treaties such as the Berne Convention. United Kingdom copyright legislation makes special provision for people who are not British citizens to qualify for United Kingdom copyright protection. The rules governing foreigners' rights to claim particular kinds of copyright (such as copyright in films) can be very complicated and reference should always be made to more detailed works and the statutory materials.

The position with design right is less generous to foreigners: for example, although United States citizens can claim United Kingdom copyright, they are not, at least not yet, entitled to (unregistered) design right. The United States is a rather special case as regards mutual recognition of intellectual property rights but it is slowly falling into line.

Any foreigner or foreign company can apply for a United Kingdom trade mark, patent or registered design and can sue for passing-off (if there is a reputation in the United Kingdom). For example, the famous Parisian restaurant, Maxim's, could maintain an action for passing-off against a restaurant in Norwich, decorated in French period style and called "Maxim's" (*Maxim's v Dye*, 1977.)

Foreign claimants are treated exactly the same way as domestic plaintiffs in litigation, but they sometimes have to provide security for the costs of litigation where domestic claimants do not.

Public International Aspects of Intellectual Property Policy

Intellectual property law has been the subject of attempts at international harmonisation for over 100 years. There are several important treaties governing intellectual property rights, which in the early days of harmonisation were principally directed at ensuring mutual recognition of intellectual property rights (see the Berne and Paris Conventions). More recently, a series of multilateral (and some bilateral) treaties have focused on the provision of minimum standards of intellectual property protection and restrictions on the exceptions and controls that governments can exercise over intellectual property rights.

The most important modern treaty is the TRIPS agreement (Trade Related Intellectual Property Rights), one of the WTO treaties. The TRIPS agreement requires members of the WTO (most of the countries of the world) to adhere to fairly tight intellectual property standards. One English judge has described the agreement as a "yoke".

Although the TRIPS agreement is not directly effective in the English courts, it has real teeth. Even the US, which provides for generous protection in many respects, has been held to have violated it by providing inadequate intellectual property protection. In the WTO, that provides a right to financial compensation or its equivalent.

Issues surrounding the TRIPS agreement and developing countries

In recent years, there have been criticisms of the TRIPS agreement, mainly originating from a perception that the standards that it requires countries to introduce would prevent developing countries from adopting the approach adopted by many developed countries in the past, namely to copy themselves into greater prosperity. There is an extensive academic debate among economists as to whether it makes sense for countries to introduce a high level of intellectual property protection when it does not have the resources to benefit. For such countries, it is said, extensive intellectual property rights are a burden not a benefit. Others, of course, maintain that such rights actually contribute to particular kinds of valuable economic activity, whether it be foreign investment or the development of local creative industries or local scientific research.

There is some truth on both sides. What can be said with some confidence is that the context in which any given intellectual property regime operates is critical to whether it delivers net benefits, and on that, the devil is in the detail. So while it may pay Kenya to have a sophisticated plant breeders rights regime (it has an extensive export industry in horticulture), it may not pay it to have a sophisticated patents regime (it may not have a sufficiently large research base for it to be an advantage and it may not attract foreign investment).

Other criticisms of the TRIPS agreement have focused on the impact of introducing rigid, Western-style, patent laws on the ability of poorer countries to obtain less expensive generic pharmaceuticals, particularly for the treatment of AIDS and other important diseases. There are moves to ensure that developing countries without manufacturing facilities of their own will be able to obtain generic pharmaceuticals from countries where there is manufacturing capacity. However, it is not clear whether this will provide an adequate answer. There are many who accept that pharmaceutical companies need money for research and development (and to pay their shareholders), but find it much harder to understand why those funds should come from those who can least afford it and who may be unable to benefit from the therapy at all if patent level prices are charged.

29. FURTHER READING AND WEBSITE REFERENCES

Useful Websites

The following websites have a great deal of useful information about intellectual property law and links to other sites with more.

Chartered Institute of Patent Agents
www.cipa.org.uk

EPO Patent Database
www.espacenet.com

European Commission Internal Market Site Map (IP subjects under heading Business) Market—Intellectual Property
www.europa.eu.int/comm/internal_market/sitemap_en.htm

European Court of Justice
www.europa.eu.int/cj/en/index.htm

European Patent Office
www.european-patent-office.org

Institute of Trade Mark Attorneys
www.itma.org.uk

Intellectual Property cases before the ECJ
www.patent.gov.uk/about/ippd/ecj/index.htm

Intellectual Property Institute
www.ip-institute.org.uk

Intellectual Property Lawyers Association (Solicitors)
www.ipla.org.uk

IP Bar Association (Barristers)
www.ipba.co.uk

Office for Harmonization in the Internal Market (Trade Marks and Design)
www.oami.eu.int

UK Government IP Site
www.intellectual-property.gov.uk

UK Patent Office
www.patent.gov.uk

World Intellectual Property Organisation (WIPO)
   www.wipo.org

British and Irish Legal Information Institute (BAILLI)
   www.bailli.org.uk
(A comprehensive yet free legal website with most decisions
since about 1996—many of the cases in this book can be found
on this.)

The Licensing Executives Society (a large association of IP
professionals)
   www.bi.les-europe.org

All European (both national and EPO) applications from 2000
onwards and many earlier patents too—including US patents.
Some data goes back as far as 1970
   Esp@cenet

ICANN
   www.icann.org

Nominet
   www.nic.uk

INDEX

243

254